Y0-AAB-105

This book comes with access to more content online.

Quiz yourself, track your progress,
and score high on test day!

Register your book or ebook at
www.dummies.com/go/getaccess.

Select your product, and then follow the prompts
to validate your purchase.

You'll receive an email with your PIN and instructions.

Digital SAT® Prep 2025/2026

A Wiley Brand

Digital SAT®
Prep 2025/2026

with Online Practice

by Ron Woldoff, MBA

Digital SAT® Prep 2025/2026 For Dummies® with Online Practice

Published by: **John Wiley & Sons, Inc.**, 111 River Street, Hoboken, NJ 07030-5774, www.wiley.com

Copyright © 2024 by John Wiley & Sons, Inc., Hoboken, New Jersey

Published simultaneously in Canada

For general information on our other products and services, please contact our Customer Care Department within the U.S. at 877-762-2974, outside the U.S. at 317-572-3993, or fax 317-572-4002. For technical support, please visit https://hub.wiley.com/community/support/dummies.

Wiley publishes in a variety of print and electronic formats and by print-on-demand. Some material included with standard print versions of this book may not be included in e-books or in print-on-demand. If this book refers to media such as a CD or DVD that is not included in the version you purchased, you may download this material at http://booksupport.wiley.com. For more information about Wiley products, visit www.wiley.com.

Library of Congress Control Number is available from the publisher.

ISBN 978-1-394-25827-7 (pbk); ISBN 978-1-394-25829-1 (ebk); ISBN 978-1-394-25828-4 (ebk)

SKY10075480_051824

Contents at a Glance

Introduction 1

Part 1: Getting Started with the SAT...5
CHAPTER 1: What to Expect with the SAT 7
CHAPTER 2: Strategies for Success...15

Part 2: Owning the SAT Reading and Writing Section 21
CHAPTER 3: Raising Your Best SAT Reading and Writing Score.....................23
CHAPTER 4: What Are They Saying: Sentence Completion and Grammar Questions............37
CHAPTER 5: Thinking Fast: Critical Thinking and Data Questions.........................51

Part 3: Owning the SAT Math Section 67
CHAPTER 6: Raising Your Best Math Score 69
CHAPTER 7: Simplifying Numbers and Operations 73
CHAPTER 8: Solving Algebra and Functions 93
CHAPTER 9: Drawing Geometry and Trigonometry 131
CHAPTER 10: Measuring Statistics and Probability 159

Part 4: It's All You: Acing the SAT Practice Exams 169
CHAPTER 11: Practice Exam 1 171
CHAPTER 12: Practice Exam 1: Answers and Explanations 203
CHAPTER 13: Practice Exam 2 221
CHAPTER 14: Practice Exam 2: Answers and Explanations 251
CHAPTER 15: How Did You Do? Scoring Your Practice SAT 269

Part 5: The Part of Tens 275
CHAPTER 16: Ten Mistakes That Others Make That You Won't.......................277
CHAPTER 17: Ten Ways to Get the Most from Practice SATs........................281

Index...285

Table of Contents

INTRODUCTION...1
   About This Book..1
   Icons Used in This Book 2
   Beyond the Book..3
   Where to Go from Here 3

PART 1: GETTING STARTED WITH THE SAT..5

CHAPTER 1: **What to Expect with the SAT**...7
   Thinking About the ACT 7
   So . . . What's on the Digital SAT?..8
   Working the Online, Adaptive SAT 9
   Signing Up before Sitting Down: Registering for the SAT 10
      How to register 10
      When to take the test 10
   Accommodating Special Needs 11
      Learning disabilities...11
      Physical issues 12
      Financial help 12
   Making the SAT Work for You as a Foreign Student...12
   Examining Your Mind: What the SAT Really Looks For..13
   Scoring on the SAT..14
      Composite score 14
      Score reports 14

CHAPTER 2: **Strategies for Success**..15
   Planning Your Prep Time 15
      Starting early: The long-term study time 16
      Moving along: The medium-term study time 17
      Getting closer: The short-term study time...17
   The Exam Is Tomorrow: What to Do the Night Before Your SAT 18
   Show Time: What to Do the Day of Your SAT 18
      Starting out that morning..19
      Taking control of the tension...19
      Focusing during the test..19
   It Isn't You: Testing under Adverse Conditions 20

PART 2: OWNING THE SAT READING AND WRITING SECTION........21

CHAPTER 3: **Raising Your Best SAT Reading and Writing Score** 23
   Understanding SAT Reading and Writing...23
   Managing Your Time with Reading Strategies..24
   Finding the Right Answer, Fast, with More Strategies 25
   Putting the Strategies to Use with Practice Questions...26
      Detail questions...27
      Inference and main idea questions 28
      Writer's purpose questions 29

Practicing with Reading Passages 30
    Social studies 30
    Science 32
    Literature 33
    Poetry 35

CHAPTER 4: What Are They Saying: Sentence Completion and Grammar Questions 37
Completing Sentences and Using In-Context Vocabulary 37
Killing It Softly: The SAT Grammar Review 40
    Grammar and punctuation 40
    Transitions 41
    Verb matching 42
    Verb tension 43
    Parallel structure 43
    Pronoun cases 44
    Punctuation 44
    Words in context 45
Practice Questions 46
Practice Answers 49

CHAPTER 5: Thinking Fast: Critical Thinking and Data Questions 51
Starting with the Question Formats 51
Applying the Strategies 52
Exploring the Question Formats 52
    Purpose of the underlined sentence 52
    Overall structure of the text 53
    Paired reading 54
    Interpreting data 55
    Strengthening or weakening a claim 56
    Using quotations for support 57
    Completing the text logically 58
    Interpreting Research Questions 59
Practice Questions 61
Practice Answers 65

PART 3: OWNING THE SAT MATH SECTION 67

CHAPTER 6: Raising Your Best Math Score 69
Taking On SAT Math 69
Starting with Formulas 70
Typing Your Answers 71
Refreshing the SAT Math Topics 71

CHAPTER 7: Simplifying Numbers and Operations 73
Simplifying the Basics 73
    Starting with types of numbers 73
    Using order of operations 75
Simplifying Numbers and Operations 76
    Simplifying prime numbers 76
    Simplifying percents 76
    Simplifying ratios 78
    Simplifying conversions 80
    Simplifying exponents 81

Simplifying square and cube roots 86
Simplifying imaginary *i* 88
Simplifying projections 90

CHAPTER 8: **Solving Algebra and Functions** 93
Solving for *X* 93
Solving for x with a number 93
Solving for x with a y 94
Solving for *x* in a radical 95
Solving for *x* in a fraction 96
Solving for *x* in a reciprocal fraction 97
Solving for More Than One *X* 98
Solving an absolute value 98
Solving a quadratic 100
Solving the difference of squares 103
Solving an expression 105
Setting Up Equations 107
Setting up a story 107
Setting up a sum of numbers 108
Setting up interest 109
Setting up rates of change 112
Graphing Coordinate Geometry 114
Graphing a line 115
Graphing two lines 118
Graphing an inequality 120
Graphing a parabola 121
Graphing a circle 125
Graphing a function 127

CHAPTER 9: **Drawing Geometry and Trigonometry** 131
Drawing Basic Shapes 132
Drawing angles 132
Drawing triangles 135
Drawing rectangles and squares 140
Drawing trapezoids and parallelograms 140
Drawing circles 143
Drawing overlapping shapes 144
Drawing parts of circles 145
Drawing 3-D Shapes 147
Drawing rectangular solids and cubes 147
Drawing cylinders and cones 149
Drawing spheres 150
Solving Trigonometry Problems 151
Solving right triangles with SOH CAH TOA 152
Solving unit circles and radians 154
Solving trigonometric equations 157

CHAPTER 10: **Measuring Statistics and Probability** 159
Measuring the Mean, Median, and Mode 159
Measuring the mean 159
Measuring the median and mode 160
Measuring the range 161
Measuring Probability 162
Measuring Graph Data 163

    Measuring bar graphs. 163
    Measuring circle or pie charts 164
    Measuring line graphs 164
    Measuring scatter plots 165
    Measuring multiple graphs .166

PART 4: IT'S ALL YOU: ACING THE SAT PRACTICE EXAMS 169

CHAPTER 11: Practice Exam 1 171
  Section 1: Reading and Writing .173
    Module 1 173
    Module 2 182
  Section 2: Math 193
    Module 1 193
    Module 2 197

CHAPTER 12: Practice Exam 1: Answers and Explanations 203
  Section 1: Reading and Writing .203
    Module 1 203
    Module 2 206
  Section 2: Math 209
    Module 1 209
    Module 2 214
  Answer Key 220

CHAPTER 13: Practice Exam 2 221
  Section 1: Reading and Writing .223
    Module 1 223
    Module 2 233
  Section 2: Math 242
    Module 1 242
    Module 2 246

CHAPTER 14: Practice Exam 2: Answers and Explanations 251
  Section 1: Reading and Writing .251
    Module 1 251
    Module 2 255
  Section 2: Math 258
    Module 1 258
    Module 2 263
  Answer Key 267

CHAPTER 15: How Did You Do? Scoring Your Practice SAT 269
  Finding Your Reading and Writing Score 269
  Finding Your Math Test Score 271
  Recording Your Overall Scores .273
    First practice exam 273
    Second practice exam. 273
    Third practice exam. 273
    Fourth practice exam 273

PART 5: THE PART OF TENS 275

CHAPTER 16: **Ten Mistakes That Others Make That You Won't** 277

You Won't Cheat 277
You Won't Neglect Your Break...277
You Won't Pack Sugary Snacks 278
You Won't Panic Over the Time Limit 278
You Won't Run Out of Steam 278
You Won't Rush Through the Questions 278
You Won't Get Stuck on a Question 279
You Won't Stress Over the Answers 279
You Won't Change Your Morning Routine 279
You Won't Dwell on Previous Modules...................................279

CHAPTER 17: **Ten Ways to Get the Most from Practice SATs** 281

Practice an Entire SAT Exam in One Sitting 281
Practice Not Making Mistakes under Pressure 281
Practice with the Bluebook App 282
Practice with Others in the Room 282
Practice as a Dress Rehearsal 282
Practice Your Competitive Edge 283
Practice Your Test-Taking Strategies..................................283
Practice Managing Your Time 283
Practice Finding Your Areas of Focus 284
Review your Practice SAT Answers and Explanations 284

INDEX 285

Introduction

Years ago, during an early gig as a consultant, I sat at a desk that had a *For Dummies* book on the shelf. The book was something office related, like *SQL For Dummies.* I took a sticky note and wrote the word "Ron" with a black marker, then placed the note over the word "Dummies" on the spine of the book, so it read, "SQL For Ron." It fit nicely.

Since starting my test-prep company, I've had students who would go on to do great things, and many have had amazingly successful careers. You, too, are in this group of future success stories. How do I know? Because you're on your way to a good school for a college degree, which will open lots of doors, and you're oh-so-close to getting started. You just need to get past this one hurdle called the SAT.

The SAT challenges your ability to conjure up everything you've covered in high school — some stuff you haven't touched in years. Really all you need is a refresher, some strategies, and practice. This book has all that and more: It goes beyond rehashing what you've learned (and forgotten) by providing exam-specific strategies and tips for answering questions quickly and getting through the exam. There are examples, practice questions, and practice exams to help you build your skills, identify areas you need to work on, and build your confidence for test day.

I know deep in my heart that each person I work with can do well on this exam. Right off the bat, I aim for 100 percent success with each student. You're a little rusty here, haven't seen that there, could use a few tips, but you'll pick it up fast and do just fine. Success on the SAT is like anything else: If you know what to do, and you practice, you'll be fine. I get you started with some review and guidance, and you take it from there.

About This Book

Digital SAT Prep 2025/2026 For Dummies with Online Practice is a whirlwind tour of the SAT. This book takes you through each section of the exam, explaining what the test-makers are looking for and how you can deliver it. This book starts at the very beginning to cover all the basic math and verbal concepts, and because you have the capacity, it then challenges you with SAT-level questions. This book also shows you how to approach the questions, avoid common mistakes, and master the intuitive tricks that help you knock it out of the park.

To earn a top score on the SAT, you have three goals:

1. **Know what's on the exam.**

   That's in this book, so read the whole thing. No matter how well you know a topic, you can discover strategies and avoid common traps, and the SAT has a way of asking a question that's different from what you're used to — or what you learned in the classroom. This book has hundreds of tried-and-true strategies so you can cut through the muck and get the most points on the SAT.

2. Strengthen your weak areas.

Turn to specific sections for targeted information. This book is organized to make it easy for you to find strategies and practice for specific question types that you have trouble with.

For more practice exams and a bonus set of math questions, see the "Beyond the Book" section below.

3. Prepare for the test-taking experience.

You'll need practice exams to get ready for the experience. Packaged with this book are four online practice exams: two in this book, and all four online. When your exam is around the corner, take one or two practice exams in real-life, dress-rehearsal settings. Flip to Part 5 for ten ways to build your skills from the practice exams.

Basically, this book does it all: It prepares you for the exam by bringing your skills from the basic level to the SAT level. What else is there?

There's vocab.

To help you with vocab, as you read through this book, you'll notice that some words have a style all their own. Each SAT vocabulary word in this text appears in *this font,* followed directly by its *connotation* (meaning). Fortunately, the SAT doesn't hammer vocab like it used to, and most of the vocab on the exam is in context, so it's easier to work with. That said, a good way to learn SAT vocab is to encounter it in a question and see what it means along with how it's used. When you get stuck on a vocab word, write it down. This is an effective complement to studying from a list or flash cards.

Icons Used in This Book

Here's how to decode the icons that appear in the margins of this book:

TIP

The Tip icon points out helpful hints about strategy — what all-star test-takers know and rookies need to learn.

WARNING

The Warning icon identifies the sand traps that the SAT writers are hoping you'll fall into as you take the test. Take note of these warnings so you know what to do (and what not to do) as you move from question to question on the real SAT.

REMEMBER

The Remember icon connects a previously discussed strategy to the topic or example at hand.

PLAY

The Play icon indicates an example practice question within the regular chapter text.

Beyond the Book

Besides all the ways this book can help you perform well on the SAT, there are even more online, including these.

- » **Cheat Sheet:** At www.dummies.com, type "Digital SAT Prep 2025-2026 For Dummies cheat sheet" in the search box and you'll find the book's cheat sheet, which gives you last-minute details that you'll want to have at your fingertips, including a rundown of how to get the most points on each SAT section.

- » **Practice questions:** You'll find about 400 SAT-type questions in the practice exams, plus about 50 bonus SAT-style math problems, all online to help you build your competence and confidence. Focus on areas where you need practice and verify that you're up to speed in other areas. You can select the level of difficulty and answer the questions through untimed and timed quizzes, so you can work at your own speed and gain experience working under pressure.

Register online for access to the additional tests and practice:

1. **Register your book or e-book at Dummies.com to get your PIN. Go to** www.dummies.com/go/getaccess.

2. **Select your product from the drop-down list on that page.**

3. **Follow the prompts to validate your product, and then check your email for a confirmation message that includes your PIN and instructions for logging in.**

TIP

If you do not receive this email within two hours, please check your spam folder before contacting us through our Technical Support website at https://support.wiley.com/ or by phone at 877-762-2974.

Now you're ready to go! You can come back to the practice material as often as you want — simply log on with the username and password you created during your initial login. No need to enter the access code a second time.

Where to Go from Here

Get started! No matter what you do next, start simple. You have exactly what you need right here in your hands, so breathe deep and turn the page. It's all you.

1

Getting Started with the SAT

IN THIS PART . . .

Getting to know the SAT

Seeing how the SAT measures your performance

Planning your study time

IN THIS CHAPTER

» Choosing between the ACT and the SAT

» Seeing what the SAT covers

» Scheduling your study time for the SAT

» Accommodating for special needs

» Doing amazing even if English isn't your first language

» Understanding what the SAT looks for

» Getting the SAT scoring

Chapter **1**
What to Expect with the SAT

T he best and easiest way to reduce your anxiety and own the SAT is to become familiar with it. Knowing what to expect means you can plan for it, so nothing on exam day is a surprise.

In this chapter, you find the basics of the SAT, including when, where, and how often you should take it. This chapter also tells you what sort of scores you receive, explains how to deal with special needs, and gives you a peek into the structure of the actual exam. If English isn't your first language, there are tips on getting the edge over your primarily English-speaking competition.

Thinking About the ACT

Most 11th and 12th graders take one of two, or both, giant exams on their way to college. One is the SAT, and the other is the ACT. Most colleges accept both, but you should check with your target schools just to be sure. When you call or email the college admissions office, among your other questions, ask the following:

» Do you require an exam score with my application?

» If so, do you accept both the SAT and the ACT?

» Do you need me to write the exam essay?

You take the ACT as a paper-based test, but at some testing centers, you have the option to take it on the computer. The paper-based and computer-based versions of the ACT are exactly the same in terms of length, types and numbers of questions, difficulty level, and scoring algorithm.

At the time of this writing, the ACT takes between four and five hours, while the SAT has been shortened to just over two hours. It's possible that in response to the revised SAT, the ACT will change even more, with reduced numbers of questions and shorter reading comp passages. At this time there is no indication of other changes to the ACT, so here's a rundown of the differences between the current ACT and the recently revised SAT.

The SAT and the ACT are similar in overall difficulty. The math is about 90 percent the same, but SAT math goes more in depth than ACT math, while ACT math covers more topics. (ACT math has logarithms, for example, which SAT math does not.) Some students may find ACT math easier.

The ACT also has a Science Test, which the SAT does not. To compensate, the SAT has science-based questions mixed into the Reading and Writing section, but not to the extent of the ACT Science Test. Students who struggle with science may prefer the SAT.

The ACT also ends with an optional essay question, which the SAT does not.

SAT Reading and Writing covers similar topics to ACT Reading and Writing however, the SAT combines these into a two-part module that runs slightly over an hour, while the ACT separates Reading and Writing into two tests, or three tests with the optional essay, totaling about two hours (or close to three hours with the essay). The SAT doesn't have an optional essay, so the entire exam is about two and a half hours, while the ACT can run over five hours if you include the essay.

Basically, it sounds like the digital SAT is a better bet, but I would expect the ACT to respond with its own shorter, digital version sometime soon. In the meantime, for more on the ACT overall, pick up *ACT Prep 2025/2026 For Dummies with Online Practice* by Lisa Zimmer Hatch and Scott A. Hatch (published by Wiley).

Besides contacting your target schools and checking their websites, you can find more on the application requirements by checking a college guide. A *college guide* is a *compendium* (thorough collection) of school listings and admission requirements. Many libraries and bookstores carry college guides, and you can also talk with your college counselor, who may also have one.

TIP

If college isn't in your immediate future, you may want to take the SAT just to get it out of the way, while the test topics are still fresh in your head. If your plans include a stint in the armed forces or the Peace Corps before hitting higher education, you can keep your options open by taking the SAT before you go. Then when you're ready to get back into the classroom, you'll have some scores to send to the college of your choice. As of this writing, your SAT scores are officially valid for five years, but that could change, or the college you apply to may require newer scores. Just keep that in mind.

So . . . What's on the Digital SAT?

What are you getting into here? Well, it's nothing you can't handle, but it helps to know what's coming up. Here is the digital SAT testing experience, in this order.

>> Reading and Writing section: Two 32-minute modules consisting of 27 questions each, totaling 64 minutes for 54 questions.

>> Ten-minute break.

>> Math section: Two 35-minute modules consisting of 22 questions each, totaling 70 minutes for 44 questions. You're provided with an on-screen calculator for both modules.

Table 1-1 provides a quick overview of what's on the exam.

TABLE 1-1 **Digital SAT Breakdown by Section**

Section	Number of Questions	Time Allotted
Reading and Writing Module 1	27 questions	32 minutes
Reading and Writing Module 2	27 questions	32 minutes
Break	—	10 minutes
Math Module 1	22 questions	35 minutes
Math Module 2	22 questions	35 minutes

Each section mixes in a few unscored "trial" questions, which are impossible to discern from the actual, scored questions. This is good — it means you don't get an extra, unscored "trial" module.

Note that the paper-based practice SATs from CollegeBoard.org have more questions in each section (33 questions per Reading and Writing module; 27 questions per Math module), but no stated time limit. These practice SATs are excellent for preparing, but they don't reflect the actual testing experience.

Working the Online, Adaptive SAT

Within each module, each question counts exactly the same toward your score: The more questions you get right, the higher your score for that module. An easy question is worth the same as a hard question. Because you can move back and forth within each section, one strategy is to skip around and answer all the easy questions first, then go back and work the hard questions. If you like this idea, *try it out on a practice test* before exam day.

On the computer version of the exam, the *second* Reading and Writing or Math module becomes easier or harder based on your performance on the *first* one. For example, if you do extremely well on the first Math module, the SAT thinks you're good at math, so it makes the second Math module harder. Even if you don't get as many right answers in the second Math module, your score will be good because the questions were harder. Your score will definitely be higher than the score of someone who bombs the first Math module — so the SAT thinks they're not good at math — but does great in the second Math module, because the questions were much easier.

Signing Up before Sitting Down: Registering for the SAT

The SAT is given at multiple times at select high schools and testing centers throughout the United States and in English-speaking schools in many other countries. This section explains how and when to register for an exam and the acceptable methods of payment.

How to register

You can register for the SAT online, by mail, or, if you've taken the SAT before, by phone.

Online registration is simple: Go to www.sat.collegeboard.org/register to create an account, sign up, and choose a test center and date. You need to have a credit card or PayPal account and a digital photo of yourself ready to upload. Be sure the photo meets the College Board's standards: a headshot where your whole face is visible and you're the only one in the photo. Head coverings are okay if they're religious in nature.

You can also register by mail. At the time of this writing, you have to register by mail if you're younger than 13 or older than 21 or if you need to take the exam on a Sunday for religious reasons.

You can also ask your school guidance counselor for a registration form. If you're homeschooled, call the nearest public or private high school, or call the College Board Customer Service Center for help. If you register by mail, you'll have to attach a photo and enclose registration payment (credit card number, a check from a United States bank, or a bank draft).

The College Board Customer Service line within the U.S. is 866-756-7346 and outside the U.S. is 212-713-7789. Hearing-impaired test-takers can call the TTY Customer Service number, which within the U.S. is 888-857-2477 and outside the U.S. is 609-882-4118. You can also contact the College Board by mail at this address: College Board SSD Program, P.O. Box 8060, Mount Vernon, IL 62864-0060.

TIP

However you register, you'll be asked whether you want to sign up for the Student Search Service. Answer yes and fill out the questionnaire. Colleges, universities, and some scholarship-granting organizations receive information about you from this service. Expect lots of emails and letters — a little annoying, perhaps, but it's good to know that the schools are interested in you. You may also discover a school or scholarship that you weren't aware of but that meets your needs perfectly.

WARNING

Scammers are interested in you, too. Don't send personal or financial information to any organization unless you know it's legitimate. You know this, of course, but exam registration and college application is a new game. Not sure something is legit? Call the College Board Customer Service line to check.

When to take the test

The SAT is typically offered seven times a year, and you can take it as often as you want. Ideally, you take it two or three times, but the door is open if you want another chance. Most high schoolers follow this pattern.

>> **Start in the fall of your sophomore year:** Here you take the PSAT/NMSQT, which stands for Preliminary SAT/National Merit Scholarship Qualifying Test, and is sort of a junior SAT, for the first time. For you as a 10th grader, this exam doesn't count for much other than a practice and eye-opener of the series of exams to come. See Chapter 2 for more on the PSAT.

>> **Continue in the fall of your junior year:** Here you take the PSAT/NMSQT again, only this time it counts. If you do well, it opens the door to many scholarship opportunities and special programs. No pressure now.

>> **In the spring of your junior year:** Take the SAT as a first run, which serves as a practice test, though you can send in your scores if you're pleased with them. Note that you can also practice with an unscored practice exam, but this experience isn't quite the same as the real thing. Some juniors take the SAT twice during the spring.

>> **Again in the fall of your senior year:** The SAT strikes again, but this time you're ready, and you should do well enough to use these scores for your application. You also have the chance for a few tries. If you're an early decision candidate, you should take the test in October or November.

>> **Finally, in the winter of your senior year:** You have one more chance to get it right, or if you did get it right, you have one more chance to get that scholarship. By now you're a pro, so success should be right in your hands. There may be some juniors in the room with you.

REMEMBER

The SAT is typically given on a Saturday, but there are exceptions for those who can't on Saturday for religious reasons. If you fall into that category, your SAT may be on a Sunday or a Wednesday following a Saturday SAT day. Get a letter from your religious leader on letterhead and mail it in with your registration form.

TIP

Register early to select a test site. When you register, you may request a test site, but if it's filled, you get an alternate. So don't delay — send in the form or register online as soon as you know when and where you want to take the exam. You'll probably want to test at your own high school, if possible, where the campus setting is familiar to you.

Accommodating Special Needs

Like many products and services, the SAT stresses fairness and equal access for all students, including those with special needs. Even if you don't think you belong in this category, skim this section. You may discover an option that will help you "show what you know" when it matters most.

Learning disabilities

If you have a learning disability, you may be allowed to take the SAT under special conditions. The first step is to get an Eligibility Form from your school counselor. (Homeschoolers, call a local high school.) You may also want to ask your college counseling or guidance office for a copy of the *College Board Services for Students with Disabilities* brochure. If your school doesn't have one, contact the College Board directly or check the testing agency's website (https://accommodations.collegeboard.org).

TIP

Once you're certified for accommodations on any College Board test (an AP, an SAT Subject Test, or the PSAT/NMSQT), you're certified for all College Board tests, unless your need for accommodation arises from something temporary, as described in the next section. If you fall into that category, see the next section for more information.

File the form well in advance of the time you expect to take the test. If the College Board grants you the accommodation, you'll be eligible for extra time on the SAT, which could mean an extra 50 percent of time for each test. So if a regular test-taker has 32 minutes per verbal module, for example, an extended-timer gets 48 minutes.

Physical issues

At no additional charge, the SAT also provides wheelchair accessibility, large-print tests, and other accommodations for students who need them. Be sure to submit your Eligibility Form early so that the College Board can request documentation and get things ready for you. You can send paper documentation or file an Eligibility Form online. Check out `https://accommodations.collegeboard.org` for details.

If a physical issue (say, a broken arm) occurs shortly before your scheduled SAT and you can't easily take the exam at a later date, call College Board Customer Service, explain the situation, and have your physician fill out the forms requesting whatever accommodation you need.

TIP

Questions about special needs? Your high school's counselor or principal can help, or you can check the preceding link or email the College Board (ssd@info.collegeboard.org).

Financial help

If you need financial help, you can apply for a fee waiver, available to low-income high school juniors and seniors who live in the United States, Puerto Rico, and other American territories. (United States citizens living in other countries may also be eligible for fee waivers.) The College Board also gives you four extra score reports for free, along with four request forms for college application fee waivers. The College Board does what it can.

If you're worried about paying for school later on, there are loans, grants, scholarships, and other programs to help you achieve success in college and hopefully your career. There are many, many opportunities and places to look, so talk to your school counselor. That's what the counselor is for!

You can also check with your school counselor for fee-waiver applications. (As with everything SAT, if you're a homeschooler, call a local high school for a form.) And be careful to avoid additional fees when you can. You run into extra charges for late or changed registration and for some extras — super-speedy scores, an analysis of your performance, and the like. (See the section, "Scoring on the SAT," later in this chapter for more information on score-reporting options.)

Making the SAT Work for You as a Foreign Student

This is an opportunity for you to stand out among your high school peers and represent with honors the country where you are a national! A high score on this exam is certainly within your reach, even if English is not your first language, if you know what to do and practice your skills.

For the SAT Reading and Writing section, you may get stuck on some of the academic vocabulary. To work on this, as you practice SAT-level reading, underline and look up any word you don't know. After a while, you'll know enough of the words.

Also, the vocabulary strategy for all SAT-taking students helps you as well: As discussed in this book's intro, be sure to learn any word in *this font*, which is an SAT vocabulary word followed by its *elucidation* (definition).

You also have probably studied the mechanics of English more than your native English-born counterparts, so you may have a better academic understanding of sentence structure and verb form than they do. I have observed many, many times in a class with both English-only and non-native English speakers that after a refresher of the basics of this test, the non-native English speakers often do much better than the native English speakers!

One thing that you can do right now is start reading books in English. Pick movies or novels that you love in your own language and read the English versions. You'll be more into the story, and you'll know the gist of events well enough to pick up the English style of writing. Most importantly, you'll learn the placement of grammar and the style of expressive writing.

For the SAT Math section, the math doesn't change from language to language, so if you can crack the basic language used to put forth the problem, you should do just fine. There may be some minute differences (for example, 2,345.67 in one language may appear as 2.345,67 in another), but the basics are the same, and the small differences are easy to master. Just be sure to practice using SAT materials.

Examining Your Mind: What the SAT Really Looks For

The exam attempts to measure the skills you need to succeed in school and in the workplace. It's not a measure of how smart you are, nor is it a measure of how well you do in school. It measures how adaptable you are, and especially how well you prepare for a giant exam.

TIP

The college application essay is a great place to put your scores in perspective. If your SAT score struggles from a special circumstance, such as a learning disability, a school that doesn't value academics, a family tragedy, or any other reason, you may want to explain your situation in an essay. A good essay gives the college a way to interpret your achievement and to see you, the applicant, in more detail. For help with the college admission essay, check out *College Admission Essays For Dummies* by Jessica Brenner (Wiley).

The SAT doesn't test facts you studied in school. You don't need to know when Columbus sailed the Atlantic or how to calculate the molecular weight of an atom. Instead, the SAT takes aim at your ability to follow a logical sequence to comprehend what you've read and write grammatically well in Standard English. The math portion checks on the math skills you have picked up during your years in high school. The point is that the SAT isn't a giant final exam or a review of high school. It's a test of your *skills, not* your *knowledge.*

Use this to your advantage. The skills for the Reading and Writing section, covered in Part 2, are easy to learn and just take practice to master. The skills for the Math section are also of a limited scope and are captured in Part 3 of this book. In other words, pretty much everything you need to know for the SAT fits into a medium-sized book. There may be an occasional "oddball" question as the SAT steps outside its defined scope of topics, but these questions are very few and very far between.

One *caveat* (disclaimer) to the preceding claim: Everything you need to know for the SAT is right here in this book, *assuming* you already have a basic grasp of English and math. This claim assumes that you have certain skills at the basic high school level: You can read and understand a narrative in English, you can construct a complete sentence in English, and you can execute basic math, such as long division and adding fractions. If any of these topics is an area where you struggle, there are literally thousands of books and resources available to you, many free online or at a library. You can also check with your school for any type of remedial program, including student tutors. This is something you can easily fix and place into the past, and it'll help you far beyond this exam.

Scoring on the SAT

The SAT gives colleges an in-depth look at your skills and performance. If you take the exam more than once, as most students do, you can use the detailed information from your score reports to craft a personalized study program and zero in on the skills you need to fine-tune.

Composite score

Your exam score, called the *composite score*, is the score that everyone is worried about. It's the sum of the Reading and Writing section (200 to 800 points) and Math section (also 200 to 800 points). The maximum composite score is 1600, and the minimum is 400, which you get for showing up.

TIP

You can run through the basics of converting your correct answers to a tangible SAT score in Chapter 15, following the practice exams in Part 4.

Score reports

At the time of this writing, the SAT provides four score reports, which can be sent to your choice of schools. (*Yikes?* Not really. More like, *Yes!*) If you want to send out more reports to more schools, you can do so for a nominal fee. Check the College Board website at www.collegeboard.org for current prices. You can request additional score reports when you sign up for the exam, when you take the exam, or after the fact. At the time of this writing, your scores are good for five years.

After you get your SAT scores, you can order a Question-and-Answer Service (QAS), which shows each question from the exam, which answer you selected, and if applicable, the correct answer. There may be a small fee for this, and the fee waiver may apply. If you are planning to retake the SAT, this service is a lifesaver: It's like turning on a light to see your exam performance. The bad thing is that this service isn't available for some tests, but the good thing is that it *is* available with your PSAT, so use that!

Score reports arrive in your mailbox and at your high school a few weeks after your test, and in your email about a week sooner. The College Board usually posts on its website the date that the test scores will be available.

Last thing. Be sure to create a free College Board account at www.collegeboard.org, where you can check your scores and register for the PSAT and SAT. Here, along with your score, you can find how well you did in comparison to everyone else who took the exam when you did. You can also immediately access the QAS and get right to the questions. Plus, you can get the Bluebook app and practice SAT pdfs, all for free.

Chapter **2**

Strategies for Success

" All things are ready, if our mind be so," wrote William Shakespeare. When you hit test day, your preparation is the key to your success. You know this; it's why you're here. And this chapter outlines the strategies and game plans for you to prepare for the SAT and the opportunities that follow.

SAT prep can start at any point along your high school path and still be effective. In this chapter are ways to plan your studying when the test is a year away, a few months away, and right around the corner. And for those of you who suddenly realize that the test is *next week*, there is a panic-button scenario (and some suggestions on goal planning and time management). Lastly, this chapter tells you what to do the night before and the morning of SAT day, along with steps to take if you're faced with adverse conditions.

Planning Your Prep Time

As soon as you sign up for an SAT, the clock starts ticking. You have only so much time to study and practice, and suddenly the exam is tomorrow morning. The good news: I've taken many a student down this road, with great results, and here I've *curated* (collected) the best success strategies. The following sections show you how to optimize your study and practice time so you can answer the test questions quickly and easily. Note that these strategies are *in addition* to studying with this book.

Starting early: The long-term study time

You're the person who buys summer clothes in December. (Smart! That's when they're on clearance.) You also plan ahead — way ahead. This is not a bad strategy for long-term success in your life and career. When your SAT is roughly a year out, start with these strategies:

» **Sign up for challenging courses in school.** Skip the courses that require papers short enough to tweet and just enough math to figure out how many minutes remain before your next vacation. Go for subjects that stretch your mind. Specifically, stick it out with math at least through Algebra II. If high school is in your rearview mirror, check out extension or enrichment adult-ed courses. Colleges will appreciate this initiative along with your SAT scores.

» **Get into the habit of reading.** Instagram, TikTok, and YouTube don't do the trick. Instead, take on academic journals, established news sources, and any publication aimed toward an adult or college-level audience. The more you read challenging material, the more you build your ability to comprehend it. This will help you in so many ways in life, but on the SAT, it helps you understand vocabulary, analyze reasoning, and deconstruct evidence. Take note of unfamiliar words and check the words online. Also notice how an author makes a point — through description, citing experts, word choice, and so forth. This helps you understand the passages and writing methods of the Reading and Writing section.

» **Take a critical eye.** Read the school or local paper, websites, or any publication, and look for reasoning techniques. They're everywhere, and once you spot them, you see them all over. Is the sales pitch, persuasive argument, or editorial using statistics, emotion, anecdotes, or humor to make its point? As a side benefit, you learn to see through these tactics and challenge the logic.

» **Revisit your math.** Resist the urge to burn your geometry books the minute the semester is over. Keep your math notebooks and especially your old exams. Revisit the questions, especially the ones you missed, because these are the topics you'll see on the SAT. Research shows that memory improves when concepts are reviewed after a period of time, and this will help when the SAT asks you to factor a quadratic, which you may not have done for a couple of years.

» **Take the practice exams in Part 4 of this book.** Work your way through all those questions and then check the answers and explanations to everything you got wrong, skipped, or wobbled on. After identifying areas of focus, you know where you have to practice. There are also free practice exams at www.collegeboard.org.

» **Build up your grammar.** The grammar review in Chapter 4 covers *almost* all of what you need for the Reading and Writing sections, but the SAT likes to throw the occasional "no one is expecting" question. For a more thorough, in-depth review of English grammar, pick up *English Grammar Workbook For Dummies* or *Grammar: 1001 Practice Questions For Dummies* (both authored by Geraldine Woods and published by Wiley).

» **Take the PSAT/NMSQT.** This "mini-SAT" gives you a chance to experience test conditions. It may also open the door to some robust scholarships, including the National Merit Scholarship (the "NMS" in the title of the test). The PSAT is a good preview of the SAT, and when you get your scores, you get to see the questions you missed along with the right answers — which, as stated in Chapter 1, is like turning on a light to see your exam performance.

This is a good, early start. Now continue on to the medium-range plan as the time before your SAT shortens.

Moving along: The medium-term study time

As the SAT moves along its timeline to your door — or something like that — here's the medium-term phase of your plan. This is where you should be when the exam is three to six months out. Don't worry if you didn't start earlier. You have time, and these steps make a huge difference.

>> **Continue sharpening your reading skills.** College-level reading skills matter, so continue reading college- and professional-level materials and looking up words that you don't know. *Peruse* (read carefully) the daily newspaper, either online or in print, and check out the way that stories are told and statistics appear. Also read the editorials and think about how the author argues a point and whether you agree with it.

>> **Work on your writing.** Send a story in to the school newspaper or send letters or emails to a publication editor. Writing for an audience ups your writing game, because you pay much closer attention to your reasoning and grammar. Do this a few times, and you're a pro! This is especially true with the sort of questions that challenge your writing skills, because there are plenty of those that you have to answer correctly on the SAT.

>> **Get an exam study-buddy.** Not a tutor. A tutor is good, but you can also benefit from practicing the SAT with someone on your own level. You get stuck on a question that your friend knows, while your friend needs help that you can provide. The studying process gets a little less tedious, and you'll be glad to know that you're not the only one in the room who doesn't know all the answers.

>> **Revisit the practice exams in Part 4 of this book.** Pay special attention to the questions that you missed before, or if this is your first round, mark those missed questions for review later on. Also check any question that puzzled you or took too much time, even if you guessed the right answer! After you know which sort of question is likely to stump you, read the chapters that explain how to answer those questions.

>> **Revisit your PSAT/NMSQT.** Just as with the practice exams, you need to revisit your performance on an SAT-style exam, and the PSAT is helpful because it shows how you do in an actual exam setting. Plus, you need to make sure that you can handle the topics that you missed on that exam, such as critical thinking, verb parallelism, or coordinate geometry. See the sidebar titled, *Should you take the PSAT/NMSQT?* at the end of this chapter for more on this preliminary exam.

Keep following this plan, and you'll be in fine shape for the SAT. Now to shift your process for the final stretch.

Getting closer: The short-term study time

The SAT is weeks away! Whether you've been following the progression or are starting now, these steps can make a nice difference and add quite a few points to your score.

PLAY

>> **Work or revisit the practice questions in the chapters of this book.** If you can answer the question easily, you're good — but if you struggle with a question, review the chapter pages that show you how to answer it. Look for the questions with the Play icon (shown to the left), and check out the online practice questions that go with this book.

>> **Work at least one practice exam from Part 4 or www.collegeboard.org.** Do your diligence and keep practicing! Get your stamina ready for the SAT marathon, plus get a sense of what's on the exam. Review your practice exam afterward, so you know where to focus. Best case, review it with a friend who is also taking the SAT and has taken the same practice test. Check out Chapter 17 for good ways to use the practice exam to boost your score.

>> **Clear your calendar of all unnecessary activity so you can study as much as possible.** It's time to prioritize, and it's just for a few weeks. Anything else can wait. Right now is crucial, and an hour in the weeks before your exam is worth a *lot* more than an hour in the weeks after. That movie or golf game can wait.

>> **Download and practice with the Bluebook testing app.** This app is free to download from the College Board's website (www.collegeboard.org), and it's the best way to experience what the actual exam is like at a testing center or high school. Here you can take the digital SAT practice test and explore the online calculator, the reference screen with all the formulas, and the ability to annotate text and cross off wrong answers. Make sure you know how the app works. Don't discover these features on exam day — practice using them now.

>> **Check the device requirements.** As of this writing, you can take the digital SAT on your own laptop or tablet, provided it meets the requirements described on the College Board's website. If you don't have a device that meets these requirements, you can borrow one from your school — provided your school has one to spare.

The Exam Is Tomorrow: What to Do the Night Before Your SAT

Your SAT is tomorrow. Scared? That's normal. When you walk into that testing room, *everyone* is scared — except you're more prepared than they are. The fear is normal, so don't deny it. Just accept that tomorrow is a big day and do what you can to control it. More on handling anxiety and taking control coming up in this chapter, but for now, here's what you do on the night before the SAT.

Most important: *Don't study anything.* Instead, get your rest. You've prepared for months (or weeks), and you've built your skills and addressed your gaps. Right now, you need to build your strength, so *get some rest.* There's always one more thing to review, but now is the time to shift focus from studying to conserving energy.

Don't go out. There'll be another party or game. Stay home and relax, maybe read or watch a movie. (No binge watching! You need your sleep.) Have a good, wholesome dinner and avoid anything intense like sushi or spicy food. The last thing you need on exam day is an upset stomach.

Resist the urge to contact friends who are also taking the test. If they're nervous too, their anxiety is not going to help you relax. Instead, *mitigate* (reduce the effect of) your anxiety by taking control of the situation. Take control of the morning by setting your phone alarm and asking your parents or guardians to wake you just in case, so you're not worried about oversleeping. Take further control by getting your stuff together (detailed in the next section) and placing it all in one spot, so it's ready to go and you're not worried about forgetting something. As you take control of the situation, your confidence will follow.

Show Time: What to Do the Day of Your SAT

Whatever your normal morning routine is, do the same on this day. Along these lines, eat something good that you're used to, that has protein (eggs, cheese, meat, tofu, and so on). Stay away from sugary foods (donuts, sugary cereals, and the like) because sugar gives you a surge of energy and then a rush of fatigue. You don't want to crash in the middle of the math section.

If disaster strikes — fever, car trouble, hurricane — and you suddenly can't take the SAT, call the College Board at (866) 630-9305 and request that they transfer your fee to the next available date.

Starting out that morning

Be sure to have the following items with you. Get them together the night before.

» **Admission ticket for the SAT:** Don't leave home without it! You can take a picture, print it, or email it to yourself. Either way, just make sure you know where it is. (If your ticket hasn't arrived, check with the College Board, ideally a week or so before the test.) Without your ticket, you can't get in, and you'll have to do this whole routine over again.

» **Photo ID:** The SAT accepts your driver's license, school ID, passport, or almost any other official document that includes your picture. The SAT doesn't accept your Social Security card, credit card, or anything without your picture. If you're not sure what to bring, ask your school counselor or check the College Board website at www.collegeboard.org.

» **Water bottles:** Bring a couple of chilled water bottles to drink during your breaks. Don't bring anything sugary like soda or juice, because you'll crash and get even more thirsty. If you want electrolytes, such as a smart water, make sure it's a drink that you've tried before. If it gives you a headache, you don't want to discover that on the day of the test.

» **Some snacks:** Bring healthy snacks in your backpack, so you don't have to wait in the vending-machine line for a lousy selection. You can eat during your break, and your water bottles can keep them cold.

After you arrive at the test center, take out what you need and stow the rest of the stuff in a backpack under your seat.

WARNING
Your phone must be completely powered off and put away when you take your exam. You're not allowed to bring a laptop or tablet. Nor can you bring scrap paper, books, or other school supplies (including rulers, compasses, and highlighters). Leave them behind. Also no smartwatches. Check www.collegeboard.org to confirm everything you can and can't bring.

Taking control of the tension

You'll probably feel nervous when you arrive at the test center. This is normal, and it's okay. If you're prepared, then once you start the exam, you'll realize that it's all the stuff that you practiced, and you should feel better. Try a couple of stretches and head shakes to chase away tension. During the exam, wriggle your feet and move your shoulders up and down whenever you feel yourself tightening up. If you roll your neck, be sure to close your eyes and not to face the other students so you don't risk a charge of cheating. And take a few deep breaths to calm yourself.

Focusing during the test

Keep your eyes on your own screen. If you glance around the room, you may see someone who has already finished. Then you'll panic: *Why is he done, and I'm only on Question 2?* You don't need this kind of idea rattling around in your head. Besides, that student may have skipped to the end. Also, wandering eyes open you to a charge of cheating.

TIP
Hardly anyone gets a perfect score, so don't expect to. And you don't have to, anyway. All you need to do is score higher than many other test-takers, and with these strategies and practice, you will! Once you're in college and/or have a scholarship, the SAT doesn't matter anymore. But for now, you're not trying to get *all* of them right — you're trying to get *most* of them right.

It Isn't You: Testing under Adverse Conditions

Your test isn't actually given by the College Board. It's given by an administrator, or a proctor, qualified by the College Board, and this proctor is required to adhere to certain standards. If something odd happens during the test that you believe negatively affected your score, such as construction noises, no working air conditioning, or anything else that shouldn't be the case, register a complaint with College Board Customer Service right away for a chance to have those scores cancelled and for you to retake the exam, at no charge. Complaining to the testing center staff does no good: You must communicate directly with the College Board. You don't have much time to register this complaint, so don't delay: Talk to your parents or guardians and call (866) 630-9305 as soon as you get home. You can also talk to your school counselor that following Monday. It's likely that other students have the same complaint that you do, and by bringing this to your counselor, you have a stronger case.

REMEMBER

Schools tend to freeze the heck out of the testing rooms, so being chilly isn't grounds for registering a complaint! It does mean that you should prepare by wearing layers that you can remove if needed. Note that you may not be allowed to wear a jacket or a cap, but a sweater is okay.

SHOULD YOU TAKE THE PSAT/NMSQT?

The PSAT used to be short for the *Preliminary Scholastic Aptitude Test,* but now PSAT just means *Pre-SAT.* The NMSQT part still stands for something — *National Merit Scholarship Qualifying Test.* Though it has a two-part name, the PSAT/NMSQT is just one test, but it performs both functions of preparing you for the SAT and screening you for a host of available scholarships. If you're a super brain, the PSAT/NMSQT may move you into the ranks of semifinalists for a National Merit Scholarship, a *prestigious* (high-status) scholarship program, or give you entry to other special programs. You don't have to do anything extra to apply for these scholarships and programs. Just take the test, and if you make the cut, the National Merit Scholarship Program and other organizations will contact you. Some students who do not score well enough to become scholarship semifinalists will receive a Letter of Commendation, which also looks good on your college applications. Even if you're not sure that you'll win a scholarship or receive a letter, you should still take the PSAT/NMSQT. It mirrors the SAT, and though the PSAT is slightly shorter, it gives you a feel for the actual SAT and your performance on a standardized exam.

2

Owning the SAT Reading and Writing Section

IN THIS PART . . .

Knowing the questions on SAT Reading and Writing

Learning and practicing proven strategies

Building your skills with practice questions

IN THIS CHAPTER

» Knowing what to expect on SAT Reading and Writing

» Finding tried-and-true ways to manage your time

» Using proven strategies to answer each question correctly

» Mastering the subject content of reading passages

Chapter 3

Raising Your Best SAT Reading and Writing Score

SAT Reading and Writing isn't like what you're used to. It's composed of short excerpts from works of literature (novels, short stories, poems) and college-level journal articles on literature, science, social studies, and work or careers, each followed by a single question. You're asked to identify such mind-bending concepts as the purpose of a phrase or what's implied by a sentence or a paragraph. The SAT starts with Reading and Writing, so you're also doing this at eight on a Saturday morning.

TIP

If the depth of your regular reading is Instagram and Discord, you're going to struggle with the nuance and complexity of the passages on the SAT. Bring up your reading skills and grammar recognition by reading *Time* magazine, the *New York Times*, the *Wall Street Journal*, or any regular publication aimed at adults, at least once a week, starting now. Besides helping you with the exam, these steps will ease your transition into college where much of your reading and writing will be at this level.

Understanding SAT Reading and Writing

SAT Reading and Writing consists of 54 questions divided into two 27-question modules. (Note that the paper-based practice tests from collegeboard.org has 66 questions split into two 33-question modules, but the online test you take has 54 questions.) Each passage has one to two paragraphs, graphs, or data sets, and a single question. You have 32 minutes per module for 64 minutes total. Here's what to expect on this test.

» **Sentence Completion Questions:** Each question contains one to three sentences with a blank space indicating a missing word. Your task is to follow the logic of the text so that you can choose the best word to fill in the blank. Answering these questions depends on your knowledge of vocabulary and your ability to use the clues in the context of the sentence to find the best word to fill in the blank. There are about six or seven of these questions.

» **Standard English Convention Questions:** Paragraphs of one to three sentences measure your ability to edit text within the conventions of Standard English. A single question after each passage tests your understanding of sentence structure, usage, and punctuation.

» **Critical Reading Questions:** Short excerpts from different content areas are followed by a question that tests your understanding of the writer's craft and structure and/or the information and ideas in the text. The excerpts are taken from literature (prose and poetry), social science, history, and natural science. Some questions are accompanied by a chart or graph, while others are based on a paired set of texts, and the questions may ask you to compare, contrast, or synthesize ideas.

» **Research and Graphics Questions:** Some passages, typically science but sometimes social studies, are based on charts, graphs, or diagrams (often, but not always, accompanied by text), similar to those that appear in textbooks. Some texts are accompanied by graphs or charts, and you analyze the data or integrate information from the text and graphic.

Managing Your Time with Reading Strategies

The biggest challenge is answering all the questions before your time runs out. To address this, use these simple, tried-and-true strategies to answer the most questions and get them right.

1. First read the question.

Each passage is followed by a single question, so see what kind of question it is. This way, you know what you're looking for when reading the passage. If the question asks about Standard English conventions, you know to focus on the grammar. If the question is on critical thinking, you know to focus on the passage's logic.

Look for keywords in the question. Whether the question asks for the writer's main point or purpose, or the choice that *weakens* or *counters* the writer's claim, this clues you in to what to look for while reading the passage.

2. Then read the passage.

Armed with what the question looks for, read the passage and look for grammar or reasoning, based on the task. On the paper practice test, you can mark the text, but on the real exam, you can highlight and annotate right on the screen.

The Bluebook app allows you to highlight and annotate text, so practice using these features with the app.

3. Save the time-intensive questions for last.

Each question in the module is worth the same points, whether you answer it in one minute or five. You don't want to work through the time-intensive questions and then run out of time before reaching the fast questions! If the question looks like it's too time-consuming, mark it for review and come back to it after you've answered the fast questions.

The Bluebook app has a built-in timer, so keep track of how much time you've used and how much time you have left. With 32 minutes per module, you should be halfway through the module (about question 14) at the 16-minute mark.

4. Follow the one-minute-per-question rule.

Imagine this. You take five minutes to answer a tough question, you get it right (which you find out later), and then you run out of time before reaching the last three questions of the module! Who won: you or that tough question?

I'd say the question won: It cost you three right answers at the end. Don't fall for this trap. Instead, if you're stuck on a question, skip it and come back to it later. (Note that this strategy also applies in the Math module.) Follow these steps:

1. Guess an answer. If time runs out before you return to this question, at least you threw a mental dart for a 25 percent chance of getting it right.

2. Mark the question for review. This way, of course, you know which question to return to.

Most students are faster with the Sentence Completion and Standard English Convention questions than they are with the Critical Reading and Research and Graphics questions. This may also be true for you, but try it out on a practice test to be sure.

If you want to return to a question, click Mark for Review right on the screen, above the question. Then you can check the Review screen from anywhere in the module to see a list of questions showing which ones you've marked for review or you've left to answer.

Don't mark for review every question that you have any doubt on! When you have five minutes remaining, and the review screen shows 20 questions marked for review, you have no idea which answers are probably right and which ones are complete guesses that you need to go back to. Instead, mark the question for review *only* if you make a guess.

3. Go on to the next question. Follow the one-minute-per-question rule and complete the module.

If you end up not returning to the question marked for review, at least you (maybe) lost only one point, which is better than losing the handful of points at the end of the module.

Almost no one gets a perfect score. Your job isn't to answer *all* the questions correctly: It's to answer *more* questions correctly than most of the other test-takers. If you missed a question, they may have also missed that question.

Finding the Right Answer, Fast, with More Strategies

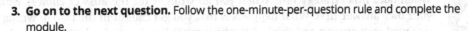

It's all about the strategies, right? With 32 minutes to answer 27 questions per module, you have slightly over a minute per question. With these strategies, that's all you need to find the right answer, or rather, eliminate wrong answers.

1. Cover the answer choices.

Place your hand or scratch paper on the screen to cover the answers. Seems silly, right? But this way, you're not tempted to glance at the answers. Sure, the right answer is there, but three trap answers are also there. Dodge these traps and *focus on the question.*

2. Answer the question yourself.

After reading the question and the passage, answer the question in your own words, *without* looking at the answer choices.

3. Cross off the wrong answers.

Your answer won't match the right answer. It doesn't have to. What it *will* do is make three answer choices appear so far out in left field that they couldn't possibly be correct. Here's what you do:

(a) Move your hand or paper down just a little to show Choice (A).

You're covering the answers, remember? Now show just the first answer. Based on your own answer, could this be right? That answer is hardly ever *yes*. More often it's either *not a chance* or *I'm not sure*. If it's *not a chance*, use the software to cross it off. (The Bluebook app allows this.) If it's *I'm not sure*, leave it. **Don't spend time on it.** Either cross it off or leave it, and *move on*.

(b) Move your hand or paper down a little more to show Choice (B).

Here's the thing. Sometimes an answer is so clearly, impossibly wrong that you can cross it off as soon as you read it. If you're not sure, leave it. Either way, move *quickly* to either cross off or leave each answer choice.

(c) Same thing with Choices (C) and (D).

One at a time, either cross off or leave the answer. Typically, you'll have three crossed off and one remaining, so go with the remaining answer and get to the next question. If you have two answer choices remaining, quickly check them to see which is more likely. If you can't tell, that's okay: Take a guess, mark the question for review, and *move on*.

WARNING

When does this strategy fail? When you go straight for the answer choices without thinking of your own answer first. What happens is that you get caught in the trap of wrong answers, where you read each answer and think, "Maybe *that's* it," and spend valuable time going back and forth to the passage. Don't do that!

Also, *don't doubt your own answer when you read the answer choices.* Sure, the correct answer may contain more depth and detail than your answer — but so may the three wrong answers. *Trust yourself* to answer the question well enough! No matter how far off your own answer is, it'll be good enough for you to eliminate three wrong answers.

REMEMBER

It's okay to miss a question here and there — but it's *not okay* to spend five minutes on one question and then run out of time with a bunch of questions unanswered.

Putting the Strategies to Use with Practice Questions

Strategies take practice. You're not used to them, and it's easy to mess up the first few times. That's okay. Practice the strategies, get them wrong, forget certain steps — *before* exam day. That's what practice is for.

This excerpt is from the science text, *The Dancing Mouse: A Study in Animal Behavior*, by Robert M. Yerkes.

As a rule the dancing mouse is considerably smaller than the common mouse. All the dancing mice had black eyes and were smaller as well as weaker than the common gray house mouse. The weakness, indicated by their inability to hold up their own weight or to cling to an object, curiously enough does not manifest itself in their dancing; in this they are tireless. Frequently they run in circles or whirl about with astonishing rapidity for several minutes at a time.

Detail questions

Detail questions are often *keyword* questions, where you look back in the text for keywords from the question.

PLAY

For example: Which choice best states an unexpected quality of the dancing mouse?

Cover the answer choices! Which detail in the passage was surprising or unexpected?

(A) The dancing mouse is smaller and weaker than the common mouse.

(B) The dancing mouse has black eyes.

(C) The dancing mouse can dance energetically.

(D) The dancing mouse cannot cling to an object.

How did you do? Did you cross off Choices (A), (B), and (D)?

(A)	Smaller and weaker	Cross this off: True, but nothing in the text indicates that this is unexpected.
(B)	Black eyes	Cross this off: True, but nothing in the text indicates that this is unexpected.
(C)	Dance energetically	Leave this one: The text states that the weakness of the dancing mouse does not **curiously** carry over into its dancing.
(D)	Cling to an object	Cross this off: True, but nothing in the text indicates that this is unexpected.

While the descriptions in Choices (A), (B), and (D) are true statements about the dancing mice, nothing in the text indicates these characteristics are surprising. But the text states that *curiously*, the weakness of the dancing mice does not extend to their dancing. The word *curiously* is your clue that Choice (C) presents something unexpected about the dancing mouse.

Here's another example where you focus on a keyword.

PLAY

According to the text, in what way does the dancing mouse not have a weakness?

Cover the answers. In what way do *you* think the dancing mouse is superior? (Never mind how that sounds.) Reread the paragraph and focus on the mouse's abilities. Skim the passage for the keyword "weakness."

It seems that the mouse only has weaknesses, but it's *tireless* in dancing. Keep that in mind now, and cross off the wrong answers:

(A) endurance

(B) muscle strength

(C) visual acuity

(D) tenacity

Did you cross off Choices (B), (C), and (D)? They're so impossible that it *has* to be Choice (A). Here's the process:

(A)	Endurance	Leave this one: "Endurance" is in the ballpark of "tireless."
(B)	Muscle strength	Cross this off: It has nothing to do with "tireless."
(C)	Visual acuity	Cross this off: It's not even close (though the passage mentions the mouse's eyes, don't misinterpret this).
(D)	Tenacity	Cross this off: *Tenacity* means "ability to cling," and though it may relate to "tireless," the passage refers to dancing, not clinging.

WARNING

The word "tireless" by itself could match "tenacity," like when you're clinging to the handles of a jet ski. Be sure to keep the context in mind when checking the answer choices.

Inference and main idea questions

An *inference* is a conclusion that you reach based on evidence, and SAT Reading and Writing has many of these questions. You get a certain amount of information, and then you have to stretch it a little. The questions may resemble the following:

>> The author implies which of the following about college admissions success and using *Digital SAT Prep 2025-2026 For Dummies*?

>> Which of the following statements would the author most likely agree with regarding college and career path?

Inference questions require a certain amount of reading between the lines and thinking about what the writer implies. Read the passage, and do what you did before: Cover the answer choices, answer the question yourself, and cross off wrong answers.

Try this inference question, based on these sentences about the westward journey of settlers during the 19th century.

PLAY

During the arduous cross-country trek, the women generally do the driving, while the men and boys bring up the rear with horses and cattle of all grades, from poor, weak calves to fine, fat animals, that show they have had a good living where they came from.

With which statement would the travelers described in this passage probably agree?

Cover the answers! Of course, you can't predict "which one," but you *can* think of what the answer *could* be. What do *you* think the travelers' attitude would be like? How about, "The women are sick of driving and the men are sick of handling animals."

Now: Cross off wrong answers.

(A) Only healthy animals can survive a long journey.

(B) All livestock should be treated equally.

(C) Gender distinctions are considerations in assigning work.

(D) Many pioneers are motivated by greed.

Did you cross off Choices (A), (B), and (D)? They're so impossible that it *must be* Choice (C). Here's the detail:

(A)	Only healthy animals can survive a long journey.	Cross this off: no mention of that.
(B)	All livestock should be treated equally.	Cross this off: no mention of that either.
(C)	Gender distinctions are considerations in assigning work.	Maybe. The men handled animals and the women drove. Leave this one.
(D)	Many pioneers are motivated by greed.	This may be true, but it doesn't match your answer and it's not supported by anything in the passage.

Now for a main idea question from the same short passage.

Which of the following is closest to the main idea of the passage?

PLAY

Cover those answers. What do *you* think the main idea is? Something like, "The settlers had a difficult journey west." Keep it simple.

Now cross off wrong answers:

(A) The cattle varied in quality.

(B) The westward journey was slow and difficult.

(C) Horses brought up the rear.

(D) Women were better drivers even then.

Did you cross off Choices (A), (C), and (D)? They're so far from your answer that it *must be* Choice (B). Here's why:

(A)	The cattle varied in quality.	Cross this off: It may be true, but it's not the main idea, and it doesn't match your answer.
(B)	The westward journey was slow and difficult.	Leave this one: It's not far from your answer.
(C)	Horses brought up the rear.	Cross this off: Also true, but it's not the main idea, and it also doesn't match your answer.
(D)	Women were better drivers even then.	Cross this off: It may be true through the ages, but it doesn't match your answer.

Note a pattern in these main idea answer choices: Even the wrong answers may be true and/or stated somewhere in the passage, but being true or stated doesn't make it the *main idea*.

Writer's purpose questions

Writer's purpose questions ask you to figure out what the writer is trying to accomplish in the passage. Writers write for so many different reasons. Does the passage make a claim? Support or refute a point of view? Challenge an idea that is accepted by others? Offer a new interpretation? Your task is to determine why the writer wrote this passage.

PLAY

To cite the old proverb, "We live in interesting times." One indicator: Just pause from reading this book for a moment and reflect on the recently invented digital devices you have close at hand. Open up your smartphone or tablet and observe a cornucopia of entertainment and lifestyle apps — games, photography, music, cooking, sports — as well as social media and messaging apps that link you to friends, family, and colleagues across the globe, anytime. Most of us have instant access to the world's information via powerful, personalized search engines that fit in our pockets. Later in the book we talk to experts who now wonder about the burdens of being always connected. But how often have you wondered, "How on Earth did we live without our devices?"

Which choice best states the writer's purpose in including the proverb?

(A) To place attention on how interesting modern devices can be

(B) To show the foresight held by old wisdom

(C) To remind the reader that things have always been changing

(D) To reflect on how things today are so different

Cover the answers. In your own words, describe why you think the author quotes an old proverb in a passage about new electronics? Possibly the writer wants to remind you that even among all these new things (digital devices, etc.), all the old things were new once, so there has always been change.

Now, thinking about your answer, cross off wrong choices. Did you cross off Choices (A), (B), and (D)? You're left with Choice (C), which is close to your own answer.

Practicing with Reading Passages

SAT Reading passages come in three basic flavors: Literature, Social Studies, and Science. The Literature passages include excerpts from prose (short stories, novels, essays) and poetry. These passages aren't in any particular order, so you may have to switch gears from poetry to science just like that.

Social studies

If the passage is about social studies (history, anthropology, sociology, education, cultural studies, and so on), keep these tips in mind when you read the whole passage:

>> **Go for the positive.** The SAT usually isn't critical about its topics, so if you see a question about the author's tone or viewpoint, look for a positive spin.

>> **Note the structure.** The passage frequently presents a claim and supports it with facts, statistics, or quotations from experts. If you're asked about the significance of a particular detail in a passage, the detail is probably evidence in the case that the author is making.

>> **Identify cause and effect.** History and social studies passages often explain *why* something happens. Search for keywords such as *therefore, hence, consequently,* and others that signal a reason.

> » **Look for opposing ideas.** Experts, including historians, are into criticizing each other's interpretations of archaeological discoveries or important events. (Maybe they do this to assert themselves, but anyway . . .) Look for the opposing sides, or find the main theory and the objections to it.

To put these tips into action, here is a brief history passage taken from *To and Through Nebraska*, by Frances I. Sims Fulton, describing settlers traveling to the West during the 19th century.

PLAY

During all this time, and despite the disagreeable weather, emigrants from the cities of the Northeast to the wilderness in the West keep up the line of march, traveling in their "prairie schooners," as the great hoop-covered wagon is called, into which, often are packed their every worldly possession, and have room to pile in a large family on top. Sometimes a sheet-iron stove is carried along at the rear of the wagon, which, when needed, they set up inside and put the pipe through a hole in the covering. Those who do not have this convenience carry wood with them and build a fire on the ground to cook by; cooking utensils are generally packed in a box at the side or front. The coverings of the wagons are of all shades and materials. When oil cloth is not used, they are often patched over the top with their oil-cloth table covers, saving them from the rain.

Which choice best states the purpose of the details about the wagon?

Cover the answers. In your own words, why does the author describe the covered wagons in so much detail? Probably to give an example of how the travelers are resourceful and clever. Now cross off wrong answers:

(A) Reveal the convenience of covered wagons.

(B) Emphasize the ingenuity of the travelers.

(C) Show that the travelers were ill-equipped for life on the frontier.

(D) Contrast life in the city with life in the wilderness.

Did you cross off Choices (A), (C), and (D), leaving Choice (B) as the only possible answer? Here's the rationale. According to the passage, the travelers pack everything they need into one wagon. Some have more than others, but those who, for example, lack stoves "carry wood with them and build a fire on the ground." They protect themselves from the rain with either a wagon cover or a tablecloth.

PLAY

Which of the following best fits the theme of this passage?

Cover the answers. In your own words, what's the passage mainly about? Maybe something like, "Traveling and camping in a covered wagon." Perfect. Now cross off those wrong answers:

(A) Cooking on the frontier

(B) Chasing the gold rush

(C) Traveling in a prairie schooner

(D) Economics of the Old West

Cross off Choice (A), because even though cooking is part of it, it's not the main idea. Cross off Choice (B) which, though it may be true, isn't specific enough, and more importantly, doesn't match your answer. Choice (C) stays: Remember that "prairie schooner" is what they called the covered wagons. Cross off Choice (D), which isn't even mentioned in the passage. Choice (C) is left, so that's what you go with.

Science

Science passages don't rely on your knowledge of the topic: Everything you need to know to answer the questions is in the passages. You are expected to know the basics — for example, the Earth orbits the Sun, water boils when it's heated, cells divide — but there's no need to study the science topics to prepare for these passages. Instead, practice the strategies.

These passages cover such science topics as biology, chemistry, environmental science, physics, experiments, and various phenomena. Try this approach when reading a science passage:

» **Search out the facts.** Whether describing an experiment, survey, or observation, all the information you need to know is in the text or in the graphic element. Pay attention to numbers, including percentages, populations, and rates of growth or change.

» **Don't worry about technical terms, but do know general science vocabulary.** If you see a strange word, the definition is probably tucked into the sentence. You won't encounter a question based on the definition of *Tephritidae* unless the passage explains what it is. (It's a type of fruit fly.) You should, however, know general terms that pop up frequently in science-related material, such as *control group* (a group that doesn't participate in an experiment and serves as a point of comparison) and *catalyst* (something that causes or increases the rate of change, as in a chemical process). As you work through practice exams, jot down these general terms from the answer explanations, because you may see them again on exam day.

» **Identify the argument.** Some SAT science passages present a dispute between two viewpoints. The question may zero in on the evidence for each scientific theory or hypothesis, and then quiz you about each author's stance.

» **Notice the examples.** The SAT science passages tend to offer examples both in the text and in the graphics. The questions may ask what the examples prove.

If the question includes a graphic or chart, follow these guidelines:

» **Look at everything.** The title; the explanation on the top, bottom, or sides; the labels inside a diagram — *everything*. Don't memorize it, but notice it: Is there a pattern or contrast? Are the numbers on the side in thousands? If a graph reaches the level of 12, you need to know whether this represents 12 actual or 12 thousand.

» **Note the variables.** The *variable* is the part that changes. Some graphs include more than one — perhaps a solid line showing peanut butter sales and a dotted line tracing jelly sales.

» **Note the relationship between the graphic and the text.** Usually these work together. A bar graph may tell you how many test-takers earned scholarships, while the text may explain how one scholarship freed up funds for a new Jeep. It could happen. Anyway, together these statistics paint a clear picture.

Try this visual-elements question:

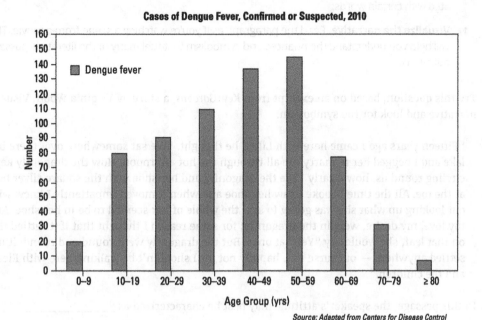

Cases of Dengue Fever, Confirmed or Suspected, 2010

Source: Adapted from Centers for Disease Control

The information in the passage supports which statement about Dengue fever?

PLAY

Cover the answers. In your own words, what do you think is up with the fever? It seems to hit middle-aged folks the hardest. Good thing you're young. Anyway, with this middle-aged point in mind, cross off the wrong answers:

(A) Infants are less likely to contract Dengue fever than the elderly.

(B) In 2010, most cases of Dengue fever occurred in people ages 40 to 60.

(C) The risk of catching Dengue fever rises with age.

(D) Dengue fever is especially dangerous for infants and children.

Choices (A), (C), and (D) are easy targets to cross off, leaving Choice (B) as the only possible answer. This is because the bars for ages 40 to 49 and 50 to 59 are higher than those for other age groups.

Literature

Questions on literature may ask you to read part of a poem or story and interpret the lines, understand a character's motivations, understand the theme, describe the structure of a text, or indicate the function of a selected line from the text.

Keep these tips in mind:

» **Look for the big picture.** Ask yourself, "What do I know about what's going on in this poem or story?" Things may be symbolic or representative, or they might stand out in the author's narrative for a reason. For example, something like, "Joan never forgot seeing the keys on the table." What's important about those keys? Pay attention to how this detail in the story reveals something about Joan's character.

>> **Stay attuned to word choice.** A literature passage is perfectly suited to questions about the author's tone (*bitter, nostalgic, fond, critical,* and so forth). Pay attention to the feelings associated with certain words.

>> **Visualize the narrative.** Read the paragraph as if you're watching a scene from a movie. This will help you understand the nuances and symbolism that fuel many of the literature passage questions.

Try this question, based on an excerpt from *Kew Gardens*, a story by Virginia Woolf. Visualize the narrative and look for the symbolism:

PLAY

"Fifteen years ago I came here with Lily," he thought. "We sat somewhere over there by a lake and I begged her to marry me all through the hot afternoon. How the dragonfly kept circling round us: how clearly I see the dragonfly and her shoe with the square silver buckle at the toe. All the time I spoke I saw her shoe and when it moved impatiently I knew without looking up what she was going to say: the whole of her seemed to be in her shoe. And my love, my desire, were in the dragonfly; for some reason I thought that if it settled there, on that leaf, she would say "Yes" at once. But the dragonfly went round and round: it never settled anywhere — of course not, happily not, or I shouldn't be walking here with Eleanor and the children."

In this passage, the speaker's attitude may best be characterized as _____.

Cover the answers. What do you think characterizes the speaker's attitude? Maybe something like, desperate for the dragonfly to make Lily say yes, but then glad it didn't? Now cross off the wrong answers:

(A) mocking

(B) confused

(C) nostalgic

(D) argumentative

Desperate and glad don't connect with Choices (A), (B), or (D), so cross those right off, leaving Choice (C) as the only possible answer. And it's right. Here's why: In this paragraph, the speaker looks at the past, remembering an afternoon when he "begged" Lily to accept his marriage proposal. He's feeling pleasure and sadness at remembering the past, which of course is *nostalgic,* Choice (C). The sadness shows in Lily's refusal, which he now sees "happily." Choice (B), confused, doesn't match because he wasn't confused: He simply changed his mind, and apparently dodged a bullet.

And, of course, SAT Literature loves symbolism. Try this one:

PLAY

In this passage, Lily's shoe most likely represents _____

Cover the answers. What do *you* think her shoe represents? Maybe a counterpart to the dragonfly that will not cooperate and also Lily's feelings. Something like that. Your answer doesn't have to be close. It just has to be something that you think of without looking at the answers. Now cross off wrong ones.

(A) Lily's desire to protect others

(B) Lily's reluctance to settle down

(C) Lily's love for the narrator

(D) the narrator's attraction to Lily

See? When you think of your own answer, even if it's far out there, it makes the wrong answers *really easy* to cross off. You should have easily crossed off Choices (A), (C), and (D), leaving Choice (B), though iffy, as the only possible answer, and the right one. See, *that* is how you turn a challenging question into an easy one.

TIP

The answer that you think of hardly ever matches the right answer exactly. That's okay — *it doesn't have to.* Your self-thought answer serves a much more important role: *It makes the wrong answers stand out like weeds in a garden.* Cross 'em off, go with the remaining one, and that's all you have time to do in the roughly one-minute-per-question that you get in the Reading and Writing section.

Poetry

Reading poetry is a little different from reading prose (sentences and paragraphs). Poetry is written in lines, typically in a *cadence* (rhythm), and it may have unusual word order.

On the SAT you may read short poems or excerpts from longer poems. Be sure to review any introductory information, as it provides helpful context to the poem.

Try this one:

PLAY

The following poem was written by British poet William Wordsworth in 1802.

My Heart Leaps Up When I Behold

My heart leaps up when I behold

A rainbow in the sky:

So was it when my life began;

So is it now I am a man;

So be it when I shall grow old,

Or let me die!

The Child is father of the Man;

And I could wish my days to be

Bound each to each by natural piety.

Which choice best describes the overall structure of the text?

Cover the answers. How would you describe the structure of the text? The speaker sees a rainbow that makes him happy always and forever (now, as a boy, still as an old man). Your answer doesn't have to be perfect: It just has to be close.

Now cross off wrong answers.

(A) The writer examines an occurrence in nature and realizes it's a sign that his life is almost over.

(B) The writer first examines his outer life and then compares that insight to his inner life.

(C) The writer finds joy in a natural phenomenon and traces that response through three time periods in his life.

(D) The writer sees a natural phenomenon and then questions its role in his life.

Cross off Choice (A): The writer doesn't think the rainbow is a sign that his life is over.

Cross off Choice (B): The writer doesn't compare his outer life to his inner life.

Keep Choice (C): The writer finds joy in the rainbow and connects it to phases in his life.

Cross off Choice (D): The writer doesn't question the role of the rainbow in his life.

And the correct answer is Choice (C). But you already knew that.

See how this works? When you think of your own answer, even if it's not even nearly anywhere close to the correct answer, it still does its job by making the wrong answers *easier* to cross off. *That* is how you turn a challenging question into an easy one. Now, build your skills by exploring the topics and practicing the strategies for the questions in the next two chapters.

Chapter **4**

What Are They Saying: Sentence Completion and Grammar Questions

N ow, start fine-tuning the strategies from Chapter 3. Stick with the one-minute-per-question rule, and remember: Almost no one gets a perfect SAT score, but as long as your score is higher than the scores of most other SAT-takers (which it will be, because you're using this book, and they're not), you'll do well enough to reach or exceed your goals in college admissions.

Completing Sentences and Using In-Context Vocabulary

To answer these questions, consider the context of the narrative, and pay attention to both the definition and the connotation (or feeling and situation) associated with the word. Remember the strategies:

1. Cover the answer choices.

2. Answer the question yourself.

3. Cross off wrong answers.

These strategies are detailed in Chapter 3 and should be automatic for SAT Reading and Writing. Try them out on this question:

PLAY

The U.S. Fish and Wildlife Service warns campers, hikers, and hunters to avoid encounters with bears. In any encounter with a bear in the wild, the behavior of the human matters. If a bear is rummaging through a trash can and takes little notice of you, then slowly leave the area and move to a safer location. If the bear appears to be more curious or aggressive and approaches, stand your ground and be prepared to use bear spray. The bear's behavior should _____ your response.

(A) ignore

(B) mimic

(C) determine

(D) follow

Now for the strategy.

> **First:** Cover the answer choices and fill in the blank yourself. Consider the context clues in the sentence. The text states that *in encounters with a bear, the behavior of the human matters.*
>
> **Next:** Think logically. If you take different actions depending on what the bear does, then the bear's behavior should let you know what you should do.
>
> **Now:** Think of the word that you would use to fill in the blank, without looking at the choices (because they're covered up, right?). You probably came up with a word like "cause." Now that you have your answer, cross off the wrong answer choices.
>
> Choice (A) is out, as you can't rely on the bear to ignore your response. Cross it off.
>
> Choice (B) isn't very logical, so cross it off.
>
> Choice (C) makes sense. If your response depends on the bear's behavior, then the bear's behavior should determine (or cause) your response. Leave it.
>
> Choice (D) doesn't work as you can't count on the bear to follow your actions. Cross it off.
>
> The remaining answer is the correct answer, Choice (C).

Nice. Now for some more.

PLAY

Images from the Hubble Space Telescope reveal a small galaxy labeled UGCA 307. It consists of a diffuse band of stars containing red bubbles of gas that mark regions of recent star formations. Appearing as just a small patch of stars, UGCA 307 is a diminutive dwarf galaxy without a _____ structure, resembling nothing more than a hazy patch of passing cloud.

(A) blurry

(B) brittle

(C) heavy

(D) defined

Use the strategy: Cover the answer choices, read the sentence, and focus on the context clues. It's important to remember you are looking for a word that describes what the structure of the galaxy is *without*. What do you know about the structure of UGCA 307?

> ❯❯ It's a small galaxy.
>
> ❯❯ It appears as a patch of stars.
>
> ❯❯ It resembles a hazy patch of passing cloud.

So, what kind of structure does UGCA 307 not have? If the galaxy resembles a hazy patch, then it is without a clear shape or a sharp outline.

Now check the answers.

(A) blurry: That is what it does look like, so it wouldn't be without a blurry structure. Cross it out.

(B) brittle: There's nothing in the text about soft or brittle, so brittle doesn't make sense. Cross it out.

(C) heavy: Again, nothing in the text about weight. Cross it out.

(D) defined: Having a defined structure is the opposite of having a hazy shape, so leave this one.

Choice (D) remains, so go with that.

The correct answer is Choice (D).

Now for another:

PLAY

Raj was _____ about performing in the student talent show. Although he was pleased and honored about being chosen, he was nervous about performing before such a large audience of his classmates, friends, and family.

(A) cheerful

(B) proud

(C) fearful

(D) ambivalent

You have several context clues in this sentence, but they seem to contradict each other:

» Raj was pleased.

» Raj was honored.

» Raj was nervous.

The missing word obviously describes Raj, so how does he feel? Seems he's both pleased and nervous, so your answer is something like *mixed up, confused,* or *unsure.*

Now cross off wrong answers.

(A) cheerful: Yes, but he's also nervous. Cross it out.

(B) proud: Yes, but he's also fearful. Cross it out.

(C) fearful: Yes, but he's also pleased and honored. Cross it out.

(D) ambivalent: If you don't know this word, the prefix *ambi-* means "both" (like ambidextrous), and Raj feels both pleased and nervous. *Ambivalent* means having mixed or contradictory feelings and is the perfect word to fit in the blank.

The correct answer is Choice (D).

As you enhance your SAT prep by reading college-level publications (you *are* doing this, aren't you?), do a quick look-up of any unfamiliar word and jot down (or just think of) what it means. This is easy enough. If you're reading online, right-click or tap the word; if you're reading print, you can actually say, "Okay Google (or Siri, or Alexa), define *nomenclature.*"

Killing It Softly: The SAT Grammar Review

This grammar review is quick and painless, and if you're pretty good at grammar, it's a good refresher and heads-up of what to expect. Here are the most commonly asked grammar topics on the SAT.

Grammar and punctuation

The conventions of Standard English questions cover the basic rules of grammar, usage, and rhetoric that you are expected to know in college. On these questions, you'll see a blank space in a text that you have to fill in with a choice that best completes the sentence according to the conventions of Standard English. Later, in the section, "Killing It Softly: The SAT Grammar Review," you'll find a further review of grammar topics to know for the exam — and for college. But for now, here are some topics to get you started.

>> **Incorrect punctuation:** Apostrophes and commas may be extra, missing, or in the wrong place. The SAT also mixes up colons and semicolons for you to sort out.

>> **Incomplete sentences:** *Run-ons* (having two subjects and two verbs) must be properly joined, and *fragments* (such as a subject but no verb — for example, "The dog.") must be completed.

>> **Misplaced modifiers:** A *modifier*, which is just an adjective in more than one word, must be near the noun that it modifies. For example, this is incorrect: "The skier went off the trail, laughing loudly." *Laughing loudly* is the modifier, so it should be near *the skier*, not *the trail*; otherwise, the sentence reads as if the *trail* were laughing. Maybe it was.

>> **Wrong homophones:** Do you turn right or turn write? Is the tree taller than or taller then the tent? There are many homophones in English, but the SAT just asks about the common ones.

>> **Wrong-tense verbs:** Make sure the verb tense expresses the right time for an event or state of being. Also check for subject-verb agreement, which especially appears in parallel structure. Oh, right — parallel structure.

>> **Parallel structure:** This means that if one noun has a few verbs, say, "the dog runs, jumps, and pants," then each verb is in the same tense. It's not always that simple, but it's always that easy.

Besides what *to* look for, here's what *not* to look for. This is the Don't Worry About list:

>> **Don't worry about spelling.** The SAT doesn't test spelling except for those homophones.

>> **Don't worry about capitalization.** The SAT very infrequently takes on capitalization. Assume that a word is capitalized properly unless a glaring mistake jumps out at you.

When you answer the conventions of Standard English questions, be sure that your answer choice completes the sentence without any grammatical error. You must be able to place the answer choice in the blank and end up with a proper result.

Ready to practice? Try this sample question.

The water beyond the mangrove trees _____ including tires, chunks of wood, and plastic trash bags.

(A) were not only was polluted but also laden with debris

(B) not only polluted but were also laden with debris

(C) not only polluted but also debris was laden there

(D) was not only polluted but also laden with debris

This sentence has one subject, *the water*, paired with two predicates, *was polluted* and *laden with debris*. The verb *was* is missing from *laden with debris*. Choice (A) uses the plural verb *were* instead of the singular verb *was* to agree with water, so cross it off. Choices (B) and (C) remove *was* from *polluted*, among other errors, so cross them off as well. Choice (D) places *was* before *not only*, so *was* applies to both predicates, and is the correct answer.

For a full-scale grammar refresher, take a look at the latest editions of *English Grammar For Dummies* and *English Grammar Workbook For Dummies* (both authored by Geraldine Woods and published by Wiley).

Transitions

A *transition* establishes the relationship between two clauses, which are usually a series of events. The question asks you to pick the transition that makes the most sense. For example, you wouldn't say, "She got in her car *because* she drove away" or "She got in her car and *however* drove away." You would say, "She got in her car and *then* drove away."

Here are some common transitions that you'll find on the SAT.

>> **Contrast:** "He loves ice cream, *but* he hates Rocky Road." Other contrast words include *however, although, otherwise, on the other hand,* and *never/nonetheless.*

>> **Joining:** "She loves music, *and* she loves the blues." Other joining words include *moreover, further, likewise, in addition,* and *besides.*

>> **A results in B:** "He watered the plants, *so* they grew tall." Other "A results in B" words include *therefore, afterwards,* and *consequently.*

>> **B results in A:** "The car was clean *after* she washed it." Other "B results in A" words are *because* and *since.*

Don't try to memorize these, but rather recognize them and the logic of the relationships they establish in the sentence. That's easier and more useful. Try it out on this practice question.

The sequoia, a type of redwood, is the largest species of tree in the world, growing as tall as 280 feet. _____ the largest specimen is General Sherman, which can be found in California's Sequoia National Park.

(A) Furthermore,

(B) Otherwise,

(C) Therefore,

(D) However,

California's General Sherman is an *example* of the giant sequoia, so out go Choices (B) and (D). The species didn't *result* in Sherman, so cross off Choice (C). The only answer left is Choice (A), *furthermore,* which is a *joining* transition and supports the example.

Verb matching

Verb matching includes singular to singular, plural to plural, and consistent verb tense. In terms of agreement, the SAT asks about:

>> Subject-verb pairs

>> Pronoun-antecedent pairs

Subject-verb agreement

A *verb* expresses action or state of being; the *subject* is whoever or whatever is *doing* the action or in the state of being. A singular subject takes a singular verb, and a plural subject takes a plural verb. Check out these examples:

>> "The *snowmobiler chases* James Bond." *Snowmobiler* is a singular subject; *chases* is a singular verb.

>> "Six more *snowmobilers join* the pursuit." *Snowmobilers* is a plural subject; *join* is a plural verb.

The SAT expands upon this with trickier arrangements, like these:

>> **There/here.** These words aren't subjects. The subject comes *after* the verb, like this: "Here are three calculators." The subject is *calculators,* matching the verb *are.*

>> **Either/or** and **neither/nor.** These words may join two subjects, so match the verb to the closest subject:

- "Neither the car nor the *tires are* in the garage." *Tires* is the closest subject, so the plural verb *are* is correct.

- "Neither the tools nor the *truck is* in the shop." *Truck* is the closest subject, so the singular verb *is* is correct.

>> **Interrupters between the subject-verb pair.** If an interrupter, such as a modifier or prepositional phrase, comes between the subject and the verb, it doesn't change the verb form.

This is correct: "The soda machine, along with the games, *is* perfect for the basement." *Along with the games* is an interrupter, so the singular subject *soda machine* stays with the singular verb *is.* An interrupter could also be set off by dashes: "The dog — after chasing the cats — is chasing a car."

REMEMBER

Two singular nouns joined by *and* make a plural. For example, "The fox and the hound *are* both inside." *The fox* and *the hound* together make a plural subject.

Noun-pronoun agreement

The noun that the pronoun refers to is called an *antecedent*. Regardless of what it's called, it's the word that a pronoun replaces. In the sentence, "The receiver chased the ball and caught it," *it* is a pronoun, and *the ball* is the antecedent because *it* stands for *the ball.* The rule on antecedents is simple: Singular goes with singular and plural goes with plural. You probably already know all the easy applications of this rule. In the *receiver/ball* sentence, you'd never dream of replacing *the ball* with *them.* The SAT-makers, however, go for the tricky combinations:

>> **Pronouns containing *one, thing,* or *body* are singular.** Match these pronouns with other singular pronouns.

"*Everyone* brought *his or her* cheat sheet." *Everyone* is singular because it has *one* in it, and it goes with the singular *his or her*. Same with *none* and *nobody*. Note that modern convention uses *they*, but if you have to select a singular pronoun on the SAT, go with *his or her*. More on this below.

» **Either, neither, each,** and **every are singular.** These words are sometimes followed by phrases that sound plural (*either of the boys* or *each father and son*), but these words are always singular.

"*Neither* of the girls brought *her* calculator." *Neither* is singular, so it goes with *her*, also singular.

WARNING

Watch out for traps based on recent changes in language. You may hear (or say) something like, "*Someone* is at the door, so let *them* in." However, *someone*, which is singular, doesn't go with *them*, which is plural, so on the SAT this would be wrong, even though in some forms of modern writing, this may be considered correct.

Verb tension

In the SAT Reading and Writing section, *tense* isn't just how you feel on the exam. It's the verb quality that indicates relative time. Remember these rules:

» **The helping verbs *has* and *have* connect present and past actions.** When you see these helping verbs, something started in the past and is either still going on or just stopped. ("Raja *has been* playing soccer all afternoon, and Suja *had been* watching until her phone rang.")

» **The helping verb *had* places one past action before another past action.** ("Asha *had scored* a goal before Raja did.")

» **The tense doesn't change for the same subject.** A sentence where the verbs change tense isn't correct. "Charise *is cooking* dinner and *watches* TV," should be, "*watching* TV." If the second verb has a different tense, it needs a new subject. More on this below, in *Parallel writing*.

TIP

A verb can also be contrary to the fact. This just means that when a statement isn't true, it's worded differently. (*If I were creating the SAT, I would dump all the grammar questions. If I had known about the grammar questions, I wouldn't have thrown my English textbooks into the pool.*) The *if* part of the sentence — the untrue part — gets *were* or *had*, and the other part of the sentence features *would*. The SAT-makers may place *if I would* or *if I was* to trip you up. Your job, of course, is to catch that and mark *if I were*. Don't worry — these aren't common.

Parallel structure

A favorite SAT question concerns *parallelism*, the way a sentence keeps its balance. The basic premise is simple: In a sentence, each verb attached to the same noun *must be* in the same tense. You can't "surf and soak up sun and playing in the sand" because *playing* is a different tense. You can "surf and soak up sun and play in the sand" without any problems — well, without any grammatical problems. Keep these ideas in mind:

» **Look for lists.** Whenever two or three verbs are in the same sentence, they may have the same subject. Check the subject and make sure the verbs match.

» **Look for paired conjunctions.** Conjunctions are joining words. Three common paired conjunctions are *either/or, neither/nor,* and *not only/but also*. When you encounter one of these pairs, make sure the verbs are in the same tense.

» **Look for two complete sentences joined together: Usually the verbs are both active or both passive.** In an active-verb sentence, the subject is doing the action ("The quarterback threw the ball.") or is in a state of being ("The linebacker is in the game."). In a passive-verb sentence, the subject receives the action of the verb ("The ball was thrown by the quarterback."). A parallel sentence needs to be consistent with active or passive verbs.

Pronoun cases

Pronouns have *case*, which refers to using *he* versus *him*, *she* versus *her*, *they* versus *them*, *it* versus . . . well, *it* is the same. Anyway, the rule is simple: Use a subject pronoun (*he, she, they*) for the subject, and an object pronoun (*him, her, them*) for almost everything else. Here's how you tell the difference:

» **Identify the subject and the object.** The *subject* is the one that's doing something, and the *object* is the target of the action. For example, if you see, "The referee penalized the player," the *referee* is the subject and the *player* is the object. In pronoun case, this sentence would read, "*He* penalized *him*."

» **Isolate the pronoun.** If you see, "The proctor gave the test to three boys and she," you may not notice the error. Cut out "the three boys," however, and you have, "The proctor gave the test to *she*." Now the error is easier to spot: The sentence should read, "The proctor gave the test to *her*."

REMEMBER

One thing: The pronoun *must* be clear. Something like, "Mary and Sandy each used the book, and she aced the exam!" won't fly.

Punctuation

Some punctuation also appears in the SAT Reading and Writing section. Here is what you need to know:

» **Join sentences correctly.** Sometimes a comma and a *conjunction* (joining word) — for example, *and, or, but,* and *nor* — do the job, and sometimes you need a semicolon. Note that a comma alone doesn't do the trick: you also need the conjunction. Transition words (*consequently, therefore, nevertheless, however*) look like they could join two sentences, but they can't — they need a semicolon. More on the semicolon next.

» **Know semicolons.** The *semicolon* (;) joins two complete sentences. It takes the place of the *comma* with *and*. "The dog ran outside, *and* the cat chased it" could also be, "The dog ran outside; the cat chased it." Typically, the SAT has a complete sentence *before* the semicolon — you need to make sure there's a complete sentence *after* it. Also, the semicolon never goes with the word *and* — it takes its place.

» **Punctuate descriptions correctly.** If the description is essential to the meaning of the sentence — you don't know what you're talking about without the description — don't use commas. If the description is interesting but nonessential, place commas around it.

- For example, don't place commas around this description, because you need the George part to clarify the sentence: "The play *that George wrote* makes no mention of the SAT."

- On the other hand, place commas around this description, because the opening date isn't essential to the point of the sentence: "George's play, *which opened last Friday*, broke records at the box office."

>> **Check apostrophes.** You may find an apostrophe where it doesn't belong, say in a possessive pronoun or in a simple, non-possessive plural.

- A possessive pronoun (*whose, its, theirs, his, hers, our,* and so on) <u>never</u> has an apostrophe.

- A conjunction joining two words (*it's, don't, isn't, aren't*) <u>always</u> has an apostrophe. This is how you tell *it's* from *its*: *It's* joins *it* and *is* and gets an apostrophe; *its* is the possessive of *it* and does not have an apostrophe.

Be clear on this: *It's* with an apostrophe is the conjunction of *it* and *is,* as in "*It's* parked outside." Also, *its* without an apostrophe is the possessive pronoun, as in "The dog pulled on *its* leash."

>> **Use colons.** The *colon* (:) does two things. It joins two complete sentences exactly like a semicolon. Sometimes the second sentence is capitalized, but it doesn't have to be. Any time a semicolon is correct, a colon works just fine. "The dog ran outside: The cat chased it." (You'll never have to choose between a semicolon and a colon if they're both correct.) The colon can also be followed by just a word or a phrase; unlike the semicolon, it doesn't need another compete sentence. This sentence is correct: "There's one topic in math that drives me crazy: probability."

The other thing the colon does is begin a list, taking the place of *such as* or *for example*. A sentence like, "There are things on the table, *such as* an SAT, a calculator, and an aspirin," can also be written as, "There are things on the table: an SAT, a calculator, and an aspirin." The list is never capitalized (unless it has proper nouns), and the colon never goes with the words *such as* or *for example* — it takes their place.

Words in context

The SAT asks about vocabulary in context, so you may see a word that *sounds* right but is considered wrong. These word pairs and homophones are frequent fliers on the exam:

>> **Affect and effect.** The SAT *affects* your life. The *effect* of all this prep is a high score. See the difference? The first is a verb and the second a noun. Once in a while, *effect* can be a verb meaning "to bring about," as in "Pressure from college *effects* change," and *affect* can be a noun that means mood, as in "The scholarship brought a nice *affect.*" But these are rare.

>> **Fewer and less.** *Fewer* is for stuff you can count (candies, teeth, cavities) and *less* is for stuff you measure (sugar, taste, toothache intensity).

>> **Good and well.** In general, *good* describes nouns, and *well* describes verbs. In other words, a person or thing is *good,* but you do something *well.* Your skills are *good,* and you study *well.*

>> **Ensure and insure.** You *ensure* something happens or doesn't happen, like practice *ensures* success. You *insure* something when you provide *insurance,* like the agent *insured* your truck and jet ski. That should be easy to remember.

>> **Farther and further.** Take something *farther* if it's literally going a distance, like my horse ran *farther* than your horse. Take it *further* for a matter of extremes, like the lawyer investigated *further*. No one messes this up.

This list obviously doesn't contain all the misused words or expressions you may encounter on the SAT tests, but these are the common offenders.

Practice Questions

PLAY

1. The following except is from *Bacteria in Daily Life* by Mrs. Percy Frankland (1903).

   Amongst some of the curiosities to be found on the shelves of microbe-museums may be mentioned bacteria which give out light, and thus, like glowworms, reveal themselves in the dark. These light-bacteria were originally discovered on the bodies of sea creatures, and cultures of them have been successfully photographed, the only source of light being that provided by the bacilli themselves. The amount of light _____ by a single bacillus might indeed defy detection by the most sensitive plate procurable, but when gathered in multitudes, the magnitude of which even eight figures fail to express, these phosphorescent bacteria enable the dial of a watch to be easily read in the dark.

   Which choice completes the text with the most logical and precise word?

   (A) evicted

   (B) eliminated

   (C) emitted

   (D) entrusted

PLAY

2. The COVID-19 pandemic disrupted businesses across the United States. Some businesses _____ the pandemic by increasing telework, adding workplace flexibilities, or changing pay. A business's response to the pandemic often depended on a particular firm's policies, which were often extended to some or all employees in the firm regardless of individual establishment size.

   Which choice completes the text with the most logical and precise word or phrase?

   (A) denied

   (B) adjusted to

   (C) conceded to

   (D) disengaged

PLAY

3. The following excerpt is from *The Decline and Fall of the Roman Empire* by Edward Gibbon (1776).

   The camp of a Roman legion presented the appearance of a fortified city. As soon as the space was marked out, the advanced guard carefully levelled the ground, and removed every _____ that might interrupt its perfect regularity. Its form was an exact quadrangle; and we may calculate that a square of about seven hundred yards was sufficient for the encampment of twenty thousand Romans.

   Which choice completes the text with the most logical and precise word?

   (A) impediment

   (B) uniformity

   (C) stability

   (D) obscurity

PLAY

4. The prosecuting attorney tried to get the testimony of a neighbor who claimed to have heard a woman's cry excluded from the trial. He claimed that since there was no corroboration of this information, it had no _____ on the case.

Which choice completes the text with the most logical and precise word?

(A) endurance

(B) conviction

(C) propaganda

(D) bearing

PLAY

5. The following is from a history of ancient Egypt.

Hatshepsut was the daughter of the great warrior king, Thutmosis I, and, according to some historians, was during her father's later years associated with him in the government. Along with Hatshepsut, he left two sons, and the elder of these, according to Egyptian law, _____ him. The son was, however, a mere youth, of a weak and amiable temper, while Hatshepsut, his senior by some years, was a woman of great energy, clever, enterprising, vindictive, and unscrupulous. She took the direction of affairs under her brother's reign, her influence paramount in every department of the government.

(A) succeeded

(B) evaluated

(C) criticized

(D) neglected

PLAY

6. The following excerpt is from *Travels in the Upper Egyptian Deserts* by Arthur Edward Pearse Brome Weigall.

The nights in the desert are as beautiful as the days, though in winter they are often bitterly cold. With the assistance of a warm bed and plenty of blankets, however, one may sleep in the open in comfort; and only those _____ this vast bedroom will understand how beautiful night may be.

Which choice completes the text so that it conforms to the conventions of Standard English?

(A) whom know

(B) who have known

(C) whom will know

(D) who knew

PLAY

7. The International Space Station is an unprecedented achievement in global human endeavors to conceive, plan, build, operate, and utilize a research platform in space. With assembly of the station at completion, continuity of visiting vehicles, and support of a full-time crew of six, the era of utilization for research by a team of global scientists _____.

Which choice completes the text so that it conforms to the conventions of Standard English?

(A) advance

(B) advances

(C) have advanced

(D) will have advanced

8. After celebrating our cousin's birthday with a lavish three-hour dinner, we were dismayed to find that it had started snowing. We headed home immediately because of the inclement weather _____.

Which choice completes the text so that it conforms to the conventions of Standard English?

(A) and it was late.

(B) and we were worried about the fact that it was getting later and later.

(C) but the snow had us worried about it being late.

(D) and the lateness of the hour.

9. The following excerpt is from *The Story of Mankind* by Hendrik Willem van Loon (1921).

We know very little about the first "true" men. We have never seen their pictures. In the deepest layer of clay of an ancient soil, we have sometimes found pieces of their bones. These lay buried amidst the broken skeletons of other animals that have long since disappeared from the face of the _____ have taken these bones and have been able to reconstruct our earliest ancestors with a fair degree of accuracy.

Which choice completes the text so that it conforms to the conventions of Standard English?

(A) earth, anthropologists

(B) earth and anthropologists

(C) earth, and anthropologists

(D) earth; and, anthropologists

10. This passage is from *Into the House of the Ancestors* by Karl Maier (Wiley).

Unlike those in some other major research centers in Africa, the scientists in Bamako are Africans, mostly Malians, but with a sprinkling of researchers from neighboring African countries. This is not a case of Europeans and Americans taking a mobile First World lab and setting it up in the African bush. _____ it is a center of scientific excellence, which is administered by Malians, and where the most immediate benefits fall to Malians, though the ramifications are invaluable to Africa and the entire world.

Which choice completes the text with the most logical transition?

(A) Rather,

(B) Therefore,

(C) Furthermore,

(D) Accordingly,

11. Breathing technique plays the most important part in the art of swimming; _____ no one ever becomes a good swimmer unless attention is paid to the matter of breathing, which must be done with regularity and precision.

Which choice completes the text with the most logical transition?

(A) but,

(B) nonetheless,

(C) conversely,

(D) in fact,

Practice Answers

1. **C.** The topic of the text is bioluminescent bacteria, or light-producing bacteria. The logic of the sentence indicates that the word that completes the text should mean "given off." Think of a word that you know that means "giving off light," and then look at the choices: The best word to complete the text is *emitted* (released or given off). It is not *evicted* (removed from a lodging) or *eliminated* (abolished or excluded) or *entrusted* (handed over to another).

2. **B.** The topic of the text is the effect of COVID-19 on businesses. The logic of the sentence indicates that the word that completes the text should mean "modified" or "made changes to." You can probably come up with a few words to fit that meaning. The best phrase to complete the text is *adjusted to* (changed to or adapted to). The best word or phrase is not *denied* (rejected) or *conceded to* (admitted to or allowed) or *disengaged* (disconnected).

3. **A.** The topic of the text is Roman encampments. The logic of the sentence indicates that word that completes the text should mean an obstacle or hindrance. Think of words that you know that mean obstacle, and then look at the choices. The best word to complete the text is *impediment* (an obstacle or hurdle). The best word is not *uniformity* (sameness) or *stability* (steadiness) or *obscurity* (insignificance or murkiness).

4. **D.** The topic of the text is the connection between the testimony and the case. The logic of the sentence indicates that the word that completes the text should mean relevance or connection. The best phrase to complete the text is *bearing*. To have a *bearing* on something means to have an effect on it. The best word is not *endurance* (strength or durability) or *conviction* (strongly held belief or verdict) or *propaganda* (slanted information).

5. **A.** The topic of the text is Egyptian history. The logic of the sentence indicates that the reign of the king Thutmosis I was followed by the reign of his son. Thus, his son *succeeded* or followed or replaced his father. The other choices, *evaluated* (appraised or estimated the value), *criticized* (found faults), or *neglected* (abandoned, ignored) do not fit the context of the sentence.

6. **B.** Choice (B) completes the text so that it conforms to the conventions of Standard English. The nominative pronoun *who* is needed because it is the subject of the verb *have known*; *whom* is incorrect because it is an objective pronoun. The tense that is needed in this sentence to convey action that began in the past and continues into the present is the present perfect *have known*. Choice (D) uses the correct pronoun *who* but the incorrect past tense verb *knew*.

7. **B.** Choice (B) completes the text so that it conforms to the conventions of Standard English. The singular form of the verb *advances* is needed to agree with the singular subject *utilization*. Choice (A) incorrectly uses the plural form of the verb *advance*. Choices (C) and (D) incorrectly use the plural form of the verb *have*.

8. **D.** Choice (D) completes the text so that it conforms to the conventions of Standard English, specifically, the conventions of parallel structure. Because the *lateness of the hour* is parallel to *the inclement weather*, it is the best choice. Choices (A), (B), and (C) incorrectly use an independent clause after the conjunction, so they are not parallel to the prepositional phrase *of the inclement weather*.

9. C. Choice (C) conforms to the conventions of Standard English because it is punctuated correctly. Two independent clauses cannot be joined with a comma — remember the dreaded comma splice? Cross out Choice (A). The same for Choice (B), which has no punctuation between the independent clauses, and Choice (D), which incorrectly uses the semicolon and the word "and."

10. A. Choice (A) completes the text with the most logical transition. A transitional word of contrast is needed to complete the logic of "This is not a case . . ." "Rather, it is . . ." The other choices do not convey this logical contrast. Choice (B) *therefore* indicates *as a result.* Choice (C) *furthermore* indicates *more information.* Choice (D) *accordingly* indicates *appropriately* or *for that reason.*

11. D. Choice (D) completes the text with the most logical transition. The second half of the sentence reinforces the first half; thus, the transitional phrase *in fact* is the most logical choice. Choices (A), (B), and (C) all indicate a contrast between the two halves, a relationship that does not fit the logic of the sentence.

Chapter **5**

Thinking Fast: Critical Thinking and Data Questions

Whether you read lengthy novels or spend hours scrolling through social media, or both, you are bombarded with information and data in some form every day. This will help your SAT performance, because on your exam, you read short passages (both fiction and nonfiction), some with tables or graphs, and answer a question on each passage. The previous chapter covered questions on grammar, main ideas, and details; this chapter takes things further with questions on critical thinking and data analysis.

Starting with the Question Formats

Critical Thinking and Data questions appear in standard formats on the SAT. These are the question types that you will encounter:

Purpose of underlined sentence asks, as the name suggests, for the purpose of a sentence underlined within a paragraph.

Overall structure of text asks about how the text was written, such as whose point of view is expressed and whether the main idea is stated or implied.

Paired reading has two paragraphs, or texts, and asks how they fit together. For example, one text could be an example of the other, a counterargument, or a response.

Using data provides data in the form of a table or a graph, along with a question on what you can infer.

Strengthening or weakening a claim describes an argument or a plan, which you strengthen or weaken based on new information from the answer choices.

Using quotations for support is a variation of strengthening or weakening a claim, where the answers are quotes instead of simply information.

Logically completing the text is easy to spot because the text is missing the ending. It's also easy to answer, because if you understand the text, then only one answer logically completes it.

These formats may overlap. For example, you may logically complete the text based on data. The important thing is that by recognizing the question format, you're one step closer to taking control of the exam and knowing exactly what to do.

Applying the Strategies

Remember those strategies that I keep repeating? And you're only on Chapter 5. Kidding, but these are the keys to your success, and they only work if you practice them, so here they are again, summarized. Be sure to apply these strategies as you practice the questions in this chapter.

Remember to stick with the one-minute-per-question rule. If you're stuck, guess an answer, mark the question for review (or circle it in this book), *move on*, and come back to it later. These strategies help you keep this timing:

>> **Cover the answer choices.** Use your scratch paper or hand to cover the screen. Focus on understanding the question and text without distraction from the answer choices.

>> **Read the question first,** *then* **the text.** This way you know what you're looking for when reading the text.

>> **Answer the question yourself.** Your answer won't match the correct answer, but it doesn't have to — instead, it makes the *wrong* answers stand out.

>> **Check each answer and cross off wrong ones.** Remember: You're *not* looking for the right answer. You're *crossing off* wrong answers.

If you answer the question yourself, then the three wrong answers stand out like apples on a pear tree. There will be one answer that you don't cross off, so go with that. It's all you'll have time to do.

REMEMBER

Exploring the Question Formats

Since the SAT uses a standard set of question formats, you can recognize and practice them. You can go into the test knowing exactly what to expect and how to get the questions right.

Purpose of the underlined sentence

In this question, a portion of the text is underlined, and your task is to determine which answer choice most accurately states the purpose of the underlined portion in the context of the whole text.

The following is adapted from an article titled "The Deadliest Atlantic Tropical Cyclones, 1492–1996" from the National Hurricane Center and Central Pacific Hurricane Center website.

PLAY

The legacies of Atlantic tropical cyclones span many cultures and thousands of years. Early evidence of these storms predates extant weather records. <u>Geologists believe that layers of sediment at the bottom of a lake in Alabama were brought there from the nearby Gulf of Mexico by storm surges associated with intense hurricanes that occurred as much as 3,000 years ago (Liu and Fearn 1993).</u> Similarly, sediment cores from the Florida west coast indicate exceptional freshwater floods during strong hurricanes more than a thousand years ago (Davis et al. 1989).

Perhaps the first human record of Atlantic tropical cyclones appears in Mayan hieroglyphics (Konrad 1985). By customarily building their major settlements away from the hurricane prone coastline, the Mayans practiced a method of disaster mitigation (Konrad 1985) that, if rigorously applied today, would reduce the potential for devastation along coastal areas (e.g., Pilkey et al. 1984; Sheets 1990).

Which choice best describes the function of the underlined sentence in the overall structure of the text?

(A) It states a hypothesis that is challenged by evidence from Liu and Fearn.

(B) It provides definitive evidence that supports a claim first found in Mayan hieroglyphics.

(C) It offers a hypothesis that geologists have proved using geological analysis.

(D) It presents a finding that may prove to support a claim in the first sentence.

First, what do *you* think the writer wants the underlined sentence to accomplish in this paragraph? The sentence starts with, "Geologists believe," telling you that geologists *aren't certain* that the sediment in the Alabama lake came from a storm 3,000 years ago.

Next, cross off the wrong answer choices.

> Choice (A) says the sentence is challenged by evidence from Liu and Fearn, but Liu and Fearn offered this evidence, so cross it off.

> Choice (B) says the sentence provides definitive evidence, but you know this isn't the case, from your own answer, so cross this one off.

> Choice (C) says the sentence offers a hypothesis that geologists have proven, which, like Choice (B), you know isn't the case. Away it goes.

> Choice (D) says the sentence presents a finding that *may* (but doesn't definitely) prove to support the claim that cyclones have been occurring for thousands of years. Leave Choice (D), and it's the only one left, so go with it.

Overall structure of the text

This question asks you to determine the organizational pattern the writer uses for the text. For example, the text may be structured as a description, a sequence, a comparison, a cause and effect, or a problem and solution.

PLAY

This passage is an excerpt from *Middlemarch*, a novel by George Eliot (1871).

> Miss Brooke had that kind of beauty which seems to be thrown into relief by poor dress. Her hand and wrist were so finely formed that she could wear sleeves not less bare of style than those in which the Blessed Virgin appeared to Italian painters; and her profile as well as her stature and bearing seemed to gain the more dignity from her plain garments, which by the side of provincial fashion gave her the impressiveness of a fine quotation from the Bible, — or from one of our elder poets, — in a paragraph of to-day's newspaper. She was usually spoken of as being remarkably clever, but with the addition that her sister Celia had more common-sense.

Which choice describes the overall structure of the text?

(A) A first-person narrator introduces herself, describes her friend Dorothy, and then begins her story.

(B) A third-person narrator describes Miss Brooke's physical appearance and her dress using biblical allusions, and then compares her to her sister.

(C) An unknown narrator comments on Miss Brooke's poverty, then her religious affiliation, and finally, her competition with her sister.

(D) The omniscient narrator compares two sisters, Miss Brooke and her sister Celia, and comments on their elaborate garments.

First, what do *you* think is the overall structure? Miss Brooke is on the level of Italian paintings, biblical quotes, and poems, plus she's clever but has less common sense than her sister.

Next, cross off wrong answers.

Choice (A) is out, as the passage doesn't have a first-person narrator. Cross it off.

Choice (B) stays, as it references Miss Brooke's biblical comparisons and her sister. Still check the other answer choices. Leave this one.

Choice (C) goes, as there's no evidence of Miss Brooke's religious affiliation or her competition with her sister. Cross it off.

Choice (D) is out, as the passage isn't a comparison of Miss Brooke and her sister Celia, plus it describes Miss Brooke's garments as being "plain," not "elaborate." Cross it off.

Paired reading

Paired reading offers two short texts. Your job, per the question, is to determine how the texts fit together. One text may be an example of the other, or a counterargument, or a supporting argument. Start with the question.

PLAY

Text 1 is an excerpt from *The Secret Life of Dust* by Hannah Holmes (Wiley). Text 2 is an excerpt adapted from the online article titled "Understand Climate Change" by the U.S. Global Change Research Program.

Text 1

One very clear message in the ice is that the Earth's climate is naturally erratic. According to the dust and gases trapped in the ice, the climate is <u>always—always—in'flux</u>. If it's not gettin' warmer, it's getting colder. Year to year the shifts may be masked by an El Niño, La Niña, a Mount Pinatubo, or some other temporary drama.

Text 2

Earth's climate is now changing faster than at any point in the history of modern civilization, primarily as a result of human activities. Global climate change has already resulted in a wide range of impacts across every region of the country and many sectors of the economy that are expected to grow in the coming decades. Thousands of studies conducted by researchers around the world have documented increases in temperature at Earth's surface, as well as in the atmosphere and oceans. Many other aspects of global climate are changing as well. Human activities, especially emissions of heat-trapping greenhouse gases from fossil fuel combustion, deforestation, and land-use change, are the primary driver of the climate changes observed in the industrial era.

How would the author of Text 2 respond to the underlined portion of Text 1?

(A) By agreeing that climate is in a constant state of change but asserting that human activities have pushed the natural climate fluctuations to more serious and impactful levels.

(B) By asserting that climate change represents a temporary shift in climate patterns and with ongoing efforts, will reverse the effects of human activities.

(C) By acknowledging that climate change is a naturally occurring phenomenon and is unaffected by human activities.

(D) By disputing that climate change represents a normal pattern of temperature variability and asserting that it is solely a response to irresponsible human activity.

First, answer the question. How would the writer of Text 2 respond to the underlined statement? Maybe the author of Text 2 would agree with the underlined portion of Text 1, but with the *caveat* (condition) that the climate in flux is changing more intensely, as a result of human activity.

Next, cross off wrong answers.

Choice (A) is possible: It recognizes that Text 2 accepts the concept of natural climate fluctuations but asserts that human activities have worsened the natural ups and downs of climate. Leave this one.

Choice (B) is out: It adds the unsupported element of climate shift being temporary. Whether this is true is irrelevant: Stay within the text itself, which doesn't mention this point. Cross it off.

Choice (C) asserts that Text 2 says that climate change is unaffected by human activities, but this is contradicted by the evidence in Text 2: "Human activities. . . are the primary driver of the climate changes observed in the industrial era." Cross it off.

Choice (D) states that Text 2 disputes the idea that climate change is a naturally occurring process, but Text 2 does not do this. Cross it off.

Choice (A) is the remaining answer and is the correct choice.

Interpreting data

This question, as the title implies, asks you to draw a conclusion from the data in a graph or chart, or combine the data with the information in the text. You may also be asked to determine what *can't* be inferred from the data. A key strategy, after reading the question, is to focus on the data *first*, and the text *second*.

PLAY

Can animals predict earthquakes? Since ancient times, strange or unusual behavior in fish, birds, reptiles, and animals has been reported. In modern times, too, people have noticed what they believe to be early warning signals from their pets. In 1975, for example, snakes awoke from hibernation just before a major earthquake in China. The snakes froze to death; the weather was still too cold for them to survive.

Many pet owners firmly believe that their dogs or cats have advanced knowledge of the terrifying event that is a major earthquake. Because many animals can see, hear, and smell things beyond the range of human senses, they may detect small changes in air pressure, gravity, or other phenomena associated with earthquakes. Animals that predict earthquakes may be reacting to the *P* wave that humans can't feel. Researchers know that earthquakes generate two types of waves, *P* waves and *S* waves. The *P* wave travels faster than the *S* wave, which is stronger and more easily felt. If animals are indeed able to warn of earthquakes, and if scientists find an effective way to monitor the animals' signals, many lives will be saved.

Estimated Number of Deaths from Earthquakes, Worldwide, 2008–2019

2008	2009	2010	2011	2012	2013	2014	2015	2016	2017	2018	2019
88,708	1,790	226,050	21,942	689	1,572	756	9,624	1,297	1,012	4,535	244

U.S. Geological Survey/ Public Domain.

Which of the following best supports the researchers' conclusion based on data from the table?

(A) This research is important because each year more and more people die from earthquakes.

(B) While the number of people who die from earthquakes is consistent from year to year, reducing the number of deaths is certainly a worthwhile goal.

(C) Monitoring animals' signals will be a valuable resource even though the numbers of people who die from earthquakes is steadily decreasing.

(D) These efforts could help avoid another year like 2010, when more than 200,000 people died from earthquakes.

First, answer the question yourself: What's the researchers' conclusion with the data? Remember to focus on the data *first*, in which 2010 and 2008 were the deadliest years for earthquake deaths. Focus on the text *second*, which concludes that animal signals could help reduce these deaths.

Next, cross off wrong answers:

Choice (A) is out, because the annual number of earthquake deaths is not increasing, so cross it off.

Choice (B) is out, because even though reducing deaths is certainly worthwhile, the number of annual deaths isn't consistent from year to year. Cross this off.

Choice (C) is out, because the annual number of earthquake deaths is not decreasing, so cross it off also.

Choice (D) stays, because it supports the data (and your answer) that 2010 was a terrible year. This is the last answer standing, and is correct.

Strengthening or weakening a claim

The text presents a claim, which you strengthen or weaken based on one of the answer choices. For example, take the claim that Myra came out of the kitchen, and the last donut was gone, so she must have eaten it. *Weaken* this claim by adding *new information* that changes the outcome (say, other people were also in the kitchen), so you can't say whether Myra ate the donut. *Strengthen* the claim by suggesting that *nothing else* happened that is relevant (say, no one else was home that day), so Myra probably *did* eat the donut.

Watch out for answer choices that are out of scope, which are always wrong. For example, if Myra has a sweet tooth, it doesn't change the evidence of whether she ate the donut.

WARNING

PLAY

The following passage is adapted from *U.S. History For Dummies*, by Steve Wiegand (Wiley).

Hopscotching from the British Isles to the Shetland Islands to the Faroe Islands, the Vikings arrived in Iceland about A.D. 870. Around 985 a colorful character known as Erik the Red discovered Greenland and led settlers there. Like so many things in human history, the Vikings' first visits to the North American continent were [probably] by accident.

Which of the following statements, if true, most weakens the claim that the discovery and visits of North American lands were by accident?

(A) The period of Scandinavian history to which the term Viking is applied extends roughly from the middle of the 8th to the end of the 10th or the first half of the 11th century.

(B) A Yale University map that supposedly offered verification of Viking explorations has been declared a forgery.

(C) Erik the Red lived in Iceland for a period of time.

(D) A newly discovered journal describes the Vikings having ambition to expand their territory by exploration and domination of new lands.

First, answer the question yourself. Keep your answer simple: It won't match the correct answer, but it'll highlight three *incorrect* answers. What would suggest that the discovery of North American lands *wasn't* by accident? Maybe that it was *on purpose*. See? Simple.

Now, cross off any answer choice that either doesn't fit with your answer or is out of scope.

Choice (A) offers some historical background, but that's it — nothing about the accidental or intentional discovery of new lands. Cross it off.

Choice (B) is interesting but out of scope. What does a university map have to do with Viking land discovery? Cross it off.

Choice (C) is also out of scope. Places where Erik the Red lived have little to do with whether North American discovery was intentional. Cross this off.

Choice (D) provides new information that the Vikings intended to visit and expand to new lands, so the discovery of Greenland and other North American lands was *not* by accident. Leave this answer, and it's the correct choice.

Using quotations for support

This is a variation of the Strengthening or Weakening a Claim question from the previous section. Not only do you strengthen or weaken the text, but you also find an example to support the text. Like all other questions in this section, read the question first, then the text, then answer the question yourself, and then cross off wrong answers.

PLAY

In a research paper, a student is reporting on the problems associated with sleep deprivation. The student has found anecdotal evidence that sleep deprivation is detrimental to physical and mental health, and that it can even be a causative factor in the onset of serious diseases.

Which quotation from an expert best illustrates the student's claim?

(A) "Lack of sleep also damages the immune system and is linked to many chronic health problems, including heart disease, kidney disease, high blood pressure, diabetes, stroke, obesity, and depression."

(B) "In a recent year, nearly 30 percent of adults reported that they slept less than six hours a night and only 31 percent of high school students got at least eight hours of sleep on an average weekday night."

(C) "Drivers younger than 25 are more likely to fall asleep while behind the wheel of an automobile."

(D) "In one study, research subjects who slept after learning a new task, retained knowledge and scored higher on tests than those who did not sleep."

First, answer the question yourself: What illustrates the claim that sleep deprivation is bad for you? Maybe that it makes you sick, or die, or crazy. Perfect answer. Now, cross off wrong answers:

Choice (A) looks good — it matches your answer and provides specifics about both physical health (heart disease, kidney disease, high blood pressure, diabetes, stroke, obesity) and mental health (depression). Leave it uncrossed, but check the other answers just to be sure.

Choice (B) is on topic and true, but it doesn't match your answer. It only says that many people have this. Cross it off.

Choice (C) is also a point related to sleep deprivation, but it doesn't illustrate the claim as well as Choice (A) does. It also doesn't match your answer. Cross it off.

Choice (D) says quite the opposite of your answer. Don't fall into "the choice that is close, but wrong" trap. Instead, cross it off.

The remaining answer is Choice (A), which is the correct answer.

Completing the text logically

With these questions, the text ends with an incomplete sentence, and you select the answer that best completes the logic of the sentence and the text. Think of what the text is trying to say, and think to yourself what makes the most sense (in other words, answer the question yourself), before crossing off wrong answers.

PLAY

The following is adapted from *Sherlock Holmes For Dummies* by Steven Doyle and David A. Crowder (Wiley). Note: Arthur Conan Doyle's Sherlock Holmes first appeared in 1887, in a series of short stories published in *The Strand Magazine*.

The public was wildly enthusiastic about Sherlock Holmes, but one man didn't share that feeling. Incredibly, it was Arthur Conan Doyle himself. He had greater ambitions in mind as a writer; he believed he'd make his mark in literature by writing historical novels. Once Doyle began to see the detective as an impediment to his work instead of part of it, he found a way to make sure Holmes never bothered him again: he killed him off. However, Doyle never realized how popular Sherlock Holmes was until he killed him. Over 20,000 people _____ .

Which choice most logically completes the text?

(A) vowed that they would never read a Sherlock Holmes story again.

(B) had never read a Sherlock Holmes story, and now they never would.

(C) canceled their subscriptions to *The Strand Magazine* in protest.

(D) preferred to read Doyle's historical novels than his detective stories.

What's the author trying to say? That Sherlock Holmes was a remarkably popular character. So what would 20,000 people do to make the point that they didn't want to read that Sherlock was killed? Maybe protest somehow.

Now cross off the wrong answers.

Choice (A) isn't logical. Never reading another Sherlock story isn't much of a protest if no more stories are being written. Cross it off.

Choice (B) isn't logical either. If the people had never read a Sherlock story, they wouldn't be concerned if the stories ended. Cross it out.

Choice (C) is logical. The 20,000 people protested Sherlock's death by canceling their subscriptions to the magazine in which the stories appeared. Leave this answer.

Choice (D) isn't logical. If people prefer to read Doyle's historical novels to his detective stories, then they're not really protesting anything. Cross it out.

Choice (C) remains and is the correct answer.

Interpreting Research Questions

Each Reading and Writing module has about five research questions, comprised of notes on a topic, usually in bullet points, followed by a question. Like all the others in this section, read the question first.

The question may ask you to:

» Emphasize a particular point about the notes.

» Emphasize the aim of the study.

» Present a study and its methodology.

» Explain the advantage of one quality over another or explain the difference between them.

» Emphasize the relative size, weight, capacity, or some other quality of two items.

» Introduce a new topic to an audience.

» Make a generalization about a study.

The steps are the same as for the other Reading and Writing questions: Cover the answer choices, read the question, read the text (in this case, bullet points), and take your best shot at what the answer looks like. Then check each answer choice, one at a time, and either cross it off or leave it as a possibility. Like the other questions, you have about a minute to get this one.

REMEMBER

The correct choice may not refer to *all* the notes. Some notes may be irrelevant.

Try this one:

PLAY

While researching a topic, a student has taken the following notes:

>> The earliest town meetings in the colonies were held in the 1630s in New England, and attendance was mandatory.

>> In the absence of a government presence, colonies held the town meetings to make rules for the community.

>> Townspeople discussed local issues of concern including schools, roads, and bridges.

>> Town meetings allowed residents to voice their opinions on public issues and to vote on laws and budgets.

>> Town meetings are considered examples of "pure democracy," because each citizen represents himself.

The student wants to make a generalization about the impact of the town meetings on American democracy. Which choice best accomplishes this goal?

(A) It is likely that town meetings served a social as well as a political purpose in the colonies as they were opportunities for hard-working citizens to gather for reasons other than religious services.

(B) Having the townspeople gather at regular intervals and directly vote on the laws governing the colony, was an example of direct democracy in action.

(C) Although New England town meetings are often described as opportunities for residents to voice their opinions of public issues such as schools, roads, and bridges, it is probable that not everyone attended and that only the men were allowed to vote.

(D) Town meetings held in the colonies are historically acclaimed as a notable model of pure self-government and self-determination that guided the foundations of the independent United States of America.

Answer the question yourself: What is the general impact of a town meeting on American democracy? Maybe the town meeting was the *precursor* (beginning) of the modern democracy model. Now cross off wrong answers:

Choice (A) describes the purpose of the town meetings, but doesn't show them as leading to democracy, so cross it off. (Remember, the online SAT allows you to cross off wrong answers.)

Choice (B) describes town meetings as leading to democracy, but it's too specific. Remember, the question asks for a *generalization*. Cross out this trap answer, or you could keep it for now while reviewing the other answer choices.

Choice (C) also describes town meetings' relevance to democracy, but it digresses into detail and problems with the model. Another non-generalization, but this one is off topic. Cross it out.

Choice (D) is rather general and describes how town meetings led to democracy. You can almost hear the music. Keep this one, and go with it, as it's better than Choice (B) and is the correct answer.

You got this. A little practice is all it takes, so here you go. You're welcome.

Practice Questions

Practice is always good, but the data questions in particular take more time at first but go faster with practice. Following are three data questions for you to sharpen those skills before visiting the complete sets of Reading and Writing questions in Part 4.

REMEMBER

Read the question, then focus on the data *first* and the text *second.* You can usually find the answer primarily in the data.

PLAY

1. The following excerpt is from *Novel Plant Bioresources* by Ameenah Gurib-Fakim (Wiley).

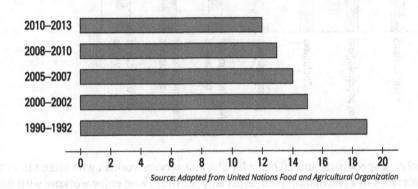

Percentage of Undernourished Persons in the World, 1990–2013

Source: Adapted from United Nations Food and Agricultural Organization

The world still faces tremendous challenges in securing adequate food that is healthy, safe, and nutritious in an environmentally sustainable manner. With the growing demand of an expected 9 billion people by 2050, it remains unclear how our current global food system will cope. Currently (2014), 868 million people suffer from hunger, while micronutrient deficiencies, known as hidden hunger, undermine the development, health, and productivity of over 2 billion people.

Which of the following most effectively uses data from the graph to support the assertions in the text?

(A) The number of people who lack important nutrients is greater in rural areas than in urban areas.

(B) The percentage of the population with an adequate amount of food rose from 1990 to 2013.

(C) The number of animal species providing food for human beings is decreasing.

(D) Over 9 billion people currently face micronutrient deficiencies.

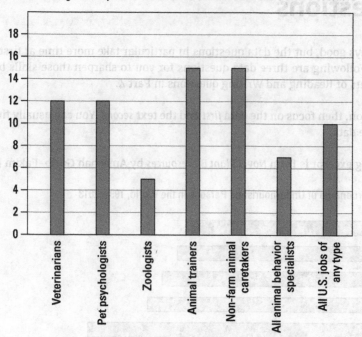

Percentage of Projected Job Growth: Animal Care and Service Workers

PLAY

2. Animal care specialists, animal behaviorists, and service workers who attend to or train animals work in a fascinating field, especially for those who enjoy working with non-human species. Entry-level workers, who need a high school diploma or its equivalent, earn around $28,000 per year, though veterinarians make about $85,000 a year. In general, higher paid careers require better education and training. Overall employment of animal behavior and service workers in all the various specialties of animal behavior is projected to _____.

Which of the following most effectively uses the data from the graph to complete the text?

(A) grow by 11 percent.

(B) decrease by 15 percent.

(C) grow by 7 percent.

(D) grow by 10 percent.

Weather Fatalities 2021

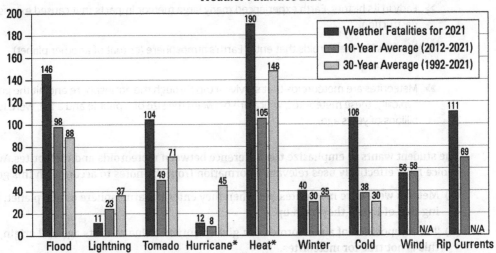

*Due to an inherent delay in the reporting of official heat fatalities in some jurisdictions, this number will likely rise in subsequent updates.
*The fatalities, injuries, and damage estimates found under Hurricane/Tropical Cyclone events are attributed only to the wind.

Source: Adapted from (www.weather.gov/hazstat/) National Weather Service -NOAA

PLAY

3. The following text is adapted from an article on the USGS website titled, "Hurricane Information."

According to a student's research on the impact of destructive weather on the U.S. population, hurricanes bring powerful winds, storm surges, torrential rains, floods, and tornadoes. A single storm can wreak havoc on coastal and inland communities and on natural areas over thousands of square miles. In 2005, Hurricanes Katrina, Rita, and Wilma demonstrated the devastation that hurricanes can inflict and the importance of hurricane hazards research and preparedness. More than half of the U.S. population lives within 50 miles of a coast, and this number is increasing. Many of these areas, especially the Atlantic and Gulf coasts, will be in the direct path of future hurricanes. Yet, while undeniably deadly, hurricanes _____.

Which choice most effectively uses data from the graph to complete the text?

(A) caused an average of 56 fatalities in the years 2012–2021.

(B) were less likely than lightning to cause fatalities in 2021.

(C) caused more deaths than tornadoes did in 2012–2021.

(D) caused fewer fatalities than heat caused over the past 30 years.

PLAY

4. The following is from the NASA's online article titled, "Meteors & Meteorites."

While researching a topic, a student has taken the following notes:

» Meteoroids are objects in space that range from dust grains to small asteroids.

» Most meteoroids are pieces that have broken off from comets, asteroids, or even other planets.

» Meteoroids are essentially "space rocks" that may contain metals.

» Early in its history, Earth experienced many large meteor impacts that caused extensive destruction.

» Meteors are meteoroids that enter Earth's atmosphere (or that of another planet) and burn up.

» Meteorites are meteoroids that survive a trip through the atmosphere and hit the ground. Typically, these meteorites, which are between the size of a pebble and a fist, were formed billions of years ago.

The student wants to emphasize the difference between meteoroids and meteorites. Which choice most effectively uses relevant information from the notes to accomplish this goal?

(A) Meteors were once meteorites but when they enter the atmosphere of any planet, including that of Earth, they burn up.

(B) The composition of a meteoroids can give scientists a clue as to its age and origin, while this is not true for meteorites.

(C) Meteorites are technically larger than meteoroids because they have to be large enough to survive the damaging effects of entering and surviving a trip through the atmosphere of an asteroid or a planet.

(D) Although meteoroid is the term for any rocky object in space that has become detached from a larger object such as a planet or an asteroid, once these objects enter the atmosphere of a planet and survive the trip, they are called meteorites.

Practice Answers

1. **B.** The data from the graph shows that the percentage of *undernourished* persons *decreases* from 1990 to 2012, which means that the percentage of *nourished* persons *increases* during this same time. Choice (A) is out because the graph and text say nothing about regional differences. Choice (C) goes because the graph and text don't discuss any specific sources of nutrition, and Choice (D) fails because according to the text, the population won't reach 9 billion until 2050, and when it does, there's no indication that all 100 percent will be suffering from undernourishment.

2. **C.** Choice (C) effectively uses data from the graph to complete the text. Be careful and accurate when you read the labels on the X (horizontal) and Y (vertical) axes on a graph. The sentence in the text states, "Overall employment of animal behavior and service workers in all the various specialties of animal behavior is projected to. . ." Locate the column labeled, *All animal behavior specialists*, which shows the 7 percent increase.

3. **D.** Choice (D) describes data that accurately completes the text. Choice (A) is not an accurate reading of the data; hurricanes caused an average of 8 deaths in 2012–2021. Choice (B) is also inaccurate; in 2021, lightning caused 11 deaths and hurricanes caused 12 deaths. Choice (C) is inaccurate because in 2012–2021, tornadoes caused 49 deaths and hurricanes caused 8. Only Choice (D) is accurate: Heat caused 148 deaths while hurricanes caused 45.

4. **D.** The question prompt indicates that the student wants to emphasize the difference between meteoroids and meteorites. Your goal is to find the relevant information from the notes that will emphasize the difference. Don't fall into the trap of thinking you must use all the information; Definitely not true! Just find the relevant notes. Choice (D) most effectively uses the relevant information to highlight the essential differences between meteoroids and meteorites — basically that meteorites are meteoroids that have survived the passage through a planet's atmosphere.

3

Owning the SAT Math Section

Exploring SAT math topics

Knowing the ways that the SAT frames math questions, and how to approach them

Spotting and dodging the SAT math traps

Answering math questions in under a minute while other test-takers get stuck

Trying not to laugh out loud

Chapter 6

Raising Your Best Math Score

O n to the math. After an hour of SAT verbal, you're doing great! You've practiced and applied the strategies from this book. Now you get a well-earned 10-minute break before running for another hour or so of math. You got this.

To boost your math score, you need to revisit topics that you may not have seen since freshman year, along with the various ways that the SAT frames the questions. Practice is good too — in fact, practice is the best way to get ahead. This section covers the topics you're likely to see along with plenty of targeted practice and review.

Taking On SAT Math

There are two math modules, back-to-back. Each module features 22 questions, for 44 questions total, both of which allow you to use the built-in on-screen calculator. One thing to note, if you practice with the paper-based tests from the College Board, those practice math modules each has 27 questions, for 54 total.

Difficulty is relative. A question that's easy for you may be challenging for your friend, and vice versa. It doesn't matter anyway, because if you know what to do, the question is easy. So what determines the question's difficulty in the context of the SAT? Difficulty is estimated from the number of students who miss the question during a trial. So a "difficult" question on the SAT is simply one where more students didn't know what to do. If you know how to approach the question, which you will after reviewing these chapters, the question is easy.

Furthermore, if you know how to approach an SAT math question, then it takes less than a minute to answer. This means that if you know what to do, you can answer all the math questions easily and without rushing. And this leads to the first two pieces of wisdom:

» **Make each question easy by knowing what you're doing.** There aren't that many topics on SAT Math. There are a few, and they're all topics that you should have seen in high school *and* are recapped here and in the following chapters. There are plenty of math topics that you don't see, such as matrices, which only appear on the ACT.

» **Don't rush, because you'll make all kinds of mistakes.** Instead, to speed up your progress through the test, make sure you don't get stuck. The way you don't get stuck is by *knowing what you're doing*. Then you'll answer all the questions easily with time to spare.

Here are more bits of wisdom (also known as SAT Math Strategies) along those same lines:

» **Don't take more than a minute on any one question.** If you don't know how to answer the question, that's okay. Here's what to do:

- Guess an answer.

- Mark the question for review.

- Move on to the next question.

- Come back to this question at the end of the module.

» **If you find yourself working a lot of math, you missed what the question is asking.** An SAT Math question is more like a puzzle than a math problem. It never takes a lot of math work, but it may take a strategic approach based on the concept. If you understand the question and set it up correctly, everything cancels and works out nicely. On the other hand, if you're working a lot of math, step back and follow the preceding strategy: Take a guess, move on, and come back to this question at the end of the module. You'll probably spot how to work the question on this second look.

» **Work the questions you know first.** A question that you answer quickly is worth the same points as one that takes you time, so work the questions you know first! Then go back to the time-consumers.

» **Write clearly on your scratch paper.** Leave enough room for large, clear drawings, and make sure your text is legible. I have students mix up 5 and *s* all the time, along with the number 1 and lower-case letter *L*. Write 5 large and the *s* small, your letter *L* as a cursive loop, like ℓ, and your *t* with the hook bottom, so it doesn't look like a plus symbol (+).

» **If you're almost out of time, click to the end and guess on 'em all.** Really, this shouldn't happen. If you practice the skills taught in the next few chapters, you'll be fine — but just in case! Take the plunge and guess through the end of the test. A wrong answer is no worse than an unanswered one, so you may as well take a shot at getting it right.

Starting with Formulas

The button marked Reference on the top right of the screen brings up a set of standard math formulas and equations to help you solve the problems. You'll probably forget it's there — almost everyone does — but these formulas, shown in Figure 6-1, are still good to know.

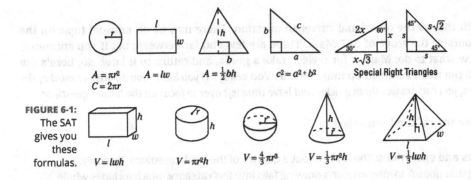

FIGURE 6-1:
The SAT
gives you
these
formulas.

$A = \pi r^2$ $A = lw$ $A = \frac{1}{2}bh$ $c^2 = a^2 + b^2$ Special Right Triangles
$C = 2\pi r$

$V = lwh$ $V = \pi r^2 h$ $V = \frac{4}{3}\pi r^3$ $V = \frac{1}{3}\pi r^2 h$ $V = \frac{1}{3}lwh$

Typing Your Answers

Of the 44 SAT Math questions, most are good ol' multiple choice, but some ask you to type your own answers. These questions are known as *fill-ins*. They work exactly the same as the multiple-choice questions, only you type in your answer instead of selecting it from a list.

The fill-in problems are normal math questions but with certain rules:

» **Don't fill in a mixed number.** If you come up with $5\frac{1}{2}$ as your answer, **don't** fill in $51/2$, because the computer will read it as "51 over 2," not "five and one-half." Instead, convert your answer to an improper fraction. Fill in $11/2$ (11 over 2) or type in the decimal: 5.5.

» **If there is more than one correct answer, just pick one.** If the answer can be either 4 or 5, just go with one and don't worry about the *other* one: The system accepts either answer as correct. That also goes for a range: If your answer is between 3 and 7, then any number between 3 and 7 is considered correct.

» **Check whether the answer needs to be rounded.** Sometimes the answer must be an integer or a decimal rounded to a certain number of decimal places.

For example, if you correctly calculate an answer of 1.75, and the question specifies that the answer needs to be rounded to *one* decimal place, then an answer of 1.75 is considered incorrect, while the rounded answer of 1.8 is considered correct.

» **If your answer is a repeating decimal, type in all the digits, rounding off the last number only.** In other words, enter .3333 or .6667 (1/3 and 2/3 expressed as decimals), not .3 or .67. Note that you don't have to round the last number; if the answer is 2/3, you can use that, or .6666, or .6667. Any of those is correct; it's probably best to just use the fraction.

REMEMBER

Don't worry if you get more than one possible answer. Some fill-in questions have several possible right answers. (Usually those problems read something like, "what is one possible value of . . .") Just pick one answer and you're set.

Refreshing the SAT Math Topics

Worried? Don't be. The important thing to know — that phrase is used a lot, but it's always true — is that *certain math topics are on the SAT, and certain math topics aren't*. If you know which ones are on the test, and the way that the SAT asks about them, then each answer in the math is within your reach. These topics are summarized below and explored in the following chapters.

TIP

The SAT Math throws the occasional curveball question. There may be an unusual topic on the edge or just outside the scope of SAT Math. These are few and far between, but if you encounter one, you know what to do: Mark it for review, take a guess, and return to it later. So, here's the wisdom of all the math summed up into one line. You ready? *If you know how to answer most of the math questions, you can answer them quickly and have time left over to focus on the harder questions.*

What are those topics? Glad you asked.

>> **Numbers and operations:** These are about a quarter of the math questions. Basically, anything that doesn't involve an *x* or a drawing falls into this category, which includes whole number operations, fractions, ratios, exponents, and radicals. Of these, ratios and exponents are typically the most commonly occurring.

>> **Algebra and functions:** These are just under half of the math questions and include anything with an *x* or any other letter that represents a number. The most commonly occurring algebra topics include linear equations, systems of equations (basically two linear equations), and parabolas.

>> **Geometry and trigonometry:** These are about a quarter of the math questions and include the typical circles and trapezoids along with 3-D shapes such as cubes and cylinders. There's some subtracting the areas or volumes of shapes, and just a little trig. The most common questions in this group involve triangles and parts of circles (like half of a wheel).

>> **Statistics and probability:** These are just a few of the math questions and involve averages and graphs, including scatter plots. The most common questions in this group are definitely the graphs.

So there you are. The secrets of SAT Math. Nice! Note that whether certain topics are more common than others varies from exam to exam, and some questions touch upon more than one topic. These assessments and any estimated priority of each math topic are based on the review of countless SATs with students. Each exam is different, and yours may have a different mix of questions or not include all the topics — but it'll be close.

Also, the math practice questions are mixed into the chapters. You find out how to work a math topic, practice with a few SAT-style questions, and go to the next topic. Go on: Four chapters, and you so got this.

REMEMBER

CALCULATING THROUGH IT

So you can use a calculator on the math. Big deal. The SAT-makers declare that you can solve every problem on the test with brainpower alone, and they're right. But there's nothing wrong with a little help. A calculator isn't the *panacea* (solution) to doing well on SAT Math — your preparation is — but it's good to have. Fortunately, the calculator is built right into the Math modules, so you don't have to worry about remembering to bring one.

Get used to how this new calculator works. Check out the free Bluebook practice software from www. collegeboard.org and explore the on-screen calculator. In the math section, click *Calc* to bring up the calculator with scientific and graphing capability, then click *Functions* to reveal a host of advanced capability, including trigonometry, statistics, and calculus.

Don't worry about learning any new functions, as almost all SAT Math questions can be answered without the calculator or with only basic functions. But, you should know how the online calculator works.

Chapter **7**
Simplifying Numbers and Operations

Now for the first step in your SAT math review. Not only do the topics in this chapter comprise about a quarter of the SAT math questions, but they are also the foundation of the questions on other SAT math topics. For example, you need to understand exponents and radicals, covered in this chapter, before you take on parabolas and trigonometry, covered in the following chapters.

Simplifying the Basics

Different types of numbers work in different ways, so here is a review of the basics and how numbers work together. In the same way that this chapter is the foundation of SAT Math, this section is the foundation of this chapter.

Starting with types of numbers

The SAT Math section refers to defined numbers such as *rational* or *imaginary* in their questions. Here's what they are.

» **Whole numbers:** A *whole number* is any number that doesn't include a fraction or a decimal and isn't negative, including 0.

» **Factors:** A *factor* is any whole number that divides neatly into another whole number. For example, 16 divides by 1, 2, 4, 8, and 16, so those numbers are factors of 16. Note that every number is a factor of itself: 5 is a factor of 5. To factor a negative number, factor out a –1 also, even though –1 isn't a whole number. For example, factors of –6 are –1, 1, 2, 3, and 6.

» **Multiples:** A *multiple* is any whole number multiplied by any other whole number. For example, multiples of 4 include 4, 8, 12, and so on. Note that every number is a multiple of itself: 7 is a multiple of 7.

» **Prime numbers:** A *prime number* is any number that has exactly two factors: itself and 1. All prime numbers are positive, and all are odd *except* for 2, which is the only even prime number. Zero and 1 aren't prime numbers.

» **Composite numbers:** Any whole number with more than two factors (in other words, not prime) is *composite*. If you can divide a number by a smaller whole number (other than 1) without getting a remainder, it's a composite number. Note that any composite number can be divided down to its primes. For example, 30, which is composite, can be divided down to its primes: $30 = 2 \times 3 \times 5$.

TIP

Speaking of divisibility, know these points:

- Any number whose digits add up to a multiple of 3 is also divisible by 3. For example, the digits of 789 add up to 24 $(7+8+9=24)$; because 24 is divisible by 3, so is 789.

- Same goes for multiples of 9. If the digits of a number add up to a multiple of 9, you can divide the number itself by 9. For example, the digits of 729 add up to 18 $(7+2+9=18)$; because 18 is divisible by 9, so is 729.

- Any number ending in 0 or 5 is divisible by 5.

- Any number ending in 0 is divisible by 10.

Consider the number 365. It's not even, so it can't be divided by 2. Its digits add up to 14, which isn't divisible by 3 or 9, so it's not divisible by those either. However, it ends in 5, so it's divisible by 5. Because it doesn't end in 0, it's not divisible by 10.

» **Integers:** Any whole number or negative whole number is an *integer*. You see integers on the number line, as in Figure 7-1. You also see non-integers on the number line, but not as often.

TIP

The farther to the right on the number line a number is, the greater it is. For example, –3 is greater than –5, because –3 is to the right of –5 on the number line.

» **Consecutive numbers:** *Consecutive* means "one after another," so *consecutive numbers* are numbers that are, well, one after another. Typically, they're just integers lined up, as in 12, 13, 14, but they can be defined and categorized. For example, consecutive *odd* numbers include 9, 11, 13, while consecutive *even* numbers of course include 6, 8, 10. If a question asks about 5 consecutive numbers starting with 7, you would write 7, 8, 9, 10, 11.

» **Rational numbers:** Any integer, along with any number that can be written as a fraction — proper or improper — or as a terminating or repeating decimal, is a *rational number*. Examples of rational numbers include $\frac{2}{3}$, a *proper fraction*; $\frac{3}{2}$, an *improper fraction*; 1.2, a *terminating decimal*; and $1.\overline{09}$ (the decimal for $\frac{12}{11}$), which is a *repeating decimal* (1.090909 . . .).

» **Irrational numbers:** An *irrational number* has decimals that never repeat or end. Practically speaking, you need to worry about only two kinds of irrational numbers:

- Radicals (such as $\sqrt{2}$ and $\sqrt{3}$)

- π, which you've seen from working with a circle

FIGURE 7-1:
The number
line.

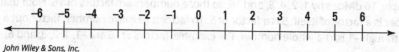

John Wiley & Sons, Inc.

You'll typically see an irrational number in its radical form or as π, not as an unwieldy decimal, but the SAT may expect you to know what it is.

» **Real numbers:** A *real number* is any number that appears on the number line. Real numbers include each type of number described previously, including those rational and irrational.

» **Imaginary numbers:** An *imaginary number* is the opposite of a real number. It doesn't appear on the number line, and though there are others in applied mathematics, there is only one that may appear on the SAT: the square root of –1, also known as *i*. This is further explored later in this chapter.

» **Undefined numbers:** An *undefined number* doesn't have a meaning. The most common undefined number, and the only one that you have to consider for the SAT, is a number divided by zero. You don't actually work with this, but if the question shows $\frac{2}{3-x}$, then somewhere in there, it's guaranteed to show $x \neq 3$ just to *make sure* that you're not dealing with that undefined number.

Here's a sample SAT question based on the concept of number basics:

PLAY

If *x* and *y* are both integers where *x* is greater than 3 and *y* is less than 2, then *x* – *y* could be

(A) 3

(B) 2

(C) 1

(D) –1

If *x* is an integer greater than 3, it must be at least 4. If *y* is an integer less than 2, it must be at most 1. To find *x* – *y*, just place those numbers: $4 - 1 = 3$, so Choice (A) is correct. Note that making *x* bigger or *y* smaller makes *x* – *y* greater than 3, so all the other choices are impossible.

Using order of operations

How many times have your folks told you to put away your phone and start your homework because you "have to get your priorities straight"? No comment on that, but here are operations priorities in math.

Consider the problem $3 + 4 \times 2$. If you add 3 and 4 first, the result is different than if you multiply 4 by 2 first. You know *PEMDAS*, remembered by "Please Excuse My Dear Aunt Sally," but actually meaning "**P**arentheses **E**xponents **M**ultiply **D**ivide **A**dd **S**ubtract," which describes the *order of operations*. When faced with a multipart problem, just follow this order.

1. **Work everything in parentheses.**

2. **Calculate all exponents.**

3. **Multiply and divide, from left to right.**

4. **Add and subtract, from left to right.**

The SAT doesn't give you ambiguous math problems such as $3 + 4 \times 2$, but you still should remember to work anything in parentheses first — usually. In Chapter 8, there are examples of questions where you leave the parentheses alone. Don't worry about it now — you'll see how it fits together — but be aware of the intended *order of operations* in a given math problem.

Simplifying Numbers and Operations

Now that you're refreshed on the basics, here's a dive into some actual math topics on the SAT.

Simplifying prime numbers

As defined in the previous section, a *prime number* is any number that has exactly two factors: itself and 1. It's always positive, and the only even prime number is 2 (whose factors are 1 and 2). Any other even number has more than two factors and isn't prime. For example, 4 is divisible by 1, 2, and 4. Zero isn't prime because it isn't positive, and 1 isn't prime because it has only one factor: 1.

The secret to working with prime numbers is just knowing that SAT Math typically asks only about prime numbers less than 20, so just know the first bunch: 2, 3, 5, 7, 11, 13, 17, 19. If you're not sure, make sure the number is *odd* (except 2 of course), and try dividing it by other odd numbers, starting with 3. If you can't divide it evenly, then the number is prime.

PLAY

If c is the smallest prime number greater than 5 and d is the largest prime number less than 15, then the value of $c + d$ is

(A) 11

(B) 13

(C) 19

(D) 20

The answer is Choice (D), 20. The smallest prime number greater than 5 is 7, and the largest prime number less than 15 is 13. Add 7 to 13 for the answer of 20.

PLAY

If a number n is the product of two distinct primes, x and y, how many factors does n have, including 1 and itself?

(A) 2

(B) 3

(C) 4

(D) 5

A prime number has only two factors: 1 and itself. Pretend in your problem that $x = 5$ and $y = 7$. Then $n = 5 \times 7 = 35$. The factors of 35 are 1, 5, 7, and 35. Because you can't break down 5 or 7, there are no other factors. As long as you pick prime numbers for x and y, you'll always get four factors for n. Choice (C) is correct.

Prime number questions aren't that common in SAT math, but they're worth knowing and understanding.

Simplifying percents

Percent, or *per cent*, if you remember your Latin, translates to *per 100*. That's why 50 percent is 50 out of 100, or one half.

Taking the percent of a number is simple. To turn a number into a percent, simply move the decimal point two spaces to the right and add the % symbol: 0.5 becomes 50, and then 50%. You can also turn a percent into a decimal by moving the decimal point two spaces to the left and dropping the % symbol, as in $60\% = 0.60$. (Other examples of percents to decimals include $12.5\% = 0.125$, $0.4\% = 0.004$, and so on.) You can also turn the percent into a fraction: 60 percent literally means, "60 per 100," or $60/100$, which reduces to $3/5$. Do you convert a percent to a decimal or fraction or leave it alone? Either way is fine, so it depends on which you're more comfortable with and on the nature of the question.

To take the percent of a percent, simply multiply the percents, or convert them back to fractions or decimals and then multiply. For example, if 50% of the chocolates are dark chocolate, and 40% of the dark chocolates have almonds, then what percent of the chocolates are dark with almonds? To multiply as percents, go with $50\% \times 40\% = 20\%$. To multiply as decimals, use $0.5 \times 0.4 = 0.2$, and as fractions, go with $\frac{50}{100} \times \frac{40}{100} \rightarrow \frac{5}{10} \times \frac{4}{10} = \frac{20}{100}$ or $\frac{1}{2} \times \frac{2}{5} = \frac{2}{10} \rightarrow \frac{20}{100}$. Any way you cut it, the answer is 20%.

For other percentage questions, fall back on the formula you mastered in grade school:

$$\frac{\text{is}}{\text{of}} = \frac{\%}{100}$$

Suppose you're asked "40% of what number is 80?" The number you're looking for is the number you're taking the percent *of*, so x will go in the *of* space in the formula:

$$\frac{80}{x} = \frac{40}{100}$$

Now cross-multiply: $40x = 8,000$. Dividing by 40 gives you $x = 200$.

You can also consider that the percent of the whole equals the part. In other words, 40% of x is 80. Set up the equation and solve for x:

$$40\%x = 80$$
$$0.4x = 80$$
$$x = \frac{80}{0.4}$$
$$x = 200$$

One subtopic of percentages is a problem that involves a percent increase or decrease. A slight variation of the percentage formula helps you out with this type of problem. Here's the formula and an example problem to help you master it:

$$\frac{\text{amount of change}}{\text{starting amount}} = \frac{x}{100}$$

The value of your investment in the winning team of the National Softball League increased from $1,500 to $1,800 over several years. What was the percentage increase of the investment?

PLAY

(A) 300

(B) 120

(C) 50

(D) 20

The correct answer is Choice (D). The key here is that the number 1,800 shouldn't be used in your formula. Before you can find the *percent* of increase, you need to find the *amount* of increase, which is $1,800 - 1,500 = 300$. To find the percentage of increase, set up this equation:

$$\frac{300}{1,500} = \frac{x}{100}$$

First reduce the fraction:

$$\frac{300}{1{,}500} = \frac{3}{15} = \frac{1}{5}$$

Then cross-multiply and divide by 5:

$$\frac{1}{5} = \frac{x}{100}$$
$$5x = 100$$
$$x = 20$$

The SAT tries to confuse you by asking about something that doesn't appear in the original question, as in this example:

PLAY

At one point in the season, the New York Yankees had won 60 percent of their games. The Yanks had lost 30 times and never tied. (As you know, there are no ties in baseball.) How many games had the team played?

(A) 12

(B) 18

(C) 50

(D) 75

The answer is Choice (D). Did you find the catch? The winning percentage was 60 percent, but the question specified the number of losses. What to do? Well, because a tie doesn't exist, the wins and losses represent all the games played, or 100 percent. Thus, the percentage of losses must be 100% – 60%, which is 40%. Put the formula to work:

$$\frac{30}{x} = \frac{40}{100}$$

Now cross-multiply: $40x = 3{,}000$ and $x = 75$

PLAY

If you invest $2,000 for one year at 5% annual interest, the total amount you would have at the end of the year would be

(A) $100

(B) $2,005

(C) $2,100

(D) $2,500

Solve the question like this: 5% = 0.05, so 5% of $2,000 = 0.05 × $2,000 = $100. But wait! Before you choose $100 as your answer, remember the original $2,000, so you now have $2,000 + $100 = $2,100. Choice (C) is correct.

Questions solely on percents aren't that common, but the percent underlies many other questions on SAT Math.

Simplifying ratios

A *ratio* compares the items of a group as a reduced fraction. For example, if there are 15 trees and 10 hammocks, then the ratio of trees to hammocks is 3:2, because the fraction $\frac{15}{10}$ reduces to $\frac{3}{2}$. Here are some further points to remember about ratios:

>> A ratio is written as $\frac{\text{of}}{\text{to}}$ or of:to.

» The ratio *of* skis *to* poles is $\dfrac{\text{skis}}{\text{poles}}$.

» The ratio *of* boats *to* trailers = boats:trailers.

» A possible total is a multiple of the *sum* of the numbers in the ratio.

You may have a ratio question like this:

At an auto show, the ratio of classic cars to concept cars is 4:5. What *could* be the total number of classic and concept cars at the auto show?

To answer this question, add the numbers in the ratio: $4 + 5 = 9$. The total must be a multiple of 9, such as 9, 18, 27, 36, and so on. Or think of it another way: The total must divide evenly into the sum of the ratio. So the total can be 27, which divides evenly by 9.

Here's an example:

PLAY

To make the dough for her signature wood-fired pizzas, Julia uses 7 cups of flour for every 5 cups of water, and she only uses whole cups. If she uses at least 10 but not more than 20 cups of water, what *could* be the total number of cups of flour and water that goes into the dough?

The answer can be 24, 36, or 48. Add the numbers in the ratio: $7 + 5 = 12$, so the total must be a multiple of 12. If Julia uses at least 10 but not more than 20 cups of water, then she uses 10, 15, or 20 cups, so multiply the multiple of 12 by 2, 3, or 4. Any answer 24, 36, or 48 is considered correct, so go with one and you're good.

Another form of the ratio question gives you the ratio and the total, and then it asks for one of the numbers. Solve it like this:

1. Put an *x* by each number in the ratio.

2. Set up an equation where these *x* numbers add up to the total.

3. Solve for *x*.

4. Place the number for *x* back into the equation.

Go through this once and it makes sense.

PLAY

A salad uses 2 Campari tomatoes for every 3 artichoke hearts, for a total of 20 items. How many tomatoes and artichoke hearts are in this salad?

1. 2 to 3 becomes $2x$ and $3x$

2. Set up the equation as $2x + 3x = 20$

3. Solve for *x*:

$$2x + 3x = 20$$
$$5x = 20$$
$$x = 4$$

4. Place 4 in for *x* in the equation:

$$2x + 3x = 20$$
$$2(4) + 3(4) = 20$$
$$8 + 12 = 20$$

So, there are 8 tomatoes and 12 artichoke hearts.

PLAY

Given that there are 30 days in April, the ratio of rainy days to sunny days next April could *not* be

(A) 5:3

(B) 3:2

(C) 5:1

(D) 4:1

The rule for ratios states that the total must be divisible by the sum of the numbers in the ratio. Because $5 + 3 = 8$, and 30 isn't divisible by 8, Choice (A) is correct. Just to be sure, check that all the other possible sums do go into 30.

A ratio question doesn't always approach the ratio directly. Sometimes you have to spot that a ratio is involved, like in this one:

PLAY

A party supplier charges a flat rate plus a certain amount per person. If supplies for 12 people cost $140 and supplies for 20 people cost $180, then supplies for 40 people would cost

(A) $220

(B) $280

(C) $300

(D) $360

First, find the cost per person. If 12 people cost $140 and 20 people cost $180, then the additional cost of 8 people is $40 (because $20 - 12 = 8$ and $180 - 140 = 40$). Divide $40 by 8 for a person-to-cost ratio of 1 : $5. Now take the 20-person cost and add the cost of 20 more people. You know that 20 people cost $180 and that 20 additional people cost $100 (because $20 \times 5 = 100$), so add the two together: $180 + 100 = 280$, and the answer is Choice (B).

Ratio questions are fairly common in SAT math.

Simplifying conversions

Conversions refers to going from one unit of measurement to another. For example, if a mile is 5,280 feet, and there are 3 feet in a yard, how long is a mile in yards? Working with conversions is simply multiplying or dividing the total number by the conversion.

In this example, because you're converting feet to yards, divide the 5,280 feet by 3 for the number of yards:

$$\frac{5,280 \text{ feet}}{3 \text{ feet}} = 1,760 \text{ yards}$$

Here's another.

PLAY

If each quarter-inch on the map represents one mile, how much distance is represented by a 3-inch segment on the map?

(A) 3 miles

(B) 4 miles

(C) 9 miles

(D) 12 miles

If each quarter-inch is one mile, then one inch is four miles. The 3-inch segment thus represents 12 miles, for Choice (D).

Conversion questions are fairly common in SAT math, and they can be varied.

Simplifying exponents

The *exponent* is one of the most commonly asked topics on SAT math. Here are the basics, and later on are the SAT variations.

The *base* is the big number (or letter) on the bottom. The *exponent* is the little number (or letter) in the upper-right corner.

>> In x^5, x is the base and 5 is the exponent.

>> In 3^y, 3 is the base and y is the exponent.

Any base to the zero power equals one.

>> $x^0 = 1$

>> $129^0 = 1$

>> $0^0 = 1$

A base to the first power is just the base. In other words, $4^1 = 4$.

A base to the second power is the base times itself:

>> $x^2 = x \cdot x$

>> $5^2 = 5 \times 5 = 25$

The same is true for bigger exponents. The exponent tells you how many times the numbers are multiplied together. For example, 3^4 means that you multiply 3 four times: $3^4 = 3 \times 3 \times 3 \times 3 = 81$.

A base to a negative exponent is the reciprocal of the base to a positive exponent. A *reciprocal* is the upside-down version of a fraction. For example, $\frac{4}{3}$ is the reciprocal of $\frac{3}{4}$. An integer (except 0) can also have a reciprocal: $\frac{1}{3}$ is the reciprocal of 3. When you have a negative exponent, just put base and exponent under a 1 and make the exponent positive again.

>> $x^{-4} = \frac{1}{x^4}$

>> $5^{-3} = \frac{1}{5^3} = \frac{1}{125}$

The answer isn't negative. When you flip it, you get the reciprocal, and the negative goes away. Don't fall for the trap of saying that $5^{-3} = -5^3$ or -125.

Also, if a number or variable with a negative exponent, such as x^{-4}, appears in the denominator of a fraction, such as $\frac{2}{3x^{-4}}$, you can make the exponent positive and move it to the numerator, like this: $\frac{2x^4}{3}$. Note that only the part with the exponent moves, in this case x, and not the other parts of the fraction, in this case 2 and 3.

To multiply like bases, add the exponents.

» $x^3 \cdot x^2 = x^{(3+2)} = x^5$

» $5^4 \times 5^9 = 5^{(4+9)} = 5^{13}$

» $p^3 \cdot p = p^3 \cdot p^1 = p^{(3+1)} = p^4$

» $129^3 \times 129^0 = 129^{(3+0)} = 129^3$

TIP

You can't multiply numbers with *unlike* bases. (Actually, you can, by making the exponents the same, but that's rare on the SAT.)

» $x^2 \cdot y^3$ stays $x^2 \cdot y^3$

» $5^2 \times 7^3$ stays $5^2 \times 7^3$ (unless you actually multiply it out)

To divide like bases, subtract the exponents.

» $x^5 \div x^2 = x^{(5-2)} = x^3$

» $5^9 \div 5^3 = 5^{(9-3)} = 5^6$

» $x^3 \div x^7 = x^{(3-7)} = x^{-4} = \dfrac{1}{x^4}$

» $129^2 \div 129^0 = 129^{(2-0)} = 129^2$

(That last one should make sense if you think about it. Any base to the zero power is 1, and any number divided by 1 is itself.)

TIP

Did you look at $5^9 \div 5^3$ and think that it was 5^3? Falling into the trap of dividing instead of subtracting exponents is easy, especially with numbers just begging to be divided, like 9 and 3. Keep your guard up.

You should know the common powers of 2, 3, 4, and 5:

$2^2 = 4$	$3^2 = 9$	$4^2 = 16$	$5^2 = 25$
$2^3 = 8$	$3^3 = 27$	$4^3 = 64$	$5^3 = 125$
$2^4 = 16$	$3^4 = 81$		
$2^5 = 32$			
$2^6 = 64$			

Multiply exponents of exponents, like this:

» $\left(x^2\right)^3 = x^{(2 \cdot 3)} = x^6$

» $\left(5^4\right)^3 = 5^{(4 \times 3)} = 5^{12}$

You can use the common powers to give numbers like bases:

If you have $9^5 = 3^x$, meaning what exponent of 3 equals 9^5, turn the 9 into 3^2, and solve it like this:

$$9^5 = 3^x$$
$$\left(3^2\right)^5 = 3^x$$
$$3^{10} = 3^x$$

And $x = 10$. Try this one:

PLAY

In the expression $16^3 = 2^x$, the value of x is:

(A) 4

(B) 8

(C) 12

(D) 16

Give each side the same base. In this expression, 2 probably works the best:

$$16^3 = 2^x$$
$$\left(2^4\right)^3 = 2^x$$
$$2^{12} = 2^x$$
$$x = 12$$

This matches Choice (C).

Here is a variation of the theme:

PLAY

In the expression $25^x = 5^6$, what is the value of x?

(A) 2

(B) 3

(C) 5

(D) 7

Give each side the same base, which here should be 5:

$$25^x = 5^6$$
$$\left(5^2\right)^x = 5^6$$
$$5^{2x} = 5^6$$
$$2x = 6$$
$$x = 3$$

This matches Choice (B). Note that the actual math is very simple. You're not crunching huge numbers; you're using your understanding of the math to simplify and solve these fast.

You can count bases with exponents if the bases match and the exponents match. In this example, with x^3, the base is x and the exponent is 3.

» $x^3 + x^3 = 2x^3$. This works the same way as $x + x = 2x$. You're just counting them.

» $37x^3 + 10x^3 = 47x^3$. Because the bases match and the exponents match, just add the numbers (also known as numerical coefficients) to count the instances of x^3: $37 + 10 = 47$.

» $15y^2 - 10y^2 = 5y^2$. Just subtract the numbers to count the instances of y^2: $15 - 10 = 5$.

TIP

You can't count bases with different exponents or different bases. In other words, $13x^3 - 9x^2$ stays $13x^3 - 9x^2$, and $2x^2 + 3y^2$ stays $2x^2 + 3y^2$. The bases and exponents must match for you to combine them.

There's your refresher of basic exponents, but no SAT math question asks about exponents like that. Here is what you need to know to take on an actual exponent question:

You can apply the exponent to terms multiplied together. If x and y are multiplied together, as xy, and the exponent is applied to them, as in $(xy)^3$, this is the same as $x^3 \cdot y^3$.

>> You can multiply bases that have the same exponent: $a^4 \cdot b^4 = (ab)^4$.

>> Try it with real numbers:
$$2^2 \times 3^2 = 6^2$$
$$4 \times 9 = 36$$

You can multiply a base with an exponent by expressions in parentheses. Distribute the base with the exponent by each term in the parentheses. It's easier than it sounds:

>> To simplify $x^2(x^3 + 1)$, distribute (which means "multiply") x^2 to x^3 and 1 separately, for an answer of $x^5 + x^2$.

>> To simplify $a^3(a^4 + a^5)$, first multiply a^3 by a^4 (to get a^7) and then by a^5 (to get a^8) for a final answer of $a^7 + a^8$.

You can factor a base with an exponent from a pair of like bases with different exponents. This is simply the reverse of the previous step.

>> To factor $n^5 - n^3$, divide both n's by the same n with an exponent.

>> You could divide by n (which is the same as n^1): $n(n^4 - n^2)$.

>> You could divide by n^2: $n^2(n^3 - n)$.

>> You could divide by n^3: $n^3(n^2 - 1)$.

Factor the expression according to the question. For example, say $n^5 - n^3$ were to appear in a question, like this:

PLAY

The expression $\dfrac{(n^5 - n^3)}{(n^2 - 1)}$ is equivalent to:

(A) n^3

(B) n^2

(C) n

(D) 1

You can factor $n^5 - n^3$ one of the three ways shown before. Which one do you use? Well, only one of them produces a factor that cancels with $n^2 - 1$: $n^3 \left(n^2 - 1 \right)$.

Now factor n^3 out of $n^5 - n^3$ and revisit the question:

$$\frac{\left(n^5 - n^3 \right)}{\left(n^2 - 1 \right)}$$

$$\frac{n^3 \left(n^2 - 1 \right)}{\left(n^2 - 1 \right)}$$

Cancel the $\left(n^2 - 1 \right)$ from the top and bottom, and you're left with n^3, which matches Choice (A).

That is how you see exponents in SAT math. With some practice, you'll spot the trick and answer each of these in under a minute. Here are a couple for you to try. It takes longer than a minute at first:

PLAY

If $x - y = 3$, what is the value of $\frac{2^x}{2^y}$?

(A) 2

(B) 4

(C) 8

(D) 16

Suppose you had to find the value of $\frac{2^7}{2^4}$. It's 2 with an exponent of $7 - 4$, or $\frac{2^7}{2^4} = 2^{7-4} = 2^3$, like you've been doing all along. So here it's the *same thing*, only with x and y instead of 7 and 4: $\frac{2^x}{2^y} = 2^{x-y}$. *Okay, Mr. Smart Instructor*, you're probably thinking, *what the #&%! am I going to do with* $\frac{2^x}{2^y} = 2^{x-y}$. Then — snap your fingers — the question tells you that $x - y = 3$. Oh. $2^{x-y} \rightarrow 2^3 = 8$. The answer is Choice (C).

Here's another one like it. Now that you know what you're doing, your challenge is to answer this one in under a minute. Ready?

PLAY

If $b - a = 2$, what is the value of $\frac{3^b}{3^a}$?

(A) 3

(B) 9

(C) 27

(D) 81

Start with $\frac{3^b}{3^a}$. The question tells you that $b - a = 2$, so solve it like this: $3^{b-a} \rightarrow 3^2 = 9$, for answer Choice (B). How long did that take? It's the *same exact question*, but you know what you're doing, so it takes *less than a minute*.

One more. This is a prime example of how the SAT math questions *aren't math problems: they're puzzles. If you start doing a lot of math, you missed what the question is asking.* There is almost *no math* to this question.

PLAY

If $(2g - 3h)^3 = 27$, then $(2g - 3h)^{-2} =$

(A) $\dfrac{1}{9}$

(B) $\dfrac{1}{6}$

(C) 6

(D) 9

Forget the values of g and h. Look at the first equation: $(2g - 3h)^3 = 27$. Think about it like a puzzle. If something cubed is 27, what could it be? It has to be 3, because $3^3 = 3 \times 3 \times 3 = 27$. So place 3 for $(2g - 3h)$ in the second equation:

$$(2g - 3h)^{-2}$$

$$(3)^{-2}$$

$$\frac{1}{(3)^2}$$

$$\frac{1}{9}$$

Choice (A) is correct.

These questions show the many, many variations of exponent questions based on the basic rules, *each of which you can just as easily handle after working through it once.* Exponents is a common topic in SAT math, so be sure to practice.

TIP

The exponent affects only what it's touching. For example, $5x^2$ is equivalent to $5 \cdot x \cdot x$. You may wonder why the 5 isn't also squared: It's because the exponent is only touching the x. If you want to square the 5 also, put the expression in parentheses with the exponent on the outside: $(5x)^2 = 5 \cdot x \cdot 5 \cdot x = 25x^2$. This is also true with the negative sign: Put -5^2 in the calculator, and it returns -25. This is because the calculator reads -5^2 as $-(5 \cdot 5) = -25$. In other words, it squares the 5 and places the negative on it: -25. To square the entire -5, place it in parentheses and square it, like $(-5)^2$. The calculator reads this as $(-5) \times (-5)$ and returns the answer you were expecting: 25.

Simplifying square and cube roots

A *square root* refers to a quantity that, when squared, yields the starting quantity. For example, $\sqrt{16} = 4$, because $4^2 = 16$. A *cube root* is similar, except the quantity is cubed to yield the starting quantity. For example, $\sqrt[3]{8} = 2$, because $2^3 = 8$.

In math-speak, a *radical* is a root as well as the symbol indicating a root, $\sqrt{\ }$. Although most numbers have square roots that are decidedly not pretty, ($\sqrt{2}$, for example, equals approximately 1.41), most of the radicals you encounter on the SAT will either simplify nicely (such as $\sqrt{25} = 5$) or can be left in the radical form (such as $\sqrt{2}$ or $3\sqrt{5}$).

A square root always yields a positive number, because a quantity times itself is never negative. The square root of any negative number is therefore not a real number and is referred to as *i* for *imaginary*. Whereas $\sqrt{25} = 5$ represents a real number, $\sqrt{-9} = \sqrt{9} \times \sqrt{-1} = 3 \times i = 3i$ and is imaginary, covered later in this chapter.

TIP

When $x^2 = 16$, x can equal either 4 or -4, because you're not taking the square root of x^2 or 16: you're finding values of x that satisfy the equation $x^2 = 16$. $\sqrt{16}$ can only be 4, and not -4, because a square root can only be a positive number. The x^2 variation is covered further in Chapter 8.

A cube root, on the other hand, may yield a positive or negative number, because a quantity times itself three times may be positive or negative. For example, $\sqrt[3]{64} = 4$ and $\sqrt[3]{-64} = -4$, because $(-4)(-4)(-4) = -64$.

Multiplying and dividing radicals is simple, as long as they're the same type of root (in other words, square or cube). Just multiply and divide the numbers as if there's no radical: $\sqrt{5} \times \sqrt{6} = \sqrt{30}$ and $\sqrt{14} \div \sqrt{7} = \sqrt{2}$. Note that you can't add or subtract radicals. For example, $\sqrt{3} + \sqrt{5}$ stays $\sqrt{3} + \sqrt{5}$. You can, however, count radicals if they're the same: $\sqrt{3} + \sqrt{3} = 2\sqrt{3}$, in the same way that $x + x = 2x$.

To take the square root of a fraction, take the square roots of the numerator and denominator as separate numbers. For example, to take the square root of $\sqrt{\frac{4}{25}}$, take the square roots of 4 and 25 separately: $\sqrt{\frac{4}{25}} = \frac{\sqrt{4}}{\sqrt{25}} = \frac{2}{5}$

If the numerator and denominator don't square-root easily, try simplifying the fraction first: $\sqrt{\frac{50}{2}} = \sqrt{25} = 5$

You can break down any radical by factoring out a perfect square and simplifying it, like these:

$$\sqrt{27}$$
$$\left(\sqrt{9}\right)\left(\sqrt{3}\right)$$
$$3\sqrt{3}$$

and

$$\sqrt{12}$$
$$\left(\sqrt{4}\right)\left(\sqrt{3}\right)$$
$$2\sqrt{3}$$

A root can also be shown as a fractional exponent. For example, $3^{\frac{1}{2}} = \sqrt{3}$ and $5^{\frac{1}{3}} = \sqrt[3]{5}$. The denominator of the fraction becomes the *index number* (the small number outside the radical), and the numerator of the fraction stays as the exponent. For example, $7^{\frac{3}{5}} = \sqrt[5]{7^3}$.

Now try some practice:

PLAY

Which is equivalent to $5\sqrt{18}$?

(A) $15\sqrt{2}$

(B) $12\sqrt{3}$

(C) $10\sqrt{5}$

(D) $8\sqrt{6}$

Simplify $5\sqrt{18}$ by factoring out the perfect square.

$$5\sqrt{18}$$
$$5\left(\sqrt{9}\right)\left(\sqrt{2}\right)$$
$$5(3)\left(\sqrt{2}\right)$$
$$15\sqrt{2}$$

And the answer is Choice (A).

PLAY

Which of the following is equivalent to $x^{\frac{n}{p}}$ for all values x, n, and p?

(A) $\sqrt[n]{x^p}$

(B) $\sqrt[p]{x^n}$

(C) $\sqrt[n]{x^{\frac{1}{p}}}$

(D) $\sqrt[p]{x^{\frac{1}{n}}}$

See, if you know what to do, the question takes less than a minute. When the exponent is a fraction, the denominator of that fraction (in this case, p) becomes the *index number* (the small number outside the radical), and the numerator of the fraction (in this case, n) stays as the exponent. And of course, the base (in this case, x) stays the base. The correct answer is thus Choice (B).

PLAY

$3\sqrt{x} + 5 = 17$

What value of x satisfies the above equation?

Start by isolating the $\sqrt{x}$:

$$3\sqrt{x} + 5 = 17$$
$$3\sqrt{x} = 12$$
$$\sqrt{x} = 4$$

Now don't make the mistake of thinking that x should be 2; $\sqrt{2}$ doesn't equal 4. Instead, square both sides, and $x = 16$.

Square roots are fairly common in SAT math, as are cube roots to a lesser extent.

Simplifying imaginary *i*

An *imaginary* number is a number that can't exist in real math. There are others in applied mathematics, but only one that you see on the SAT, which results from the square root of a negative number.

A square root always yields a positive number because a quantity times itself is never negative. The square root of any negative number is therefore not a real number and *imaginary*, written as *i*. Whereas $\sqrt{4} = 2$ represents a real number, $\sqrt{-9} = \sqrt{9} \times \sqrt{-1} = 3i$. The italic *i* specifically refers to the square root of -1, so you'll see *i* defined either as $i = \sqrt{-1}$ or $i^2 = -1$, both of which tell you exactly the same thing.

The most common mistake while working with *i* is mixing up whether the result is positive or negative. Here's a summary of how *i* works, but *don't memorize* this table. Instead, *understand* it.

i	result
i	i
i^2	-1
i^3	$-i$
i^4	1
i^5	i

And it repeats. Because $i^4 = 1$, any power higher than 4 is simply 1 times one of the above results. What is i^{10}? Remember you multiply exponents by adding them, so it's like this:

$$i^{10} = (i^4)(i^4)(i^2)$$
$$= (1)(1)(-1)$$
$$= -1$$

Work with i the same way that you work with x. As these are true with x:

$$2x + 3x = 5x$$
$$(3)4x = 12x$$

They are also true with i:

$$3i + 5i = 8i$$
$$(2)3i = 6i$$

One other thing. SAT math typically presents i in the form of a quadratic, where you multiply the expressions using the FOIL method. Quadratics are covered further in Chapter 8, but for now, here's a refresher on that ol' FOIL.

FOIL stands for First Outer Inner Last, which basically means multiply everything in one expression by everything in the other. To multiply these expressions:

$$(x + 2)(x - 3)$$

» Start with the First terms, x times x, for x^2.

» Now the Outer terms, x times -3, for $-3x$.

» Next the Inner terms, 2 times x, for $2x$.

» Then the Last terms, 2 times -3, for -6.

» Finally, add the pieces for a final quadratic result of $x^2 - x - 6$.

On these questions, you do this with terms containing i instead of x, but it works exactly the same way, only i^2 becomes -1. Here's how the SAT offers it. You ready?

PLAY

For $i = \sqrt{-1}$, what is the value of $(4 - 3i)(2 + i)$?

(A) $6 - 2i$

(B) $8 + 2i$

(C) $11 - 2i$

(D) $13 + 3i$

Don't get mad. FOIL it:

$$(4 - 3i)(2 + i)$$
$$8 + 4i - 6i + 3$$
$$11 - 2i$$

Which piece by piece is:

$$(4)(2) = 8$$
$$(4)(i) = 4i$$
$$(-3i)(2) = -6i$$
$$(-3i)(i) = 3$$

That last one, $(-3i)(i)$, is where you need to be sure the result is 3 and not -3. Work it step by step:

$$(-3i)(i)$$
$$(-3)(i)(i)$$
$$(-3)(-1)$$
$$3$$

Now that you're sure, add them up for $11-2i$, which matches Choice (C).

Here's another one:

PLAY

If $i^2 = -1$ and $2x = 3i$, what is the value of $4x^2$?

(A) 4

(B) -4

(C) 9

(D) -9

$4x^2$ is simply $(2x)(2x)$. Because $2x = 3i$, it's also $(3i)(3i)$:

$$(3i)(3i)$$
$$(3)(3)(i)(i)$$
$$(9)(-1)$$
$$-9$$

which matches Choice (D).

You're almost guaranteed to see at least one i question in the SAT Math section. There are more i questions tied to conjugates, covered further in Chapter 8.

Simplifying projections

A *projection* is a scenario where you predict a future state based on a math formula. For example, if today an orange tree is 12 feet tall, and each year it grows 3 more feet, then how tall will it be in 5 years? If t is the unit of time, in this case a year, then in t years the tree will grow $3t$ feet. If today the tree is 12 feet tall, its future height, called h, can be projected with this formula:

$$h = 12 + 3t$$

How tall will this tree be in 5 years? Place 5 for t and simplify:

$$h = 12 + 3t$$
$$= 12 + 3(5)$$
$$= 12 + 15$$
$$= 27$$

And the orange tree will be 27 feet tall.

The SAT may ask you what the 3, the 12, or the t of the formula represent:

The 3 represents the additional number of feet per year, so that each year counted by t adds 3 feet to its height.

The 12 represents the starting height of the tree.

The t represents the time, in years, that is measured by the formula.

The SAT may also ask how the formula may change. Suppose the tree only grows 2 feet per year, instead of 3. How would you change the formula? Make the 3 into a 2, so that each year t only adds 2 feet to the tree's height:

$$h = 12 + 2t$$

That's a simple projection, and you'll see more of these with linear equations in Chapter 8. The SAT also gives a notoriously complex-looking projection formula, which is actually very simple once the shock factor wears off. This is the epitome of the SAT math question that looks like madness but (1) *is workable in less than a minute if you know what to do*, and (2) *is simple math if you don't fall for the trap.*

The formula in a projection usually has an exponent that's a fraction, and that's the part that makes you jumpy. Don't be. The fraction *always* cancels out, and the rest of the formula *always* becomes simple.

Next to the orange tree is a pomegranate tree. This tree is 5 feet high, and its height is projected with this formula:

$$h = 5 + \frac{10^{\frac{t}{2}}}{t}$$

In this equation, the t exponent is divided by 2, so do you think the SAT will ask you to project the tree's height in 9 years, or 11 years? No. It'll ask you to project 2 years, or 4 years, or some number that *cancels the fraction exponent* and *keeps the math simple.*

How tall will the pomegranate tree be in 4 years? Place 4 in for t:

$$h = 5 + \frac{10^{\frac{t}{2}}}{t}$$

$$= 5 + \frac{10^{\frac{(4)}{2}}}{(4)}$$

$$= 5 + \frac{10^2}{4}$$

$$= 5 + \frac{100}{4}$$

$$= 5 + 25$$

$$= 30$$

And the tree will be 30 feet tall.

TIP

Forget the calculator! You don't need it. In fact, the calculator makes this worse, because it takes you down a complex calculation path — the *trap* — that is *way off* from what you need to answer this question. Remember the wisdom from Chapter 6: *If you find yourself working a lot of math, check your approach.*

$$f(d) = 100 + \left(2^{\frac{d}{2}} + \frac{d}{3}\right)100$$

PLAY

This equation is a model of the projected number of seed pods given off by a certain eucalyptus tree in the spring, where d represents the number of days after the start of pollination and $f(d)$ represents the projected number of seed pods. According to the model, what is the projected number of seed pods at the end of the sixth day?

Don't be scared by the equation! Remember, the SAT gives you a number to place in that makes all the fractions cancel out. In this case, place in 6 for d, and it's almost too simple:

$$f(d) = 100 + \left(2^{\frac{d}{2}} + \frac{d}{3}\right)100$$

$$= 100 + \left(2^{\frac{(6)}{2}} + \frac{(6)}{3}\right)100$$

$$= 100 + \left(2^3 + 2\right)100$$

$$= 100 + (8 + 2)100$$

$$= 100 + (10)100$$

$$= 100 + 1,000$$

$$= 1,100$$

Here's another one.

PLAY

The population of a certain city can be modeled by the function $p(y) = 20,000\left(2^{\frac{y}{20}}\right)$, where $p(y)$ represents the population and y measures years since 2020. Based on this function, the projected population of the city in 2060 is:

(A) 40,000

(B) 60,000

(C) 80,000

(D) 100,000

Put away your calculator. SAT projections are simple, even if they look mad. The expression $2^{\frac{y}{20}}$ isn't so bad when y is a multiple of 20, and in this case it's 40 (the number of years from 2020 to 2060). This means that $2^{\frac{y}{20}}$ is really just $2^{\frac{40}{20}}$, or 2^2, which of course equals 4. So the answer is $20,000(4)$, which equals 80,000, or Choice (C). Who needs a calculator? And — how long did this one take? Guessing Less. Than. A. Minute.

Projection questions are common in SAT math, so practice until you're comfortable with them.

Chapter **8**

Solving Algebra and Functions

*A*lgebra and functions are an extension of the numbers and operations covered in Chapter 7. Topics in this chapter comprise about half of the SAT Math questions, and while numbers and operations generate only about a quarter of the SAT Math questions (as if that's not enough), it's important to understand the concepts in Chapter 7 before moving on to this chapter. The topics in this chapter build upon the foundation of the previous chapter.

Solving for *X*

Solving for *x* is just that: turning something like $2x + 3 = 5$ into $2x = 2$ and finally $x = 1$. Simple, right? But the SAT, being what it is, varies this idea in ways you haven't seen before and won't see again until your graduate admissions GMAT or GRE. But that's another story.

The SAT, still being what it is, stays within its predefined scope of math topics and sets the questions up for easy answering if you know how to answer them. This chapter takes you through these SAT-level topics and shows you how to answer each question in less than a minute.

Solving for *x* with a number

To solve for *x* or any other variable that the question asks for, move that variable to one side of the equation, and divide both sides of the equation by the coefficient. For example, where $4x = x + 6$, subtract *x* from both sides of the equation for $3x = 6$. Divide both sides by 3, for $x = 2$, and the solution is 2.

A common SAT trap is where it gives the equation $4x = x + 6$, but instead of asking you to solve for x, it asks you to solve for $3x$. Working this problem is just as simple, but you fall back on your tendency to solve for x instead of what the question is asking. Of course, $3x = 6$, but how many test-takers fall for the trap and respond that $x = 2$, which is true but the wrong answer?

Try this one:

PLAY

$2x + 8 = 12$

In the above equation, what is the value of $x + 3$?

(A) 4

(B) 5

(C) 6

(D) 7

Your reflex is to solve for x, which is fine, but be sure to adjust your answer for the value of $x + 3$ and answer Choice (B):

$$2x + 8 = 12$$
$$2x = 4$$
$$x = 2$$
$$x + 3 = 5$$

Practice this so you get used to spotting the trap. You don't want to lose these easy points by sticking with a process that has been correct for most of your math life, which is solving for x by itself.

Solving for *x* with a *y*

The SAT tries to confuse you further. Just like the projections questions in Chapter 7, these questions appear menacing but are actually simple *if you know what to do*.

The SAT gives you an equation with two unknowns, such as $3x + 4y = 18$, asks you to solve for x, and tells you what y is: $y = 3$. Just place in 3 for y and solve for x.

$$3x + 4y = 18$$
$$3x + 4(3) = 18$$
$$3x + 12 = 18$$
$$3x = 6$$
$$x = 2$$

The first time you see one of these, you might get stuck putting it together. Of course, the letters aren't always x and y. Try this one:

PLAY

If $a - b = 1$ and $\frac{b}{3} = 1$, what is the value of a?

(A) 4

(B) 5

(C) 6

(D) 7

Start with $\frac{b}{3} = 1$ and multiply it all by 3, so that $b = 3$. There! That's the hard part. Now place 3 in for b and solve that puppy:

$$a - b = 1$$
$$a - (3) = 1$$
$$a = 4$$

And the answer is Choice (A), just like that. If this question took you longer than a minute, that's okay. That's why you're here.

Solving for x in a radical

Another common question type that the SAT presents, which is also just as solvable if you know what to do, is an equation where an expression with x is embedded within a radical. Go through it once, practice a few, and you'll have it down for the exam.

Take an equation like this:

$$\sqrt{2x^2 + 7} - 4 = 1$$

Start by keeping everything under the radical on one side of the equal sign, and move everything not in the radical on the other. In this case, add 4 to both sides:

$$\sqrt{2x^2 + 7} = 5$$

Now that one side is completely under the radical, and the other is not, square both sides:

$$2x^2 + 7 = 25$$

And solve for x the way you usually do:

$$2x^2 + 7 = 25$$
$$2x^2 = 18$$
$$x^2 = 9$$
$$x = 3 \text{ or } -3$$

Here, try one:

PLAY

If $\sqrt{3x^3 + 1} - 2 = 3$, what is the value of x?

(A) 2

(B) 3

(C) 5

(D) 7

You're not laughing. You should be! Each step is simple, and you know where to start. First add 2 to both sides to get rid of the -2, then square both sides, and the rest falls into place:

$$\sqrt{3x^3 + 1} - 2 = 3$$
$$\sqrt{3x^3 + 1} = 5$$
$$3x^3 + 1 = 25$$
$$3x^3 = 24$$
$$x^3 = 8$$
$$x = 2$$

Of course, there are other variations, but if you can manage this, the others won't faze you. Keep in mind that the math is *always* simple, and SAT math is designed to work out neatly.

Solving for *x* in a fraction

The SAT places *x* (or another variable) into a fraction, like this:

$$\frac{2}{15}x = \frac{2}{3}$$

First thing: When *x* is outside the fraction, move it to the top of the fraction:

$$\frac{2}{15}x \rightarrow \frac{2x}{15}$$

The basic approach is then to cross multiply:

$$\frac{2x}{15} = \frac{2}{3}$$
$$(2x)(3) = (15)(2)$$
$$6x = 30$$
$$x = 5$$

If one side of the equation is a fraction and the other side isn't, then multiply both sides by the denominator of the fraction:

$$\frac{2x}{5} = 4$$
$$(5)\frac{2x}{5} = 4(5)$$
$$2x = 20$$
$$x = 10$$

If both sides have the same denominator, you can just eliminate the denominator (which is the same as multiplying both sides by that denominator).

$$\frac{x}{7} = \frac{43}{7}$$
$$x = 43$$

PLAY

If $\frac{x-2}{4} = \frac{x+3}{5}$, what is the value of *x*?

(A) 12

(B) 22

(C) 24

(D) 30

Cross multiply and find your answer:

$$\frac{x-2}{4} = \frac{x+3}{5}$$
$$(x-2)(5) = (4)(x+3)$$
$$5x - 10 = 4x + 12$$
$$x = 22$$

And the answer is Choice (B).

Cross multiplying always works, but sometimes there's a simpler way to solve the problem. See if you can find it with this question:

PLAY

In the equation $5 - \dfrac{2x+2}{x+1} = \dfrac{9}{x+1}$, x is equal to

(A) 0

(B) 1

(C) 2

(D) 3

Note that the two fractions have common denominators, which means they can be easily combined. In this case, add the clunky $\dfrac{2x+2}{x+1}$ to both sides:

$$5 - \frac{2x+2}{x+1} = \frac{9}{x+1}$$
$$5 = \frac{9}{x+1} + \frac{2x+2}{x+1}$$
$$5 = \frac{9+2x+2}{x+1}$$
$$5 = \frac{11+2x}{x+1}$$

Now, multiply $x+1$ on both sides and solve for x:

$$5 = \frac{11+2x}{x+1}$$
$$(x+1)5 = 11+2x$$
$$5x+5 = 11+2x$$
$$3x = 6$$
$$x = 2$$

And Choice (C) is correct.

Sometimes cross multiplying produces a quadratic (meaning you get an x^2 along with an x), but the practice questions with quadratics are held for later in this chapter.

Solving for *x* in a reciprocal fraction

The SAT presents you with a fraction and asks you to reciprocate it to the other side. In its simplest form, the question looks like this:

If $y = \dfrac{2}{3}x$, what is x in terms of y?

The most effective way to do this is to separate the fraction $\dfrac{2}{3}$, reciprocate it to $\dfrac{3}{2}$, and place it on the other side.

$$y = \frac{2}{3}x$$
$$y = \left(\frac{2}{3}\right)x$$
$$\left(\frac{3}{2}\right)y = x$$
$$\frac{3}{2}y = x$$

Technically this is multiplying both sides by the reciprocal, but the separate-and-reciprocate approach is faster with some of the complex fractions that appear on the SAT. Also, the SAT likes to muddle the question. It presents something absurd, like $y = x\dfrac{2\sqrt{3gh^4}}{5k}$, and asks for x in terms of y, which means $x = y(\text{something})$. It presents the question like this:

PLAY

If $y = x\dfrac{2\sqrt{3gh^4}}{5k}$, what is x in terms of g, h, k, and y?

(A) $x = y\dfrac{2\sqrt{3gh^4}}{5k}$

(B) $x = y\dfrac{5k}{2\sqrt{3gh^4}}$

(C) $x = 2y\sqrt{3gh^4}$

(D) $x = 10y\sqrt{3gh^4}k$

Now you *could* multiply both sides by the reciprocal, $\dfrac{5k}{2\sqrt{3gh^4}}$, and that *will work*, but isn't it easier to just take the reciprocal and move it to the other side? That gives you Choice (B) in . . . 20 seconds?

Does this always work? No. You need to make sure that the fraction is set up to work this way, because *sometimes* you have to break apart the fraction. But first check; *maybe* you can just reciprocate and move it over. Before you step into the complex math, see whether you can just reciprocate and move the fraction.

If the question presents you with $y = x(\text{something})$ and asks for x in terms of y, make sure that the x that you're separating out is both in the numerator of the fraction and isn't squared or in a radical. Of course, the question could use any set of letters, but the process is the same.

Remember that $\dfrac{2}{3}x$ and $\dfrac{2x}{3}$ are the same, as are $y = x\dfrac{\sqrt{3gh^4}}{5k}$ and $y = \dfrac{x\sqrt{3gh^4}}{5k}$.

Solving for More Than One *X*

So far, solving for x has meant, for the most part, that you find *one* value for x. If $3x = 15$, then you know $x = 5$, and you're good. But many questions in the SAT Math section ask what x *could* be if it has more than one possible value, such as $x^2 = 9$. In this case, x equals either 3 or -3, and you don't know which one. Note that this is usually written as $x = 3, -3$, and it's understood that x has *one* of the two possible values, but not both. These multiple values are also called the *solutions* to the equation.

Solving an absolute value

Absolute value means the distance from 0 on the number line. Because distance is always positive, absolute value is also always positive. The number or value has bars on either side, like this: $|-15|$. Because -15 is 15 away from 0, the absolute value of -15 is 15, written in math as $|-15| = 15$.

A positive number works the same way. The absolute value of 3 is written $|3|$, which equals 3, because it's 3 away from 0 on the number line. The absolute value of –5 is written $|-5|$, which equals 5, because it's 5 away from 0 on the number line.

Be sure to simplify any expression inside the absolute value bars first. If you're working with $|3-4|$, calculate that first, for $|3-4|=|-1|$, and *then* take the absolute value, which in this case is 1.

If you have an x or other unknown inside the absolute value expression, it means that the expression is that distance from 0 on the number line, and typically could be in two separate places. For example:

$$|x|=7$$

This tells you that x is 7 away from 0 on the number line, but you don't know whether it's on the positive side or negative side, which means that the x could equal 7 or –7. A couple points to glean here:

» Any x has *one* value: You don't know which one it is without more information. (With $|x|=7$, something like $x>0$ would do the trick.)

» Any absolute value is always *positive*. A distance cannot be a negative, so an equation like $|x|=-5$ is impossible, or in math, has *no solution*.

With an expression like $|x+2|=5$, you know that $|x+2|$ is 5 away from 0 on the number line, but you don't know which side. Therefore, you actually have two equations: $x+2=5$ and $x+2=-5$. Solve them separately for the two possible values of x:

$$x+2=5 \quad \text{and} \quad x+2=-5$$
$$x=3 \qquad\qquad x=-7$$

Given $|x+2|=5$, you know that x could equal either 3 or –7. Now try one.

PLAY

In the equation $|x-4|=3$, x could equal:

If $|x-4|$ is 3 away from 0, solve this as two separate equations:

$$x-4=3 \quad \text{and} \quad x-4=-3$$
$$x=7 \qquad\qquad x=1$$

Write in either 1 or 7, and you got this one right.

REMEMBER

The value of x can't be both 7 *and* 1. x has *one* value, and that's why the question reads, "x *could* equal."

WARNING

When solving an absolute value such as $|x-3|=5$, don't write it as $x-3=\pm5$, which is technically true but doesn't help you. Adding 3 to both sides always leads to $x=8$ and omits the other answer. Instead, convert the equation to $x-3=5,-5$, then add the 3s to get both possible values of x:

$$|x-3|=5$$
$$x-3=5,-5$$
$$x=8,-2$$

Solving a quadratic

A *quadratic* is an equation having an x^2 and often an x, such as $x^2+2x-15=0$. Quadratics are one of the most commonly occurring SAT math questions, and on the SAT are simpler than the ones you encounter in Algebra II. Here are some notes:

>> With a quadratic, x usually, but not always, has two possible values.

>> A quadratic results from any equation where x is multiplied by itself. For example, cross multiplying the fractions $\frac{2}{x}=\frac{x}{2}$ results in a quadratic. (In this example, the fractions cross multiply to $x^2=4$, so $x=2$ or $x=-2$.)

>> When x appears more than one time in a single equation or set of equations, each x has the *same* value at *one* time. If one x changes (as in a graphed equation), all the x's change with it.

>> You may need to know what a, b, and c are from a quadratic equation. These are simply the coefficients from the equation when it equals 0. In the equation $x^2+2x-15=0$, a, b, and c are 1, 2, and –15, respectively (because x^2 times 1 is x^2, x times 2 is $2x$, and 1 times –15 is, of course, –15).

>> On the SAT, *most* quadratics are simple enough to solve without the Quadratic Formula. You *rarely* need this, but if you do, just place a, b, and c as described earlier into the formula:

$$x=\frac{-b\pm\sqrt{b^2-4ac}}{2a}$$

>> When you draw the graph of any quadratic equation, including $y=x^2+2x-15$, in the xy-coordinate plane, the graph results in a parabola, covered later in this chapter.

There are two parts to working with quadratics. The first is multiplying the expressions, and the second is factoring them. You multiply expressions using the FOIL method, covered in Chapter 10 and reviewed here:

FOIL stands for First Outer Inner Last, which basically means everything in one expression is multiplied by everything in the other. To multiply these expressions:

>> $(x+2)(x-3)$

>> Start with the First terms, x times x, for x^2.

>> Now the Outer terms, x times –3, for $-3x$.

>> Next the Inner terms, 2 times x, for $2x$.

>> Then the Last terms, 2 times –3, for –6.

>> Finally add the pieces for a final quadratic result of x^2-x-6.

PLAY

Try this one:

The expression $(x-3)^2$ is equivalent to

(A) x^2-9

(B) x^2+9

(C) x^2+6x-9

(D) x^2-6x+9

The exponent 2 means that $(x-3)$ is multiplied by itself, so you know that this is one to FOIL. (You also know this because you read about FOIL not even a page ago.) Set it up to FOIL and go through the steps:

$$(x-3)(x-3)$$
$$x^2-3x-3x+9$$
$$x^2-6x+9$$

And the answer is Choice (D).

More common than *multiplying* expressions is *factoring* them. The numeric part of factoring is always simple: The trick is knowing the concept.

For example, given $x^2+2x=15$, solve for x.

1. **Set the equation equal to 0.**

   It *might* already be equal to 0, but here it's not, so subtract 15 from both sides:

   $$x^2+2x-15=0$$

2. **Set up your answer by drawing two sets of parentheses:**

   $$(\quad)(\quad)=0$$

3. **To get x^2, the *first* terms are x and x, so fill those in:**

   $$(x\quad)(x\quad)=0$$

4. **Look at the *middle* and *last* terms of the equation:**

   What two numbers add to 2 and multiply to –15? Remember that on SAT math, *this part will be simple.* How about 5 and –3?

   $$(x+5)(x-3)=0$$

5. **Check your work and FOIL it back out:**

   Just takes a second, and it's worth knowing you did this right:

   $$(x+5)(x-3)$$
   $$x^2-3x+5x-15$$
   $$x^2+2x-15$$

   Nice! So how does $(x+5)(x-3)=0$ tell you what x could be? Treat it like two separate equations:

   $$(x+5)=0$$
   $$(x-3)=0$$

Meaning that x could equal either 3 or –5. In math that's written as $x = 3, -5$, and it's understood that x has only one of these two values. Also, when you graph the equation $y = x^2 + 2x - 15$, the resulting parabola crosses the x-axis at 3 and –5.

The SAT likes to explore variations of the quadratic. Here are a few:

PLAY

What are the solutions to the equation $2x^2 - 2x = 24$?

(A) 3,–4

(B) 4,–3

(C) 6,–8

(D) 8,–6

First set the equation equal to 0: $2x^2 - 2x - 24 = 0$. What next? Divide both sides by 2: $x^2 - x - 12 = 0$. *Now* you can factor it:

$$x^2 - x - 12 = 0$$
$$(x - 4)(x + 3) = 0$$
$$x = 4, -3$$

for an answer of Choice (B).

Here's another variation:

PLAY

If $x > 0$, what are the solutions to the equation $x^4 - 13x^2 + 36 = 0$?

(A) 2,3

(B) 4,9

(C) 8,18

(D) 16,36

Factor this one like a regular quadratic, only with x^2 instead of x:

$$x^4 - 13x^2 + 36 = 0$$
$$(x^2 - 4)(x^2 - 9) = 0$$
$$x^2 = 4,9$$

And if x^2 is 4 or 9, then x is 2 or 3, for Choice (A). Good thing $x > 0$, or this one would have four solutions: the regular 2 and 3 along with –2 and –3.

Crazy, isn't it? That question is *so simple* looking back at it. Here's another:

PLAY

What are the solutions to the equation $x - 9\sqrt{x} + 20 = 0$?

(A) 2,3

(B) 4,5

(C) 16,25

(D) 25,81

Yep. Factor it out. It works exactly the same; just keep in mind that x factors to $\sqrt{x}$ times $\sqrt{x}$.

$$x - 9\sqrt{x} + 20 = 0$$
$$(\sqrt{x} - 4)(\sqrt{x} - 5) = 0$$
$$\sqrt{x} = 4,5$$
$$x = 16,25$$

Thus, the correct answer is Choice (C).

Here's the strategy for this next one:

When a perfect square equals a perfect square, take the square root of both sides, and make the numeric side both positive and negative. You know this: $x^2 = 16$ becomes $x = 4, -4$. Here's the SAT variant:

PLAY

What are the solutions to the equation $(x-3)^2 = 25$?

(A) 4,3

(B) 5,2

(C) 6,–5

(D) 8,–2

The point of this question is that you don't *always* set it equal to 0 and factor. You could, but here it's faster to take the square root of both sides:

$$(x-3)^2 = 25$$
$$x - 3 = 5, -5$$
$$x = 8, -2$$

In that last step, you're adding 3 to both 5 and –5, for the answers 8 and –2, which match Choice (D).

TIP

As with the absolute value, when you take the root of $(x-3)^2 = 25$, *don't* use ± and write it as $x - 3 = \pm 5$. This is technically true, but you need to add 3 to both 5 and –5, and using ± has you lose the negative answer. Take the extra second and write both 5 and –5.

These are just some of the ways that SAT math varies the quadratic. First you get stuck, then you work through the answer, and then you totally understand the question. Get stuck on these questions *here, now,* when it *doesn't* matter — and have them for breakfast on Exam Day. Quadratics are among the most commonly asked topics on SAT Math, so practice all the variations.

Solving the difference of squares

A *difference of squares* is a specific quadratic where a perfect square is subtracted from a perfect square, as in $a^2 - b^2$. This expression factors to $(a-b)(a+b)$, so remember it like this:

$$a^2 - b^2 = (a-b)(a+b)$$

Of course, it could be any letters, but it doesn't matter. You don't find out what a and b are, but you don't need to. Think of it like this: $(a+b)$ times $(a-b)$ equals $a^2 - b^2$. So if $(a+b)$ is 8, and $(a-b)$ is 3, what is $a^2 - b^2$? Why, it's 24.

Note that if you FOIL out $(a-b)(a+b)$, the middle terms ab and $-ab$ cancel, and the result is simply $a^2 - b^2$.

PLAY

In its simplest form, the SAT asks about the difference of squares like this:

If $c^2 - d^2 = 15$ and $c + d = 5$, what is the value of $c - d$?

(A) 2

(B) 3

(C) 4

(D) 5

Set it up and place the values that you know:

$$c^2 - d^2 = (c-d)(c+d)$$
$$(15) = (c-d)(5)$$
$$c - d = 3$$

Making the correct answer Choice (B).

Now the SAT doesn't ask about the difference of squares *quite* like that. That would be too easy! For you, it'll *still* be too easy. Anyway, the SAT embeds the difference of squares into other math topics. Try this one:

PLAY

If $y^2 - x^2 = 16$ and $y + x = 8$, what is the value of $\frac{2^y}{2^x}$?

(A) 2

(B) 4

(C) 8

(D) 16

Start with the $\frac{2^y}{2^x}$ as you would any other divided exponent. The same way that $\frac{2^5}{2^3} = 2^{5-3}$, $\frac{2^y}{2^x} = 2^{y-x}$. Remember doing these in Chapter 7? Anyway, if $y^2 - x^2 = 16$ and $y + x = 8$, you know that $y - x = 2$, so place 2 in for $y - x$ in that exponent: $2^{y-x} \rightarrow 2^2 = 4$ for an easy, less-than-a-minute answer, Choice (B).

The difference of squares is also useful for rationalizing a fraction. *Rationalizing* means making the denominator into a rational number, which is the key to solving certain SAT fraction questions. For example, the fraction $\frac{\sqrt{5}}{\sqrt{3}}$ isn't rationalized. To rationalize it, multiply the top and bottom by $\sqrt{3}$, like this:

$$\frac{\sqrt{5}(\sqrt{3})}{\sqrt{3}(\sqrt{3})} = \frac{\sqrt{15}}{3}$$

The numerator isn't rational, but that's okay — the denominator is, and the fraction is rationalized.

When a polynomial expression is in the denominator, like $\frac{2 - \sqrt{5}}{4 - \sqrt{5}}$, rationalize it by multiplying the top and bottom by *something* that eliminates the radical on the bottom. The denominator is $4 - \sqrt{5}$, so multiply top and bottom by $4 + \sqrt{5}$, like this:

$$\frac{(2 - \sqrt{5})(4 + \sqrt{5})}{(4 - \sqrt{5})(4 + \sqrt{5})}$$
$$\frac{8 + 2\sqrt{5} - 4\sqrt{5} - 5}{16 - 5}$$
$$\frac{3 - 2\sqrt{5}}{11}$$

The top still has the irrational $\sqrt{5}$, but that doesn't matter. The bottom is fully rational, and the fraction is thus rationalized.

Try this one:

PLAY

Which of the following is equivalent to the expression $\frac{2-3i}{3-i}$? Note that $i^2 = -1$.

(A) $\frac{9-7i}{10}$

(B) $\frac{9+7i}{8}$

(C) $\frac{9+7i}{10}$

(D) $\frac{9-7i}{8}$

Rationalize this one: The denominator is $3-i$, so multiply top and bottom by $3+i$, like this:

$$\frac{(2-3i)(3+i)}{(3-i)(3+i)}$$

$$\frac{6+2i-9i+3}{9+1}$$

$$\frac{9-7i}{10}$$

And the answer is Choice (A).

This section is based on topics from earlier in this chapter and from Chapter 7, like old friends, including exponents, radicals, quadratics, imaginary i, and fractions, but with the difference of squares mixed in, like a new friend.

Solving an expression

An *expression* in math is a set of values grouped together. It's another way that the SAT packages a simple concept as a challenging question. If you cut through the façade, the actual question is simple. Sound familiar?

Say you're solving for x: $2x = 6$ becomes $x = 3$, and you know what x is because it's isolated. Do you *always* have to isolate the x? No, you can leave it in the expression, like this one: $12^x = 12^7$. You know that $x = 7$ without isolating it. Okay, here's the concept again, but on a level higher. Find the value of c:

$$x^2 - 9x + 20 = x^2 - 9x + c$$

And $c = 20$, which you know for sure even though you didn't *isolate* it. Sometimes it helps to isolate the c, by crossing off x^2 and $-9x$ from both sides, but you don't *have* to.

And there you have the basics of this topic: Two expressions equal each other, and where there's a number on one side, there's an unknown on the other, and you find the value of the unknown. Sometimes you factor one side or manipulate the equations somehow, but because this is the SAT, *you know it'll be simple even if it looks tricky.*

PLAY

In this equation, where k is a constant, what is the value of k?

$$x^2 - 8x + 15 = (x-3)(x-k)$$

(A) 5

(B) 15

(C) 25

(D) 45

Factor the polynomial on the left so it matches the one on the right:

$$x^2 - 8x + 15$$
$$(x-3)(x-5)$$

Now it looks like this: $(x-3)(x-5) = (x-3)(x-k)$.

And you know that k is 5 for an answer of Choice (A).

Here's another variation:

PLAY

In this equation, where k is a constant, what is the value of k?

$$3(x^2 - 5x + 6) = 3x^2 - 15x + 6k$$

(A) 2

(B) 3

(C) 6

(D) 18

Looks menacing, doesn't it? How are you going to isolate that k? Wait — you *don't* isolate it — just divide both sides by 3. The 3 on the left cancels, and the expression on the right divides evenly by 3:

$$\frac{3(x^2 - 5x + 6)}{3} = \frac{3x^2 - 15x + 6k}{3}$$
$$x^2 - 5x + 6 = x^2 - 5x + 2k$$

You now know that $2k = 6$ making $k = 3$, for answer Choice (B). Now be honest: *How long did that question take you?*

Another variation is where you form a quadratic and find the values of a, b, and c. You remember a, b, and c from the discussion of quadratics all those pages ago, don't you? Copied straight from there: These are simply the coefficients from the equation when it equals 0. In the equation $x^2 + 2x - 15 = 0$, a, b, and c are 1, 2, and -15, respectively (because x^2 times 1 is x^2, x times 2 is $2x$, and 1 times -15 is -15).

PLAY

In the following equation, what is the value of $a + b + c$?

$$2x(x+3) + 4(x-1) = ax^2 + bx + c$$

(A) 12

(B) 10

(C) 8

(D) 6

By now this should be second nature — for *you*, because you're getting the hang of fielding the SAT tricks. Work with the polynomial on the left so it matches $ax^2 + bx + c$, and you have your *a*, *b*, and *c*:

$$2x(x+3) + 4(x-1) =$$
$$2x^2 + 6x + 4x - 4 =$$
$$2x^2 + 10x - 4 = ax^2 + bx + c$$

You now know that *a*, *b*, and *c* are 2, 10, and –4, respectively, for $2 + 10 - 4 = 8$ and an answer of Choice (C).

You good? This is a fairly common topic on SAT Math, so be sure to practice.

Setting Up Equations

Setting up equations is the approach to an SAT math question that describes a scenario, whether a story or a set of numbers, and you set up an equation to model that scenario. Sometimes you get a numeric answer, and sometimes you get an answer in terms of an unknown.

Setting up a story

A *story* is a word problem that describes a scenario, and you use this to set up an equation. For example, if Harvey handed out twice as many Twix bars this Halloween as he did last Halloween, and last year he handed out 25 bars, you know that this year he handed out 50 bars. Or, if last year Allison handed out *n* apples, and this year she handed out three times as many as last year, you know that this year she handed out $3n$ apples. One instance gives you a numeric answer, and the other gives you an answer in terms of an unknown.

The secret to setting up an equation is finding the verb *is*, which can be in other tenses, including *has been*, *had been*, *will have been*, and so on. When you find that verb *is* — in whatever tense — write down an equal sign. That gets you started.

For example: Billy *is* 3 inches taller than Henry. You can write down, $b = h + 3$. If you're not sure where to put the +3, just ask yourself, "Who's taller: Billy or Henry? (Snap fingers.) *Billy* is taller!" So add 3 to Henry.

Now try a simple one.

PLAY

The number of marbles in Box *X* is three times the number of marbles in Box *Y*. Which of the following equations is true?

(A) $3x = y$

(B) $3y = x$

(C) $xy = 3$

(D) $\dfrac{y}{x} = 3$

Translate the sentence, "The number of marbles in Box *X* is three times the number of marbles in Box *Y*" into "*x* equals 3 times *y*," or "$x = 3y$," which matches Choice (B).

The SAT may include the equation and ask about changing it. Try this one:

PLAY

Julia works at a job where her salary, s, can be represented by the equation $s = dh$, where she earns d dollars per hour for each of h hours that she works each week. If Julia gets an <u>additional</u> r dollars per hour this week, which of the following equations represents her salary this week?

(A) $s = dhr$

(B) $s = (d+r)h$

(C) $s = d(h+r)$

(D) $s = dh+r$

If Julia earns d dollars per hour during a usual week and an extra r dollars per hour this week, then this week she earns $d+r$ dollars per hour. Multiply that by h for her weekly pay for answer Choice (B).

These are good to know, so have another:

PLAY

A copying service charges \$2.50 to copy up to 20 pages plus 5 cents per page over 20. Which formula represents the cost, c, in dollars, of copying p pages, where p is greater than 20?

(A) $c = 2.50 + 5p$

(B) $c = 2.50 + 0.05p$

(C) $c = (2.50)(20) + 0.05p$

(D) $c = 2.50 + 0.05(p-20)$

The first 20 pages cost \$2.50, so that has to be in the equation. To count the pages after 20, use the expression $(p-20)$, and multiply this by 0.05 for the charge. This matches Choice (D).

Setting up equations is up there with quadratics as one of the most commonly asked topics on SAT Math. They can be varied and challenging, so you need to practice these to keep your under-a-minute average.

Setting up a sum of numbers

A *sum of numbers* is a certain type of "setting up equations" question that students tend to get stuck on, and it's commonly asked, so it's separated out here as its own topic. Basically, the SAT describes a set of numbers, gives you the total, and asks you for one of the numbers.

The question reads something like this: The sum of two numbers is 60. The first number is twice the second number. What is the smaller number?

The secret is, don't use x and y. Setting it up as $x + y = 60$ won't help you. Instead, just use x. If the second number is twice the first number, then that one is $2x$, and the equation becomes this:

$$x + 2x = 60$$
$$3x = 60$$
$$x = 20$$

PLAY

The sum of five numbers is 60. The first number is four times the total of the other four numbers. What is this first number?

(A) 12

(B) 24

(C) 36

(D) 48

Call the first number x. If x is four times the total of the other four numbers, then the total of those four numbers is $\frac{x}{4}$. Now set up the equation:

$$x + \frac{x}{4} = 60$$

$$\frac{5x}{4} = 60$$

$$5x = 240$$

$$x = 48$$

And the answer is Choice (D).

Here, try another one:

Ms. Tan and Mr. Davis teach history and Algebra at Brandeis. If together they have 290 students, and Ms. Tan has 30 more students than Mr. Davis does, how many students does Ms. Tan have?

Say Ms. Tan works with x students. If Mr. Davis works with 30 fewer students, then he works with $x - 30$ students. Now set up the equation:

$$x + x - 30 = 290$$

$$2x - 30 = 290$$

$$2x = 320$$

$$x = 160$$

And you answer 160.

Setting up interest

Interest refers to the percent of return on a loan or investment. If you place $100 into a savings account, and in 12 months that investment is worth $105 (assuming you didn't touch it), then the additional $5 is *interest*. Start by knowing these terms.

>> **Present value (PV) or principal:** This is the starting amount of money, or the $100 in the preceding example.

>> **Future value (FV):** This is the value of the investment or loan at some future state. In SAT math, this assumes no other transaction takes place: no fees, withdrawals, and so forth. This is the $105 in the preceding example.

>> **Interest:** This is the money earned on the investment, or $5 from the preceding example.

>> **Interest rate, or i:** This is the percent of the principal that becomes interest each term, usually a year. In the preceding example, this is 5 percent. Note that if $i = 5\%$, calculate it as $i = 0.05$.

>> **Simple versus compound:** In the second year, is the 5 percent interest rate calculated on the original $100, making it *simple* interest, or the new $105, making it *compound* interest? Finance class gets carried away with this concept, but on the SAT it stays relatively straightforward: Compound means that the interest earns its *own* interest, while simple means it doesn't.

Now to see it in action. Hopefully throughout your life, you put these concepts to work *for* you, where you save or invest money that earns interest that you *own*, rather than *against* you, where you borrow money that accumulates interest that you *pay*. Digressing slightly, but the mindset of planning ahead and preparing for success with money is right in line with planning ahead and preparing for success on the SAT. Here's how it works.

Simple interest

Simple interest is calculated like this:

$$FV = PV(1+i)$$

Or using the preceding example:

$$\$105 = 100(1+.05)$$

It's easier to memorize if you *understand* it. If you start with $100, how does it multiply to $105? If you multiply the $100 by the interest rate, 5 percent or 0.05, you just get the amount of interest, $5. You need to add 1 to the 0.05, so that when you multiply this by $100, you have the total *future value* of $105.

Here's a trick. The SAT expects you to know the formula for simple interest but not compound interest. If the SAT asks a compound interest question and doesn't provide the formula, just use the simple interest formula more than once. *Usually* the interest compounds only twice, so the question doesn't take long at all.

It goes something like this:

If you place $100 into a savings account that earns 10% interest compounded annually, how much is in the account at the end of the second year, assuming the account has no other activity?

(A) $100

(B) $110

(C) $120

(D) $121

Don't worry about knowing compound interest. With only two cycles, use the simple interest formula twice. Start with the formula and place the numbers from the question to find the value of the account at the end of the *first* year:

$$
\begin{aligned}
FV &= PV(1+i) \\
&= (\$100)(1+0.10) \\
&= \$100(1.1) \\
&= \$110
\end{aligned}
$$

Now do it again for the *second* year, which starts at $110:

$$FV = PV(1+i)$$
$$= (\$110)(1+0.10)$$
$$= \$110(1.1)$$
$$= \$121$$

And the answer is Choice (D).

Compound interest

The compound interest formula is streamlined for the SAT. Here's the thing. *Don't memorize it.* Instead, *understand it.* The SAT questions on compound interest don't expect you to come up with the formula. Instead, the answer choices will be four variations of the formula, and if you *understand* it, you can spot the three wrong variations and cross them off.

Interest that compounds once a year is calculated like this:

$$FV = PV(1+i)^t$$

It's exactly the same as the simple interest formula, only the *t* exponent stands for *time*, usually counted in years. Note that this variation exists only on the SAT. Real interest compounds more often, so that formula looks like this:

$$FV = PV\left(1+\frac{i}{n}\right)^{nt}$$

where *n* is the number of times per year that the interest compounds. For example, if the interest compounds monthly, the formula looks like this:

$$FV = PV\left(1+\frac{i}{12}\right)^{12t}$$

The *i* is divided by 12 because it's the *annual* interest divided monthly. The 12*t* is because the interest compounds 12 times per year. The *t* in this case still represents years.

Note that *n* represents the number of times that the interest compounds during the time that *i* interest accumulates. If the interest rate is *monthly*, say 0.6% per month (which is 0.006), and the interest compounds once per month, then *i* isn't divided by 12 and *t* isn't multiplied by 12: The formula would look like $FV = PV(1+i)^t$, showing a monthly cycle that accumulates *i* interest.

Here's an example. See if your *understanding* is sufficient to answer the question:

PLAY

The money in a savings account increases 0.8% each month. Which of the following equations shows the future value, *FV*, of the money in the account based on the present value, *PV*, after a period of *m* months?

(A) $FV = PV(0.008)^m$

(B) $FV = PV(1.008)^m$

(C) $FV = \left(\dfrac{PV}{0.008}\right)^m$

(D) $FV = \left(\dfrac{PV}{1.008^m}\right)$

It's not a math problem, remember. It's a *puzzle*. Say you start with $100, so $PV = \$100$. If *i* is 0.8 percent, then use 0.008 (because 0.8% = 0.008, per Chapter 7). Which equation would lean in the direction of $FV = \$100 \times 1.008 = \$100.80$ after the first month? *Don't* do a lot of math. Instead, *estimate and eliminate.* If you have two or more answers that seem close, *then* do the math. But you won't.

Choice (A): $FV = \$100(0.008)^m$. No matter what m is, this won't lead to \$100.80, so cross it off.

Choice (B): $FV = \$100(1.008)^m$. If m is 1, as it would be after the first month, then this leads to \$100.80. Leave it — if you need to calculate further, you can always come back and do so.

Choice (C): $FV = \left(\dfrac{\$100}{0.008}\right)^m$. Not a chance. Run it through your calculator with $m = 1$ (in other words, the first month) and you'll see why.

Choice (D): $FV = \left(\dfrac{\$100}{1.008^m}\right)$. This is closer, but here's the thing. Because the denominator is slightly more than 1, each month the value of the account goes *down* slightly, not up. If a swimming pool has a slow leak, this type of equation would model the diminishing amount of water.

So what's left? Choice (B). And how much math did you do? Not much, right? You stopped after calculating the first month. *That's why this question takes about a minute.* And here's the thing, which is true for pretty much all the SAT math. *If you understand the question, the math is simple.* It's easy to fall into the trap of doing a lot of math, so if that happens, it's okay. *Stop working on it, move on, and come back to it later.*

Interest rate questions aren't that common, but they help you understand the rate-of-change topic that follows, so they're worth practicing.

Setting up rates of change

A *rate of change* question is a spin on the interest rate question from the previous section, where a quantity changes slowly over time. The situation can be more complicated, and you may get two or three questions based on a single scenario. The scenarios and equations are also similar to the projections questions from Chapter 7, only with more depth — and more questions.

A rate of change question describes something that grows, like the population of a city or the revenue of a business. The scenario typically provides an equation to model the rate of change, similar to the compound interest formula. Don't memorize the formula, because it changes based on the question. Instead, *understand* it.

Just look for the *starting point* and the *rate of change*. For a simple example, say that a tree is 5 feet tall and grows 3 feet each year. The SAT asks questions like these:

1. **Which equation models the tree's height after *t* years?**

    The tree's starting point is 5 and its rate of change is 3, so its height is modeled by the equation $h = 3t + 5$.

2. **What is the tree's height after 4 years?**

    $$h = 3(4) + 5$$
    Place 4 in for *t*: $= 12 + 5$
    $$= 17$$

3. **If the tree actually grows 6 feet per year, not 3, how should the equation be changed?**

    Change the $3t$ to $6t$.

A simple example indeed, but it shows the SAT questions on a rate-of-change scenario. Apply your understanding of calculating interest and the perspective of these simple questions to this example:

Questions 1–3 are based on the following information:

PLAY

Micah has a 50-pound drum of semolina in his pantry. Each week, he uses 10% of the remaining semolina in the drum for baking.

1. Which of the following equations models the amount of semolina, s, in pounds, remaining in the drum after w weeks?

   (A) $s = 50(1.1)^w$

   (B) $s = 50(0.1)^w$

   (C) $s = 50(0.9)^w$

   (D) $s = 50(1.9)^w$

2. At this rate, how many pounds of semolina will remain in the drum at the end of the second week?

   (A) 50.1

   (B) 45.3

   (C) 40.5

   (D) 35.7

3. If Micah instead obtains a 100-pound drum and each week uses 20% of the remaining semolina, then he will use exactly half of the drum

   (A) in fewer weeks than he would using 10% remaining weekly of the 50-pound drum.

   (B) in more weeks than he would using 10% remaining weekly of the 50-pound drum.

   (C) in the same number of weeks that he would using 10% remaining weekly of the 50-pound drum.

   (D) never, because at this rate he will not use half of the drum.

   1. Per the scenario, Micah uses 5 pounds of semolina in the first week, because 10 percent of 50 is 5. Try out each equation to see which leaves him with 45 pounds when $w = 1$. See, the beauty of this approach is that w is an exponent, so when it equals 1, *it goes away*. You understand the question, you make it simple, you work it in *less than a minute*.

      Choice (A): $s = 50(1.1)^w$. This increases the semolina to 55 pounds. Cross it off.

      Choice (B): $s = 50(0.1)^w$. This leaves 5 pounds. Micah *uses* 5 pounds and should have 45 left over. Cross it off.

      Choice (C): $s = 50(0.9)^w$. This leaves 45 pounds. Looks good. Don't work more math — check the next answer.

      Choice (D): $s = 50(1.9)^w$. This increases the semolina to 95 pounds. Cross it off!

      And the answer is Choice (C).

2. You already know how much semolina Micah has after the first week, plus you know the correct equation, so plug 45 in and run it again with w as 1. Or leave the 50 in there and set w as 2. Either way works. Here's the first way:

$$s = 45(0.9)^1$$
$$= 40.5$$

for an answer of Choice (C).

3. You could math this one out, but why? Instead, just *understand* it. If you have two drums of semolina, *regardless of the volume*, and you consume one at 10 percent per week and the other at 20 percent per week, which one will reach the halfway point first? Why, the 20 percent drum, so Choice (A) is correct.

SAT math questions in general, but rate-of-change questions in particular, test your *understanding* of a concept more than your ability to punch numbers. This is why the calculator isn't necessarily your friend. It helps a little, as with Question 2, but if you tried answering Question 3 with the calc, you'd *probably* get it right, but it would take a while.

Interest and rate-of-change questions borrow concepts from coordinate geometry, where you track how one number changes on its own (such as time) and causes another number to change (such as value or amount). This is a good question topic to end setting up equations and begin coordinate geometry.

Graphing Coordinate Geometry

Coordinate geometry refers to a drawing that results from one or more equations. You know the basic equation $y = mx + b$ that makes a line, and that squaring the x makes a parabola, and so on. If you forgot how this works, that's okay; it's all reviewed right here.

On the SAT, coordinate geometry is always two-dimensional. Geometry questions, with drawings, may have 3-D shapes, but *coordinate* geometry, on the SAT, does not. It exists on the x-y *rectangular grid*, also known as the *coordinate plane*, a two-dimensional area defined by a horizontal x-axis and a vertical y-axis that intersect at the *origin*, which has coordinates $(0,0)$, and form *Quadrants I, II, III,* and *IV*.

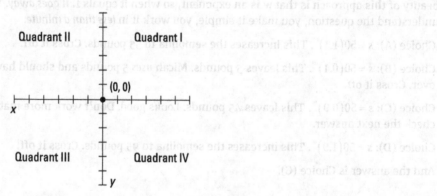

Any point on the grid has an (x, y) value, with the x indicating the horizontal position and the y indicating the vertical position. For example, this point has the coordinates $(4, 5)$:

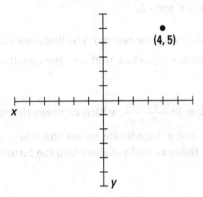

Graphing a line

A line is graphed by a *linear equation*, which is any equation with x and y and no exponents, such as $y = 2x + 1$. It can use other letters, but they're typically x and y. The equation has infinite solutions, because for any value of x, there's a matching value of y. For example, with $y = 2x + 1$, when $x = 0$, $y = 1$; when $x = 1$, $y = 3$; and so on. These x- and y-values form a line, and each x-value and matching y-value falls on the line:

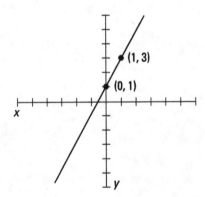

A linear equation is usually given in the *slope-intercept* form $y = mx + b$, where m is the slope and b is the y-intercept, which is the y value when $x = 0$ and the line crosses the y-axis. With the line $y = 2x + 1$, the slope is 2 and the y-intercept is 1.

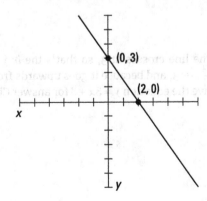

Look at the second drawing above. How do you find the equation from the line itself? Place the slope and y-intercept as the m and b, respectively, into the equation $y = mx + b$. Start with the y-intercept, which is where the line crosses the y-axis. In the drawing, the line crosses the y-axis at 3, making $b = 3$, so place that into the equation: $y = mx + 3$.

Now for the m, which is the slope. This can be found using *rise over run*: The line rises 3 and runs 2, and because it goes down, the slope is negative, so $m = -\frac{3}{2}$. Place that into the equation, and you have the answer: $y = -\frac{3}{2}x + 3$.

The slope can also be found using the *slope formula*, $m = \frac{y_2 - y_1}{x_2 - x_1}$, which captures the *rise over run* from any two points on the line. $y_2 - y_1$ refers to one y-coordinate minus the other, and $x_2 - x_1$ refers to one x-coordinate minus the other. Place these x- and y-values into the formula:

$$m = \frac{y_2 - y_1}{x_2 - x_1}$$
$$= \frac{(0) - (3)}{(2) - (0)}$$
$$= -\frac{3}{2}$$

And you have the same result: $m = -\frac{3}{2}$.

Try this one:

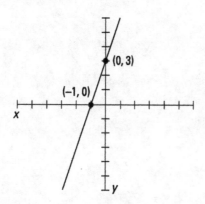

PLAY

Which of the following is the equation of the above line?

(A) $y = \frac{1}{3}x - 3$

(B) $y = -3x + 3$

(C) $y = -\frac{1}{3}x - 3$

(D) $y = 3x + 3$

Start with the bare-bones equation $y = mx + b$. The line crosses at 3, so that's the b: $y = mx + 3$. Using *rise over run*, the line rises 3 and runs 1, for $\frac{3}{1}$, or 3, and because it goes upwards from left to right, the 3 is positive. Place that for m, and you have the equation $y = 3x + 3$ for answer Choice (D).

A couple of notes before you dive into the practice questions:

>> **Parallel lines have the same slope.** They may cross the y-axis at different points, but if they have the same slope, they're parallel.

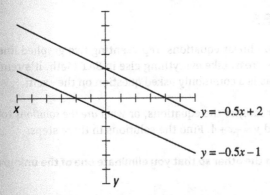

>> **Perpendicular lines have the negative reciprocal slope.** Take the slope, reciprocate it, multiply it by –1, and the resulting line is perpendicular. The y-intercepts don't matter, even though in this drawing, they match.

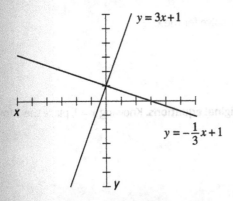

>> **Linear equations don't have to use the *slope-intercept* form.** The slope-intercept form is your friend $y = mx + b$, but an equation such as $3x + 2y = 6$ counts also. To convert it to the *slope-intercept* form and find the slope and y-intercept, just solve for y:

$$3x + 2y = 6$$
$$2y = -3x + 6$$
$$y = -\frac{3}{2}x + 3$$

>> **Linear equations don't need *both x and y*.** They can have just one or the other. If there's just an x, as in $x = 3$, then the line goes straight up and down, crossing the x-axis at 3 (and the slope is undefined). If there's just a y, as in $y = 5$, then the line is flat, crossing the y-axis at 5 (and the slope is 0).

>> **Linear equations don't have to use *x and y*.** They can use any letters. Remember the tree example from the section "Setting Up Equations"? The tree is 5 feet tall and grows 3 feet each year: $h = 3t + 5$. If you graph this, the line would have a y-intercept of 5 and a slope of 3.

>> **If it has a radical or an exponent, it's not a line.** The exponent or radical introduces a curve. In applied math it could be many things, but on the SAT it's typically a parabola or circle. There are other ways to curve the line, but these are typically what you see on the SAT.

Practice working with linear equations, because you'll see plenty of these on the SAT. Also, this topic is the foundation to understanding the other topics in the "Graphing Coordinate Geometry" section, so it's worth practicing.

Graphing two lines

An SAT question may present two linear equations, representing two graphed lines, and ask you to find the point where the lines cross. Like everything else in SAT Math, it's remarkably simple if you know what to do. Also, this is a commonly asked question on the exam.

The SAT asks, *which ordered pair satisfies* the equations, or *what are the solutions* to the equations. Take the equations $y = 2x + 1$ and $y = -x + 4$. Find the solutions in three steps:

1. **Subtract one equation from the other so that you eliminate one of the unknowns.** In this example, eliminate the *y*:

$$y = 2x + 1$$
$$\underline{-(y = -x + 4)}$$
$$0 = 3x - 3$$

2. **Solve for the other unknown.** Here, solve for the *x*:

$$0 = 3x - 3$$
$$-3x = -3$$
$$x = 1$$

3. **Place that value into one of the original equations.** Knowing $x = 1$, place the 1 for *x* in either one of the original equations:

$$y = 2x + 1$$
$$= 2(1) + 1$$
$$= 3$$

And you have the answer: $x = 1$ and $y = 3$. This means that when you graph the two lines, they cross at the coordinates $(1, 3)$:

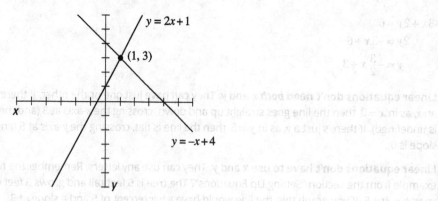

A couple of variations, which aren't common on the SAT, but you may be expected to understand:

» The equations have *infinite solutions* if they both draw the same line, because any pair of *x*, *y* coordinates that works for one equation also works for the other. If you try to solve this one, you end up with something like $0 = 0$.

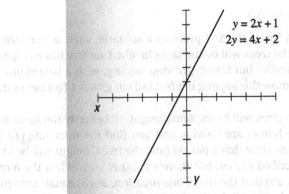

$$y = 2x + 1$$
$$2y = 4x + 2$$

» The equations have *no solutions* if they're parallel, because there is no pair of *x*, *y* coordinates that works for *both* equations. If you try to solve this one, you end up with something like $0 = 1$.

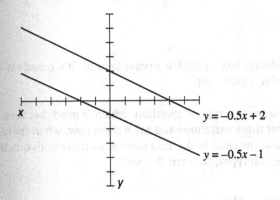

$$y = -0.5x + 2$$
$$y = -0.5x - 1$$

PLAY

Try one:

What is the solution to the equations $y = 2x + 3$ and $y = 3x + 7$?

(A) $(4, 5)$

(B) $(4, -5)$

(C) $(-4, -5)$

(D) $(-4, 5)$

Set them up and subtract them:

$$y = 2x + 3$$
$$-(y = 3x + 7)$$
$$\overline{0 = -x - 4}$$
$$x = -4$$

Then place -4 for x in one of the original equations:

$$y = 2x + 3$$
$$= 2(-4) + 3$$
$$= -8 + 3$$
$$= -5$$

And you have your answer: $(-4, -5)$, for Choice (C).

A word-problem variant of this question is where the SAT presents a scenario, such as two trees growing at different rates, and asks when the trees will be the same height. One tree has a height projected as $h = 3t + 5$, and the other is a smaller but faster-growing sapling, with a height projected as $h = 4t + 2$. From the equation, you know this sapling is 2 feet tall but grows 4 feet per year.

The SAT then asks you at what year the two trees will be the same height. It's exactly the same as with the (x, y) coordinates, only here, the letters are t and h, and you find the matching (t, h) coordinates. The answer is t, representing the time that's passed (and the trees' height will be h). You could use the subtraction method described earlier, but there's another way. When the h of one equation equals the h of the other, it means that the *rest* of one equation, $3t + 5$, equals the *rest* of the other, $4t + 2$. So set those equal to each other and solve for t:

$$3t + 5 = 4t + 2$$
$$-t = -3$$
$$t = 3$$

Note that a question like this always has a positive answer because it's based on a real-life scenario. A tree wouldn't be negative 3 years old.

So now you have two ways to solve this type of question, which is good, because the SAT varies this topic many ways. Encounter these variations and solve them now, when there's no pressure, so when the pressure's on, you know what to do. This topic is up there with quadratics as one of the most commonly asked question types, so learn this well.

Graphing an inequality

Graphing an inequality can be based on a linear or curved equation. Either way, the concept is the same. The SAT takes a simple equation, such as $y = 2x + 1$, and turns it into an inequality.

» If y is *greater* than the expression, as in $y > 2x + 1$, then the inequality includes the region *above* the line, regardless of the slope.

» If y is *less* than the expression, as in $y < 2x + 1$, then the inequality includes the region *below* the line, again regardless of the slope.

» If it is an *or equal* inequality, as in $y \geq 2x + 1$ or $y \leq 2x + 1$, then the region *includes* the line and the line is solid; otherwise, with > or <, the region does *not* include the line and the line is dashed.

» If it is a *horizontal* line that is *greater* than the expression, as in $y > 3$, then the inequality includes the region *above* the line; and if the horizontal line is *less than* the expression, as in $y < 2$, then the inequality includes the region *below* the line.

» If it is a *vertical* line that is *greater* than the expression, as in $x > 5$, then the inequality includes the region *to the right* of the line; and if the vertical line is *less than* the expression, as in $x < 4$, then the inequality includes the region *to the left* of the line.

The SAT doesn't expect you to measure anything carefully. Like most other topics, these questions are based on your understanding of the concepts. The SAT presents you with a scenario and asks you which inequality models it best.

For example, try one with the new sapling:

PLAY

Bill plants a two-foot-tall sapling that is expected to grow *at least* 4 feet per year. Which of the following inequalities best models its growth?

(A) $h > 4t + 2$

(B) $h < 4t + 2$

(C) $h \geq 4t + 2$

(D) $h \leq 4t + 2$

Cross off the wrong answers. If each year the sapling grows 4 feet or more, its height wouldn't be *less than* the expression, so eliminate Choices (B) and (D). If it grows *at least* 4 feet, then it *could* grow 4 feet, or it could grow more, so the greater-than sign is out, taking with it Choice (A). This leaves Choice (C), with the appropriate greater-than-or-equal-to sign.

Graphing an inequality isn't that common, but the scenario can be intricate. As complex as the scenario gets, remember the underlying concept is always simple. Any time you choose from equations, you *always* find the right answer by *crossing off wrong answers*.

Graphing a parabola

A *parabola* is a U-shaped curve that results from an equation where *x* is squared. For example, this is the graph of $y = x^2$:

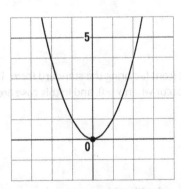

The parabola's *vertex* is the bottom center. If you were to drop a ball bearing into the U-shape, the vertex is where the ball bearing would rest. In the preceding drawing, the vertex is $(0,0)$. The official formula for a parabola is $y = a(x - h)^2 + k$, where these rules apply:

>> The vertex is at the coordinates (h, k).

>> The larger the *a*, the narrower the parabola. Don't worry about the *a* much — it's rarely asked on the SAT, but know the concept.

For example, here's the parabola graph of the equation $y = 3(x-2)^2 + 1$:

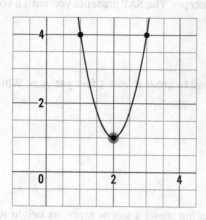

Note that it's narrower than the graph of $y = x^2$, and its vertex is $(2,1)$. Also, the h appears negative in the equation. This parabola may also appear in the form of $f(x) = 3(x-2)^2 + 1$, where $f(x)$ takes the place of y. Variations of $f(x)$ are covered later in this chapter under "Graphing a function," but for now just treat it like this: $f(x) = y$.

The parabola equation has three forms:

» The *vertex form*, $y = (x-2)^2 - 1$, where the *xy*-coordinates of the vertex are in the equation. For example, here you know that the coordinates of the vertex are $(2,-1)$, because the *x*-coordinate appears negative, but the *y*-coordinate appears as is.

» The *standard form*, $y = x^2 - 4x + 3$, which you get from multiplying out the vertex form:

$$y = (x-2)^2 - 1$$
$$= (x^2 - 4x + 4) - 1$$
$$= x^2 - 4x + 3$$

» The *factored form*, $y = (x-3)(x-1)$, which you get from factoring the standard form. This form tells you the *x*-intercepts of the graph, which occur when $y = 0$, and in this case are 1 and 3:

$$y = x^2 - 4x + 3$$
$$= (x-3)(x-1)$$

These are three forms of the same equation, which graphs like this:

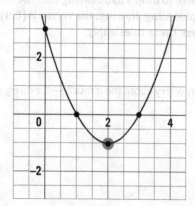

One key thing to remember is that the *factored form* gives you the x-intercepts. If the SAT asks for the x-intercepts, you can convert the standard form to the factored form by factoring it just as you would a quadratic, covered earlier in this chapter. Try this one:

PLAY

At what two points does the graph of the equation $y = x^2 - 3x - 28$ cross the x-axis?

(A) $(3,0)$ and $(7,0)$

(B) $(4,0)$ and $(7,0)$

(C) $(-3,0)$ and $(7,0)$

(D) $(-4,0)$ and $(7,0)$

The graph crosses the x-axis where $y = 0$, so place 0 for y and factor it out. Remember when factoring this quadratic, you're looking for two numbers that add to –3 and multiply to –28.

$$0 = x^2 - 3x - 28$$
$$0 = (x+4)(x-7)$$

$y = 0$ when $x = -4$ and $x = 7$, for answer Choice (D).

Here's a common variation on the theme:

PLAY

At what two points does the graph of the equation $y = x^2 - x - 2$ cross the line where $y = 4$?

(A) $(2,4)$ and $(3,4)$

(B) $(-2,4)$ and $(3,4)$

(C) $(2,4)$ and $(-3,4)$

(D) $(-2,4)$ and $(-3,4)$

Place 4 for y and solve it as you would a quadratic, meaning you set the equation equal to 0, factor it out, and find the values of x.

$$y = x^2 - x - 2$$
$$(4) = x^2 - x - 2$$
$$0 = x^2 - x - 6$$
$$0 = (x-3)(x+2)$$

$y = 4$ when $x = -2$ and $x = 3$, for answer Choice (B).

The SAT may give you a quadratic equation (which graphs into a parabola) in the *standard form* and ask for the vertex. There are two ways to find this. The first is to convert the standard form to the vertex form by *completing the square*, like this:

1. **Start with the standard form.**

   For example, $y = x^2 - 4x - 5$.

2. **Divide *b* (the x-coefficient) by 2.**

   In this case, divide –4 by 2, for –2.

3. **Place *x* and the result of Step 2 into parentheses squared.**

   $$(x-2)^2$$

4. **Take the square of the result from Step 2 and subtract it from _c_ (the number without the _x_) in the original equation.**

The –2 squared becomes 4, and you subtract this from –5 in the original equation for –9.

5. **Set _y_ equal to the results of Steps 3 and 4.**

You have $(x-2)^2$, so place the –9 to the right, for a result of $y = (x-2)^2 - 9$.

Here are the steps as a single set:

$$y = x^2 - 4x - 5$$
$$= (x-2)^2 - 4 - 5$$
$$= (x-2)^2 - 9$$

And you know that the vertex of this parabola is $(2,-9)$.

The second method is to find the _axis of symmetry_, which is basically the _x_-value of a line that goes down the middle of the parabola, and using that _x_ to find _y_. Both methods are useful depending on the variation of the question, but the axis of symmetry is simpler for just finding the vertex:

1. **Start with the standard form.**

In this case, $y = x^2 - 4x - 5$.

2. **Set up $\frac{-b}{2a}$.**

In this example, this is $\frac{-(-4)}{2(1)} = \frac{4}{2} = 2$ so the axis of symmetry is $x = 2$.

3. **Place this value of _x_ into the equation.**

$$y = x^2 - 4x - 5$$
$$= (2)^2 - 4(2) - 5$$
$$= 4 - 8 - 5$$
$$= -9$$

And you know again that the vertex is $(2,-9)$. Finding the axis of symmetry is easier, but completing the square can be useful on some questions.

The parabola is extremely common on the SAT, but converting from standard to vertex form is not nearly as common. This process becomes easy _fast_ with just a little practice, and you'll need it for certain graphing-circles questions in the next section.

Try this one:

PLAY

In the quadratic equation $y = x^2 + 2x - 8$, what are the coordinates of the vertex of the parabola?

(A) $(-1,-9)$

(B) $(-1,9)$

(C) $(1,-9)$

(D) $(1,9)$

Try this by completing the square:

$$y = x^2 + 2x - 8$$
$$= (x+1)^2 - 1 - 8$$
$$= (x+1)^2 - 9$$

From the vertex form of the equation, you know that the vertex is $(-1,-9)$, but also try this by finding the axis of symmetry:

$$\frac{-b}{2a} = \frac{-(2)}{2(1)} = -\frac{2}{2} = -1$$

And placing the x-value into the equation:

$$y = x^2 + 2x - 8$$
$$= (-1)^2 + 2(-1) - 8$$
$$= 1 - 2 - 8$$
$$= -9$$

Either way, you find that the vertex is $(-1,-9)$, for answer Choice (A).

TIP

When graphing an equation, the *solutions* are the values of x that cause y (or $f(x)$, covered later) to equal 0 and make the graph touch or cross the x-axis.

Graphing a circle

Many shapes can be graphed from equations, but the graphed shapes that appear on the SAT are primarily the line, the parabola, and the circle.

Standard form

This is the *standard form* of the equation of a circle:

$$(x-h)^2 + (y-k)^2 = r^2$$

In this equation, the h and the k are the x- and y-coordinates of the center, and r is the radius. Say you have a circle with a center at coordinates $(-3, 2)$ and a radius of 4. Its equation is:

$$(x+3)^2 + (y-2)^2 = 4^2 \text{ or } (x+3)^2 + (y-2)^2 = 16:$$

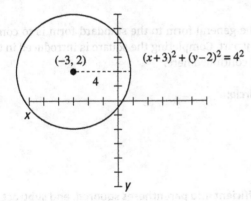

TIP

The r^2 at the end is one place the SAT tries to trip you up. If the equation of a circle is $(x+3)^2 + (y-2)^2 = 16$, the radius is **4**, not **16**.

Here's one for you to try.

PLAY

Which of the following is the equation for the graph of a circle having a center of $(-1,-7)$ and a radius of 6?

(A) $(x-1)^2 + (y-7)^2 = 6$

(B) $(x+1)^2 + (y+7)^2 = 6$

(C) $(x-1)^2 + (y-7)^2 = 36$

(D) $(x+1)^2 + (y+7)^2 = 36$

If the center of the circle is $(-1,-7)$, then inside the parentheses should be +1 and +7, so cross off Choices (A) and (C). Next, if the radius is 6, then the equation should equal 36, so cross off Choices (A) again and (B). You're left with Choice (D), which is the right answer.

General form

So far you've been working with the *standard form* of the equation of a circle. There's also the *general form*, which is just taking the standard form and multiplying everything out.

$$(x+3)^2 + (y-2)^2 = 5^2$$
$$(x^2 + 6x + 9) + (y^2 - 4y + 4) = (25)$$
$$x^2 + y^2 + 6x + 4y + 13 = 25$$
$$x^2 + y^2 + 6x + 4y = 12$$

The general form of the same circle is $x^2 + y^2 + 6x + 4y = 12$. Unlike the standard form, which tells you the secrets of the circle's center and radius, the general form doesn't offer much in the way of clear information about the circle.

The SAT gives you the general form of a circle, say $x^2 + y^2 - 2x + 6y = 6$, and asks for the coordinates of the center, or the radius, or something about the circle that's clear in the standard form but obscured in the general form. You need to convert the equation back to the standard form.

The way to convert the equation from the general form to the standard form is to complete the squares separately for the x part and the y part. Completing the square is introduced in the previous section, "Graphing a parabola," and continued here.

1. **Start with the general form of the circle:**

$x^2 + y^2 - 2x + 6y = 6$

2. **Place the x's and y's together:**

$x^2 - 2x + y^2 + 6y = 6$

3. **Place the single x and half the x-coefficient into parentheses squared, and subtract the square of that number.**

Square the –1 and subtract the result: $(x-1)^2 - 1$

4. **Do the same with the y.**

Square the 3 and subtract the result: $(y+3)^2 - 9$

5. **Move the numbers to the right side of the equation.**

In this case, add 1 and 9 to both sides:

$$(x-1)^2 - 1 + (y+3)^2 - 9 = 6$$
$$(x-1)^2 + (y+3)^2 = 16$$

6. **Convert the number on the right to its squared form:**

The 16 becomes 4^2.

Here are these steps as a single set:

$$x^2 + y^2 - 2x + 6y = 6$$
$$x^2 - 2x + y^2 + 6y = 6$$
$$(x-1)^2 - 1 + (y+3)^2 - 9 = 6$$
$$(x-1)^2 + (y+3)^2 = 16$$
$$= 4^2$$

Ready to try one? This variation is somewhat common.

PLAY

Which of the following are the center and radius of the graph of the equation $x^2 + y^2 - 6x + 10y = -18$?

(A) $(4,-6)$ and 3
(B) $(3,-5)$ and 4
(C) $(6,-10)$ and 16
(D) $(5,-8)$ and 18

Convert the equation from the general form to the standard form, and you can find the center and radius:

$$x^2 + y^2 - 6x + 10y = -18$$
$$x^2 - 6x + y^2 + 10y = -18$$
$$(x-3)^2 - 9 + (y+5)^2 - 25 = -18$$
$$(x-3)^2 + (y+5)^2 = 16$$
$$= 4^2$$

From the standard form of the equation, you know that the center is $(3,-5)$ and the radius is 4, for answer Choice (B).

You will probably see at least one graphed circle on your SAT, so prepare for it.

Graphing a function

A *function* is any kind of graphed equation that uses $f(x)$ instead of y. The equation $y = 3x - 5$ is exactly the same as $f(x) = 3x - 5$, and the value of x goes into the parentheses. So, if $x = 4$, the equation looks like this: $f(4) = 3(4) - 5$. Also, a function may use different letters, such as $g(h)$.

The SAT doesn't always give you the equation for a function. It may give you just a few values in a table, like this:

x	$f(x)$
2	3
3	8
4	5
5	11

The values may not have a pattern, so don't worry about finding one. Just know that when $x = 2$, $f(x) = 3$, and when $x = 5$, $f(x) = 11$. You won't be asked what happens when x is 3.5 or 6 or anything like that: It'll only be what's in the table.

Try this one:

PLAY

For which value of x shown in the table is $f(x) = g(x)$?

x	$f(x)$	$g(x)$
2	3	6
3	8	14
4	5	5
5	11	2

(A) 2

(B) 3

(C) 4

(D) 5

When $x = 4$, both $f(x)$ and $g(x)$ equal 5, making $f(x) = g(x)$ for answer Choice (C).

Here's another one:

PLAY

What is the value of $g(f(2))$?

x	$f(x)$	$g(x)$
2	3	6
3	8	14
4	5	5
5	11	2

(A) 2

(B) 5

(C) 6

(D) 14

From the table, when $x = 2$, $f(x) = 3$, so replace $f(2)$ with 3 in the equation. Now with the $f(2)$ out of there, you have $g(3)$, which per the table is 14. It goes like this:

$$g\big(f(2)\big)$$
$$g(3)$$
$$14$$

The answer is Choice (D).

The SAT takes this one level higher. Here's how it works. Say you have this function:

$$f(x) = x^2 + x - 12$$

From quadratics all those pages ago, you know that the equation factors into this:

$$f(x) = (x+4)(x-3)$$

This means that $(x+4)$ and $(x-3)$ are *factors* of $f(x) = x^2 + x - 12$. It also means that when $x = 3$ or $x = -4$, $f(x) = 0$. This is also written as $f(3) = 0$ and $f(-4) = 0$.

So put all these together:

» $f(x) = x^2 + x - 12$

» $f(x) = (x+4)(x-3)$

» $f(3) = 0$ and $f(-4) = 0$

» $(x+4)$ and $(x-3)$ are *factors* of the equation.

Understand this concept back and forth, and you'll quickly answer correctly a question that everyone around you gets stuck on and finally gets wrong.

Try this one based on the equation that you just explored, $f(x) = (x+4)(x-3)$.

PLAY

For the function $f(x)$, the value of $f(3) = 0$. Which of the following must be true?

(A) $(x-3)$ is a factor of $f(x)$

(B) $(x+3)$ is a factor of $f(x)$

(C) x is a factor of $f(x)$

(D) 3 is a factor of $f(x)$

If $f(3) = 0$, then the function $f(x)$ must look something like this: $f(x) = (x-3)(\text{something})$. The something part doesn't matter, but the $(x-3)$ causes the function to work like this when $x = 3$:

$$f(x) = (x-3)(\text{something})$$
$$f(3) = (3-3)(\text{something})$$
$$= (0)(\text{something})$$
$$= 0$$

If the function looks like $f(x) = (x-3)(\text{something})$, then $(x-3)$ is a factor of $f(x)$, for answer Choice (A).

Here's another one based on a new equation but the same concept:

PLAY

For the function $f(x)$, the value of $f(-5) = 0$. Which of the following must be true?

(A) $(x-5)$ is a factor of $f(x)$

(B) $(x+5)$ is a factor of $f(x)$

(C) x is a factor of $f(x)$

(D) 5 is a factor of $f(x)$

If $f(-5) = 0$, then the function $f(x)$ must look something like this: $f(x) = (x+5)(\text{something})$, making $(x+5)$ a factor of $f(x)$ for answer Choice (B).

The second question is repetitive, but you'll be glad it's repetitive when you see its twin on the exam and answer it in . . . 20 seconds? Placing bets here. But the SAT offers this in different forms, so try one more:

PLAY

Given the function $f(x) = \dfrac{5x}{x^2 - 4x + 4}$, which is not a possible value of x?

(A) 4

(B) 2

(C) 0

(D) −2

The denominator $x^2 - 4x + 4$ factors to $(x-2)(x-2)$, which means that $x = 2$ makes the denominator 0. A fraction can't bottom in 0, so 2 can't be a value of x. Choice (B) is correct.

That last question is the same idea as in the previous two questions but packaged differently. That shouldn't stop you. The $f(x)$ question is on the Top Ten SAT Math Topics list, so be ready.

IN THIS CHAPTER

» **Understanding how the SAT packages geometry questions**

» **Answering these questions quickly and easily**

» **Dodging common tricks and traps**

» **Simplifying the questions**

» **Getting the answers right**

Chapter 9

Drawing Geometry and Trigonometry

The geometry and trigonometry on SAT Math, like the other topics on this test, go fairly in depth but have limited scope. There are topics you could see, and topics you won't see, and this boundary stays consistent with little exception.

Keep in mind that on the digital exam, you can click Reference to pop open a box of formulas and information, like this:

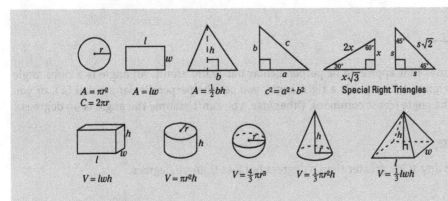

$$A = \pi r^2$$
$$C = 2\pi r$$
$$A = lw$$
$$A = \tfrac{1}{2}bh$$
$$c^2 = a^2 + b^2$$

Special Right Triangles

$$V = lwh \qquad V = \pi r^2 h \qquad V = \tfrac{4}{3}\pi r^3 \qquad V = \tfrac{1}{3}\pi r^2 h \qquad V = \tfrac{1}{3}lwh$$

There are 360 degrees of arc in a circle.

The number of radians of arc in a circle is 2π.

There are 180 degrees in the sum of the interior angles of a triangle.

The triangle ratios are especially good to know. Of course, no one ever remembers that the formulas are there, so this chapter has tips and tricks to remember them.

Drawing Basic Shapes

Basic shapes include squares, trapezoids, triangles, which get particularly complex with side-length ratios, and circles, which get tricky but manageable with arcs and sectors. Simple strategies and some memorization are the keys here, all contained in this section.

Drawing angles

Any two lines or segments that meet or cross make an *angle*, which is the space between the lines. Understanding angles is easy when you know the different types of angles and a few key concepts.

Finding an angle is usually a matter of simple addition or subtraction. In addition to the rules in the following sections, these three rules apply to angles:

>> Angles can't be negative.

>> Angles can't be 0° or 180°.

>> Fractional angles, such as $44\frac{1}{2}$ degrees or 179.5 degrees, are rare on the SAT. Angles are typically round and whole numbers. If you're placing a number for an angle, use a whole number, such as 30, 45, or 90.

Right angle

Right angles equal 90 degrees and are represented by perpendicular lines with a small box where the two lines meet.

TIP Watch out for lines that appear to be perpendicular but really aren't. An angle is a right angle *only* if the description tells you it's a right angle, you see the perpendicular symbol ($\perp$), or you see the box in the angle (most common). Otherwise, you can't assume the angle is 90 degrees.

Acute angle

An *acute angle* is any angle greater than 0 degrees but less than 90 degrees.

45°

TIP *Acute* means sharp or perceptive, so an acute angle is sharp.

Obtuse angle

An *obtuse angle* is any angle greater than 90 degrees but less than 180 degrees.

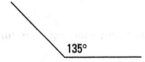

Obtuse doesn't mean the opposite of *sharp* in a physical sense, so a dull knife wouldn't be *obtuse*, but it does mean the opposite of perceptive, so an obtuse person is . . . well, not sharp.

Angles around a point total 360 degrees, no matter how many angles there are.

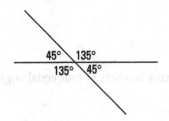

Complementary angles

Complementary angles together form a right angle: 90 degrees.

Supplementary angles

Supplementary angles together form a straight line: 180 degrees.

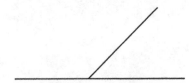

Just remember that *c* stands for both *corner* (the lines form a corner) and *complementary*; *s* stands for both *straight* and *supplementary*.

Vertical angles

Vertical angles are the opposite angles where two lines cross and have equal measures.

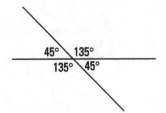

Vertical angles are across the *vertex* (the point where intersecting lines cross) from each other, regardless of whether they're side by side or above and below.

Transversal angles

A *transversal* is a line that cuts through two other lines. *Transversal angles* are formed where the transversal intersects the other two lines.

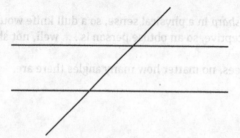

A transversal cutting through two parallel lines forms two sets of four equal angles. This is also relevant to the *parallelogram* later in this section.

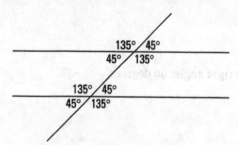

Angle concepts are mixed into other geometry and trigonometry topics, but angle-only questions come in two basic flavors. One is based on supplemental angles totaling 180°, and the other is based on angles around a point totaling 360° with the vertical angles being equal. Here they are:

In the following image, the angles are supplementary. What is the value of *x*?

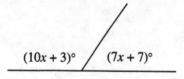

(A) 3

(B) 7

(C) 10

(D) 14

Supplementary angles total 180°, so set up an equation where the two angles total 180, drop the degree symbol, and solve for *x*:

$$(10x+3)+(7x+7)=180$$
$$17x+10=180$$
$$17x=170$$
$$x=10$$

And that makes Choice (C) the correct answer. Remember, an SAT Math question is always simple if it's set up correctly.

PLAY

In this drawing, if $a + c = 100°$, what is the value of e?

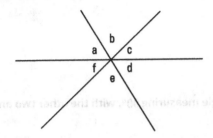

(A) 60°

(B) 80°

(C) 100°

(D) 120°

Supplementary angles total 180°, and vertical angles are equal. Find angle b, and you know angle e:

$$a + c + b = 180$$
$$100 + b = 180$$
$$b = 80$$

Because $b = e$, each is 80 for Choice (B).

Questions on angles aren't that common in SAT Math, but angles underlie almost all the other topics in this chapter.

Drawing triangles

These are some standard types of triangles:

» An *equilateral* triangle has <u>three</u> equal sides and angles.

Equilateral

» An *isosceles* triangle has <u>two</u> equal sides and angles.

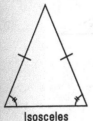

Isosceles

» A *right* triangle has one angle measuring **90°**, which appears as a right-angle box in the drawing.

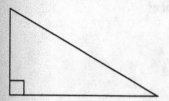

» An *isosceles right* triangle has one angle measuring **90°**, with the other two angles each at **45°**.

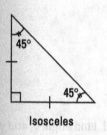

Isosceles

» **In any triangle, the largest angle is opposite the longest side.** Similarly, the smallest angle is opposite the shortest side, and the medium angle is opposite the medium-length side.

Note: In a right triangle, this largest angle is the right angle because the other two angles are each less than 90 degrees. The longest side, opposite the right angle, is the *hypotenuse*.

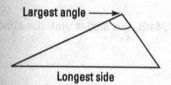

Largest angle ⟶

Longest side

» **In any triangle, the sum of the lengths of two sides must be greater than the length of the third side.** This is written as $a + b > c$, where a, b, and c are the sides of the triangle.

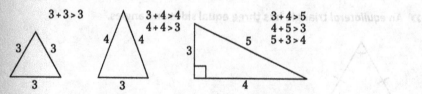

$3 + 3 > 3$

$3 + 4 > 4$
$4 + 4 > 3$

$3 + 4 > 5$
$4 + 5 > 3$
$5 + 3 > 4$

» **In any type of triangle, the sum of the interior angles is 180 degrees.**

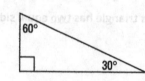

» *Similar* triangles have the same angles but are different sizes.

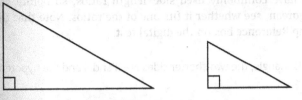

This also means that the side-length ratios are the same. Note that the term *similar* may also apply to other shapes:

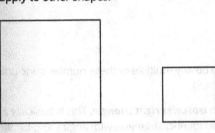

Calculating the area of a triangle

Find the area of a triangle with $A = \frac{1}{2}bh$, where b is the *base* and h is the *height*, sometimes called the *altitude*. The *height* is the distance from any angle to the opposite base. It may be a side of the triangle, as in a right triangle:

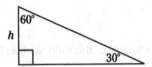

The height may also be inside the triangle, in which case it's often represented by a dashed line and a 90-degree box:

The height may also be outside the triangle, also represented by a dashed line and a 90-degree box:

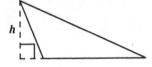

Using the Pythagorean Theorem

The *Pythagorean Theorem* states that you can find the length of any one side of a right triangle with the side lengths of the other two sides by using the formula $a^2 + b^2 = c^2$, where a and b are the shorter sides and c is the hypotenuse, opposite the 90-degree angle and the longest side of the triangle. Note that this theorem *only* works on a right triangle.

Saving time with common right triangles

Certain right triangles have commonly used side-length ratios, so before you place two side lengths into the Pythagorean, see whether it fits one of the ratios. Note that these triangles and ratios are in that pop-up Reference box on the digital test.

>> **3:4:5 triangle.** In this triangle, the two shorter sides are 3 and 4 and the hypotenuse is 5.

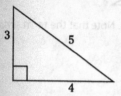

This is a ratio, so the side lengths can be any multiple of these numbers, including 6:8:10 (2 times 3:4:5) and 9:12:15 (3 times 3:4:5).

>> **45-45-90 triangle, also known as an *isosceles right triangle*.** This is basically a square cut from corner to corner, resulting in two identical triangles with angles 45°, 45°, 90° and a side-length ratio of $1:1:\sqrt{2}$.

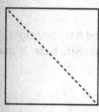
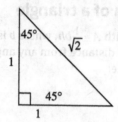

The side lengths of this triangle may appear as any multiple of this ratio, such as $5:5:5\sqrt{2}$.

>> **30-60-90 triangle.** This is basically an equilateral triangle cut perfectly in half, resulting in mirrored triangles with angles 30°, 60°, 90° and a side-length ratio of $1:2:\sqrt{3}$.

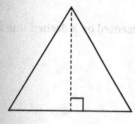
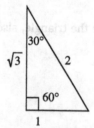

The 30-60-90 makes a regular appearance on the SAT. Just keep in mind that the hypotenuse is twice the length of the smallest side, and if you forget, it's right there in the Reference box.

If a math question reads, "Given a 30-60-90 triangle of hypotenuse 20, find the area" or "Given a 30-60-90 triangle of hypotenuse 100, find the perimeter," you've got this because you can find the lengths of the other sides:

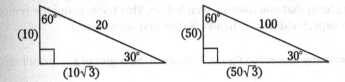

Also, if an SAT question asks for the height of an equilateral triangle, you can use the 30-60-90 triangle to solve it.

TIP

All right, enough talking . . . er, writing. Try these:

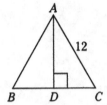

In this equilateral triangle, the length of segment *AD* is

(A) 6

PLAY

(B) 9

(C) $6\sqrt{2}$

(D) $6\sqrt{3}$

In the 30-60-90 triangle formed by *ABD*, the hypotenuse is 12 and the base is 6 because it's half the hypotenuse. Segment *AD* is the height, which is $6\sqrt{3}$, Choice (D), according to the ratio.

Try another one:

The measure of one angle of an isosceles triangle is 80°. What *could* be the measure, in degrees, of one of the other two angles?

PLAY

An isosceles triangle has one unique angle and two twin angles, for a total of 180°. If the 80° angle is the unique angle, then the other two angles are 50° and 50°. *Or*, if the 80° is one of the twin angles, then the other twin is also 80° and the third angle is 20°. Which is it? Doesn't matter. Enter either 20, 50, or 80 to get this one right. Don't worry about the degree symbol.

Triangles are among the most common math topics on the SAT, plus these concepts underlie other upcoming math topics, including trapezoids and trigonometry.

Drawing rectangles and squares

Of course, you know what rectangles and squares are. The SAT, being what it is, brings you this basic topic in some form that you haven't seen before. This book, being the remedy for the SAT, shows you what to expect and how to handle it. But first some basics:

» **A *quadrilateral* is any four-sided figure.** The sum of the angles of any quadrilateral is 360 degrees.

» **A *rectangle* is a quadrilateral with four right angles,** which makes the opposite sides equal. The area of a rectangle is *length* × *width*, where *length* is the longer side and *width* is the shorter side. The area can also be found with *base* × *height*, where *base* is the bottom and *height* is, well, height, regardless of which is longer.

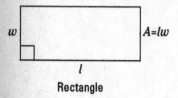

Rectangle

» **A *square* is a rectangle with four equal sides.** The area of a square is s^2, where *s* refers to a side length.

» **A *regular* shape is any shape having equal sides and angles.** For example, an equilateral triangle is a regular triangle, and a square is a regular quadrilateral.

Simple, right? Here's what the SAT does with it:

PLAY

In a certain rectangle, if the length and width were both reduced by 50%, how would the area of the rectangle change?

(A) The area would decrease by 25%.

(B) The area would decrease by 40%.

(C) The area would decrease by 50%.

(D) The area would decrease by 75%.

Draw a rectangle and give the side lengths simple numbers, preferably even numbers since you'll be dividing them by half, such as 8×10, for an area of 80. Now perform said division by half, so the new side lengths are 4×5 for a new area of 20, which is a 75% decrease from the original area. The answer is Choice (D).

Drawing trapezoids and parallelograms

You know these shapes as well, but here's a review of how they work and how to manage them on the SAT.

>> A *parallelogram* **is a quadrilateral where opposite sides and angles are equal, but the angles aren't necessarily right angles.** It's like a rectangle that got stepped on. The area of a parallelogram is *base × height*, where the *base* is the top or bottom (same thing) and the *height* is the *distance* between the two bases. As in a triangle, the height is represented by a dashed line with a right-angle box.

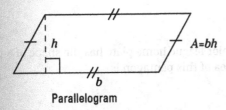

Parallelogram

>> A *rhombus* **is a parallelogram with four equal sides.** It's like a square that also got stepped on. The rhombus is measured by the distance between the angles, known as *d* for *diagonal*. The area of a rhombus is $\frac{1}{2} diagonal_1 \times diagonal_2$, or $\frac{1}{2}d_1d_2$ for short.

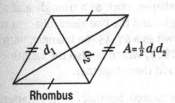

Rhombus

>> A *trapezoid* **is a quadrilateral where two sides are parallel and two sides are not.** The area of a trapezoid is $\frac{1}{2}\left(base_1 + base_2\right) \times height$, or $\frac{1}{2}\left(b_1 + b_2\right)h$, where the bases are the two parallel sides, and the height is the distance between them. If you're not sure how to remember this, it's just base times height, but you average the bases first. Or you can click the Reference button for the pop-up with the equations.

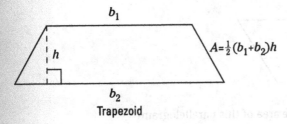

Trapezoid

>> **Other polygons that you may see include the** *pentagon*, **the** *hexagon*, **and the** *octagon*, having five, six, and eight sides, respectively. If you have to measure the area, just cut these into smaller shapes. The SAT always gives you enough detail to solve the problem.

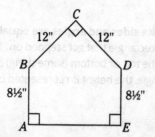

PLAY

As shown in the diagram, an official major league home plate has the shape of a pentagon. Given the measurements shown, the area of this pentagon is

(A) $144 + 12\sqrt{2}$

(B) $96 + 12\sqrt{2}$

(C) $84 + 96\sqrt{2}$

(D) $72 + 102\sqrt{2}$

The secret is to split the pentagon into separate shapes, such as a triangle and a rectangle. Look at the triangle, BCD. Because angle C is a right angle, and the two sides adjacent to C are the same length, BCD is an isosceles right triangle, also known as a 45-45-90 triangle, with the side-length ratio $s : s : s\sqrt{2}$. Therefore, the hypotenuse BD is $12\sqrt{2}$, which is also the length of the rectangle. Now find the areas of these separate shapes and add them together.

The triangle's base and height are each 12. Sure, it's rotated, but that doesn't matter: $\frac{1}{2}(12)(12) = 72$. The rectangle has a base and height of $12\sqrt{2}$ and $8\frac{1}{2}$, respectively, which multiply to $\left(12\sqrt{2}\right)\left(8\frac{1}{2}\right) = 102\sqrt{2}$. Fortunately, that matches an answer: Choice (D). Note that the SAT doesn't make you calculate the exact answer.

Here's another one.

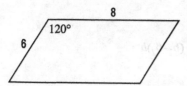

PLAY

Which of the following is the area of this parallelogram?

(A) 24

(B) 48

(C) $24\sqrt{3}$

(D) $48\sqrt{3}$

How does the 120° help you? If you draw a line from that top corner straight down to the bottom of the shape, you introduce a 30-60-90 triangle. Told you triangles are mixed into everything.

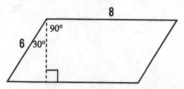

The area of a parallelogram is *base × height*. You know the base is 8, and with the 30-60-90 triangle side-length ratio of $1 : 2 : \sqrt{3}$, you now know the height is $3\sqrt{3}$ (because this new triangle has side lengths $3 : 6 : 3\sqrt{3}$). Multiply these together: $8 \times 3\sqrt{3} = 24\sqrt{3}$, for answer Choice (C).

As you can see, these questions are just puzzles, and the actual math is simple. Also, again, you don't calculate the exact answer.

Drawing circles

Of course, you know circles, but the SAT varies these up too. Like everything else SAT, and so often repeated because it's always so true, any trick is easy for you to handle if you've seen the trick before. But first, some basics:

» **The *radius* goes from the center of the circle to the outer edge.** The radius is the same length no matter where it touches the outer edge.

Radius

» **Two *radii* (not in a line) create an isosceles triangle.** This makes sense because an isosceles triangle has two equal sides.

» **A *chord* is a line segment that goes through the circle.** A chord goes all the way through the circle.

» **The *diameter* is a chord that goes through the *center* of the circle.** It's also twice the length of the radius.

Diameter

» **The *circumference* is the distance around the circle.** Find the circumference, *C*, by using either $C = 2\pi r$, where *r* is the radius, or $C = \pi d$, where *d* is the diameter, because the diameter is twice the radius.

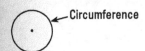

» **Pi, shown by the Greek letter π, is the ratio of the circumference to the diameter.** If you take the circumference of any circle and divide it by its diameter, the result is always approximately 3.14, represented by π.

» **Don't memorize the value of π.** Just know that it's slightly more than 3.

>> **The *area* of a circle is** $A = \pi r^2$. If you forget any of these equations, click the Reference button at the top right of the digital Math Test.

$A = 16\pi$

>> **A *tangent* is a line or other shape that touches the circle at exactly one point.** A tangent line touching a radius of the circle forms a 90-degree angle.

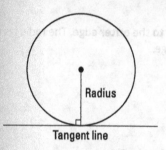

Radius

Tangent line

You know these concepts, and now you've refreshed how they work. The secret is to be fluid in converting one measure to another, such as a radius to circumference or area. Here's an SAT-style question on circles:

The radius of circle A is twice the radius of circle B. How many times greater than the area of circle B is the area of circle A?

PLAY

(A) Two times greater

(B) Three times greater

(C) Four times greater

(D) Six times greater

Pick a radius for circle A, such as 6. If that's twice the radius of circle B, then circle B has a radius of 3. Now find the areas. Place 6 and 3 for the radii of the two circles to find their areas: $\pi r^2 = \pi(6)^2 = 36\pi$ and $\pi r^2 = \pi(3)^2 = 9\pi$. Because 36π is four times greater than 9π, the answer is Choice (C).

It's a basic concept that the SAT turns sideways to throw you off. Of course, any question like this one is easy for you now.

Drawing overlapping shapes

The SAT places two shapes, with one overlapping the other, like a dinner plate on a placemat.

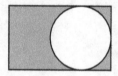

The SAT then asks you for the area of the placemat not covered by the dinner plate, or in SAT terms, the area of the shaded portion of the drawing. The way that you solve this is so simple that you need to try not to laugh out loud when you see this on the exam.

1. **Find the areas of the two shapes, separately.**

2. **Subtract the smaller area from the larger area.**

3. **Leave your answer in terms of π.**

The question gives you the numbers that you need to answer this one. In the placemat example, it tells you that the circle touches the edges of the rectangle, which measures 4×7. You can thus derive that the circle has a diameter of 4, for a radius of 2. Now to go through the steps:

1. **The rectangle area is $4 \times 7 = 28$ and the circle area is $\pi r^2 = \pi(2)^2 = 4\pi.$**

2. **Subtract the shapes for $28 - 4\pi$.**

3. **And you're done.**

You'll hardly ever have to calculate the actual value of 4π to subtract from 28. Instead, just pick $28 - 4\pi$ from the list of answers, stop laughing, and go on to the next question.

Try this one:

PLAY

A circle of radius 3 is inscribed within a square. What is the area of the shaded region?

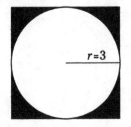

(A) $36 - 3\pi$

(B) $36 - 6\pi$

(C) $36 - 9\pi$

(D) $36 - 12\pi$

If the circle has a radius of 3, its diameter is thus 6, meaning the side of the square is also 6. Yes, the next part is even easier. The area of the square is $6 \times 6 = 36$, and the area of the circle is $\pi r^2 = \pi(3)^2 = 9\pi$. Subtract them for $36 - 9\pi$, which looks nicely like answer Choice (C).

Overlapping shapes are somewhat common on the SAT Math, so make sure you have this topic down by practicing.

Drawing parts of circles

To draw part of a circle, just draw the whole circle and take the fraction of the circle. Here are the basics and the exact steps:

>> **An *arc* is part of the circumference,** like an *arch*. The degree measure of an arc is the same as its *central angle*, which originates at the center of the circle.

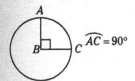

>> A *sector* is part of the whole circle, like a slice of pizza. The *arc* is the leftover crust of the pizza (if you don't eat it), and the *sector* is the slice itself. The degree measure of a sector is the same as that of an arc.

Here's how you find the length of an arc:

1. Find the circumference of the entire circle.

2. Put the degree measure of the arc over 360 and reduce the fraction.

3. Multiply the circumference by the fraction.

Here's how you find the area of a sector:

1. Find the area of the entire circle.

2. Put the degree measure of the sector over 360 and reduce the fraction.

3. Multiply the area by the fraction.

Finding the area of a sector is exactly like finding the length of an arc, except for that first step. Now try a couple:

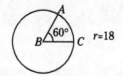

PLAY

Find the length of minor arc *AC*.

(A) 36π

(B) 60

(C) 18π

(D) 6π

Start with the circumference of the whole circle: $2\pi r = 2\pi(18) = 36\pi$. Don't multiply 36π out. Next, put the degree measure of the arc over 360: $\frac{60°}{360°} = \frac{1}{6}$. Finally, multiply the circumference by the fraction: $36\pi \times \frac{1}{6} = 6\pi$, for answer Choice (D).

TIP

The *degree measure* of the arc is not the *length* of the arc. The length is always a portion of the circumference, typically with π in it. If you chose Choice (B) in this example, you found the degree measure instead of the length.

PLAY

If point *B* is at the center of the circle, what's the area of the shaded sector?

(A) $\frac{1}{4}\pi$

(B) 16π

(C) 32π

(D) 64π

Start with the area of the whole circle: $\pi r^2 = \pi(8)^2 = 64\pi$. Next, put the degree measure of the sector over 360: $\frac{90°}{360°} = \frac{1}{4}$. Finally, multiply the area by the fraction: $64\pi \times \frac{1}{4} = 16\pi$, which matches answer Choice (B).

You got this, right? Parts of circles are fairly common on the SAT, so be sure you have this down, along with its variations.

Drawing 3-D Shapes

Almost every SAT has a couple questions dealing with a box, cylinder, sphere, or cone. The equations for these 3-D shapes are included in the Reference pop-up box, but here's a review of what you need — because everyone forgets to check the Reference box.

Drawing rectangular solids and cubes

Any rectangular solid — also known as a *rectangular prism* — on the SAT is a perfect shoebox: Each side is a rectangle, and each corner is 90°. This keeps it easy.

>> **Volume of a rectangular solid:**

Rectangular solid

The same way that the area of a rectangle is *length × width*, the volume is the area multiplied by the height, for *length × width × height*, or $V = lwh$.

>> **Surface area of a rectangular solid:**

The official equation, where *l* is length, *w* is width, and *h* is height, is $2\left[(lw)+(lh)+(wh)\right]$. Have fun memorizing that one. Instead, *understand* it. A rectangular solid is six rectangles, so measure the surface area of each rectangle. The front and back are the same, so measure one and multiply by two. Same goes for the top and bottom and left side and right side. Fortunately, rectangular solid surface area questions are rare, so don't worry about that equation.

>> **Volume of a pyramid:**

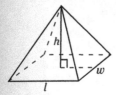

A pyramid has a square base and four identical triangular sides. Like a rectangular solid, find the volume by multiplying the length, width, and height, but with a pyramid, you divide all this by 3: $\frac{1}{3}lwh$.

>> **Surface area of a pyramid:**

There is no sensible formula for finding the surface area of a pyramid, and fortunately these questions are practically nonexistent. If you do get one, you know what to do: Find the areas of each triangle and the square base, and add 'em up.

>> **Volume of a cube:** $V = s^3$

Cube

A cube is exactly like a rectangular solid, only the *length, width,* and *height* are the same, so they're called *edges,* or *e.* Technically, the volume of a cube is the same as that of a rectangular solid, *length × width × height,* but because they're all edges, it's *edge × edge × edge,* or e^3.

>> **Surface area of a cube:**

Cube surface area questions are more common, and fortunately, simpler. Say a cube has an edge length of 2, so each side has an area of e^2, which in this case is 4 (because it's a square). With six sides, the surface area is 6×4, which is 24. This is also known as $6e^2$.

What's also common is that the SAT gives you the volume of a cube and asks you for the surface area, or vice versa. Whether you get the volume or the surface area, the secret is to backsolve and get the *edge,* then calculate what the question is asking.

PLAY

A certain cube has a volume of 27. What is its surface area?

If the volume is 27, backsolve this to get the edge:

$$e^3 = 27$$
$$e = 3$$

Now place the edge length of 3 into the surface area equation:

$$A = 6e^2$$
$$= 6(3)^2$$
$$= 54$$

And the surface area is 54.

PLAY

A certain cube has a surface area of 24. What is its volume?

If the surface area is 24, backsolve this to get the edge:

$$6e^2 = 24$$
$$e^2 = 4$$
$$e = 2$$

Now place the edge length of 2 into the volume equation:

$$V = e^3$$
$$= (2)^3$$
$$= 8$$

And the volume is 8.

The SAT, of course, goes into other variations, but they're all based on the same concept and just as easily learned.

Drawing cylinders and cones

You may be asked to find the volume of a cylinder or cone, but rarely the surface area. A question asking for the surface area also provides the surface area equation, and your task will simply be to place the numbers into the equation. The volume questions, however, are more common, and the equations are in the Reference pop-up box.

Volume of a cylinder

Cylinder

A cylinder on the SAT is also called a *right circular cylinder*, where it's like a can of soda. Each base is a circle, and each angle is 90°. The volume of a cylinder is simply the area of the circle — one of its bases — times its height. The area of a circle is πr^2, times the height h, making the volume $\pi r^2 h$.

Volume of a cone

A cone has a circular base and sides that taper to a point. Its volume is the same as the cylinder, only divided by 3: $\frac{1}{3}\pi r^2 h$.

If a cylinder has a radius of 3 and a height of 4, you can place these into the equation and find its volume:

$$V = \pi r^2 h$$
$$= \pi (3)^2 4$$
$$= 36\pi$$

What's more common is that the SAT gives you the volume and radius and asks for the height, or it gives you the volume and height and asks for the radius. Either way, just take the numbers from the question and place them into the equation.

What is the radius of a cylinder having a volume of 48π and a height of 3?

(A) 3

(B) 4

(C) 6

(D) 8

Take the volume equation and place the numbers that the question gives you:

$$V = \pi r^2 h$$
$$(48\pi) = \pi r^2 (3)$$
$$16\pi = \pi r^2$$
$$16 = r^2$$
$$4 = r$$

And the answer is (B).

These questions are no more challenging than any you've seen so far, except that the arrangements are different. Once you get used to the arrangements, taking on these questions is no problem.

Drawing spheres

Like cylinder and cone questions, most sphere questions ask for volume but rarely surface area. The volume equation is given in the beginning graphic, and the surface area equation, if needed, is given with the question.

A *sphere* is a perfectly round ball, like a basketball. Like a circle, it has a radius, so for its volume, simply place the radius into the equation: $\frac{4}{3}\pi r^3$.

Here are two to try:

PLAY

Which of the following is the volume of a sphere that has a radius of 3?

(A) 72π

(B) 54π

(C) 36π

(D) 18π

Place the radius into the volume equation. Remember, on the SAT, the math is simple:

$$V = \frac{4}{3}\pi r^3$$
$$= \frac{4}{3}\pi(3)^3$$
$$= \frac{4}{3}\pi 27$$
$$= 4\pi 9$$
$$= 36\pi$$

And the answer is Choice (C).

Here's another one, because you haven't had enough already. Just like on the real exam.

PLAY

$$A = 4\pi r^2$$

The surface area of a sphere can be found with the above equation. What is the surface area of a sphere that has a radius of 5?

(A) 25π

(B) 50π

(C) 75π

(D) 100π

Place the radius into the surface area equation:

$$A = 4\pi r^2$$
$$= 4\pi(5)^2$$
$$= 4\pi 25$$
$$= 100\pi$$

And the answer is Choice (D). Even if you haven't worked a sphere surface area question, which is most people except those who often engage the SAT, this question took you less than a minute, right? Be honest.

Solving Trigonometry Problems

Unlike the ACT, which typically has at least five trig questions among its 60 math questions, the SAT usually has only one or two trig questions in its 44 math questions. The scope of SAT trigonometry is also narrower, and this is a topic that you can move lower on your priority list. That said, if you got this far, you'll have no problem with these topics. This section covers what you need to know, even if you've never studied trigonometry.

Solving right triangles with SOH CAH TOA

SOH CAH TOA stands for

$$\text{Sine} = \frac{\text{Opposite}}{\text{Hypotenuse}}$$

$$\text{Cosine} = \frac{\text{Adjacent}}{\text{Hypotenuse}}$$

$$\text{Tangent} = \frac{\text{Opposite}}{\text{Adjacent}}$$

Opposite, adjacent, and *hypotenuse* refer to the sides of a right triangle in relation to one of the acute angles. For example, consider this right triangle:

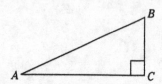

As you know, side *AB* is the *hypotenuse* (opposite the right angle and the longest side of the right triangle). For angle *A*, side *BC* is *opposite*, and side *AC* is *adjacent*. For angle *B*, they switch: Side *AC* is opposite, and side *BC* is adjacent.

Use SOH CAH TOA to quickly find the sine, cosine, or tangent of any acute angle in the right triangle.

> **To find sin A (the sine of angle A), use the SOH part of SOH CAH TOA.** Place the length of the side opposite angle *A* (in this case, side *BC*) over the hypotenuse (side *AB*).
>
> $$\sin A = \frac{\text{Opposite}}{\text{Hypotenuse}}$$
>
> $$\sin A = \frac{BC}{AB}$$

> **To find cos A (the cosine of angle A), use the CAH part of SOH CAH TOA.** Place the length of the side adjacent to angle *A* (in this case, side *AC*) over the hypotenuse (side *AB*).
>
> $$\cos A = \frac{\text{Adjacent}}{\text{Hypotenuse}}$$
>
> $$\cos A = \frac{AC}{AB}$$

> **To find tan A (the tangent of angle A), use the TOA part of SOH CAH TOA.** Place the length of the side opposite angle *A* over the side adjacent to angle *A*.
>
> $$\tan A = \frac{\text{Opposite}}{\text{Adjacent}}$$
>
> $$\tan A = \frac{BC}{AC}$$

 SOH CAH TOA only works with a *right triangle* and only with an *acute angle*, not the right angle.

TIP

Because sine and cosine are always a shorter side over the longer hypotenuse, sine and cosine can never be greater than 1. Tangent, however, can be greater than 1. You don't need to know the common values of sine and cosine, but these can be handy:

>> $\sin 90° = 1$ and $\sin 0° = 0$

>> $\cos 90° = 0$ and $\cos 0° = 1$

Find the sine of angle A in this right triangle:

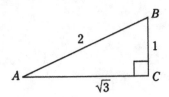

(A) 2

(B) $\sqrt{3}$

(C) 1

(D) $\frac{1}{2}$

Using the SOH in SOH CAH TOA, you know that the sine of angle A comes from the opposite (1) over the hypotenuse (2), for an answer of $\frac{1}{2}$, which matches Choice (D).

Three additional ratios appear less frequently than sine, cosine, and tangent but are just as easy to find. These are cosecant (csc), secant (sec), and cotangent (cot). Basically, you find the sine, cosine, or tangent and take the reciprocal to find cosecant, secant, or cotangent. The angle is usually represented by the Greek letter theta, θ:

$$\csc \theta = \frac{1}{\sin \theta}$$

$$\sec \theta = \frac{1}{\cos \theta}$$

$$\cot \theta = \frac{1}{\tan \theta}$$

If you get mixed up as to whether cosecant or secant is the reciprocal of sine or cosine, just remember this tip: *C* in *cosecant* goes with *S* in *sine*. *S* in *secant* goes with *C* in *cosine*.

Using the same right triangle, find the cotangent of angle A:

(A) 3

(B) 2

(C) $\sqrt{3}$

(D) 1

Using the TOA in SOH CAH TOA, you know that the tangent of angle A comes from the opposite (1) over the adjacent ($\sqrt{3}$), for a tangent of $\frac{1}{\sqrt{3}}$. Take the reciprocal to find the cotangent, $\sqrt{3}$, for answer Choice (C).

PLAY

Here's another:

For this right triangle, if $\tan B = \frac{4}{3}$, find $\cos A$.

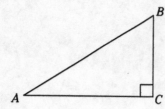

(A) $\frac{4}{3}$

(B) $\frac{5}{4}$

(C) $\frac{3}{4}$

(D) $\frac{4}{5}$

If $\tan B = \frac{4}{3}$ and tangent is opposite over adjacent (the TOA from SOH CAH TOA), then draw the triangle like this:

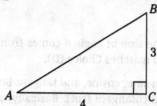

Spotting this as one of the common right triangles (covered earlier in this chapter), you automatically throw down 5 for the hypotenuse instead of using the Pythagorean Theorem.

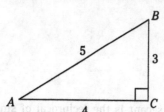

Cosine is CAH, which is adjacent over hypotenuse. Therefore, $\cos A = \frac{4}{5}$, which matches Choice (D).

Solving unit circles and radians

The *unit circle* is a circle drawn on the *x-y* graph with a center at the origin — coordinates $(0,0)$ — and a radius of 1.

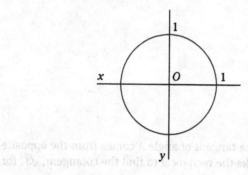

Starting with the radius of the circle at $(1,0)$, the angle θ is measured going counterclockwise.

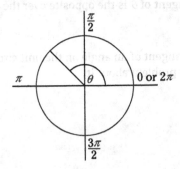

In this drawing, $\theta = 135°$. However, the angle isn't always measured in degrees; rather, it's in *radians*, which means that it's in terms of π, where $\pi = 180°$, making $135° = \frac{3\pi}{4}$.

An angle measuring $45°$ also measures $\frac{\pi}{4}$ radians. An angle measuring $270°$ also measures $\frac{3\pi}{2}$ radians. More importantly, or the way it's used on the SAT, you can tell which quadrant an angle is in from the range of radians. In other words, an angle between $\frac{\pi}{2}$ and π is in the second quadrant. For the angle θ,

» $0 < \theta < \frac{\pi}{2}$ places the angle in the first quadrant.

» $\frac{\pi}{2} < \theta < \pi$ places the angle in the second quadrant.

» $\pi < \theta < \frac{3\pi}{2}$ places the angle in the third quadrant.

» $\frac{3\pi}{2} < \theta < 2\pi$ places the angle in the fourth quadrant.

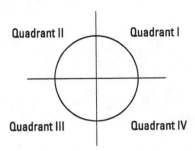

When SOH CAH TOA is applied to an angle in the unit circle, it's always for the angle θ, which comes from the radius of the circle. The *hypotenuse* is this radius, the *adjacent* is the x-value, and the *opposite* is the y-value. Consider this example, where $\theta = 60°$ and the radius meets the circle at $\left(\frac{1}{2}, \sqrt{3}\right)$, where on the xy graph, $x = \frac{1}{2}$ and $y = \sqrt{3}$.

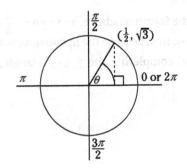

The sine of θ is the opposite over the hypotenuse, which in this case is $\frac{\sqrt{3}}{2}$. The cosine of θ is the adjacent over the hypotenuse, $\frac{0.5}{1}$, or $\frac{1}{2}$. The tangent of θ is the opposite over the adjacent, which is $\frac{\sqrt{3}}{1}$, or $\sqrt{3}$.

Knowing the quadrant and the sine, cosine, or tangent of an angle on the unit circle, you can find exactly where the angle is and solve almost any problem about it.

If $\frac{\pi}{2} < \theta < \pi$ and $\cos\theta = -\frac{3}{5}$, what is $\sin\theta$?

(A) $-\frac{4}{5}$

(B) $-\frac{3}{5}$

(C) $\frac{3}{5}$

(D) $\frac{4}{5}$

The first expression, $\frac{\pi}{2} < \theta < \pi$, places the angle in the second quadrant, and $\cos\theta = -\frac{3}{5}$ means the ratio of the x-value of the endpoint to the radius is $-\frac{3}{5}$. Because the hypotenuse (or radius) is always positive, the x-value is negative. The $\sin\theta$, being the opposite over hypotenuse, is therefore $\frac{4}{5}$, and the correct answer is Choice (D).

Try another:

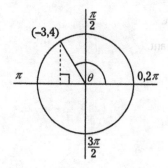

If $\frac{3\pi}{2} < \theta < 2\pi$ and $\sin\theta = -\frac{4}{5}$, what is $\cos\theta$?

(A) $\frac{4}{5}$

(B) $\frac{3}{5}$

(C) $-\frac{3}{5}$

(D) $-\frac{4}{5}$

The expression $\frac{3\pi}{2} < \theta < 2\pi$ places the angle in the fourth quadrant, and $\sin\theta = -\frac{4}{5}$ means that the ratio of the y-value to the hypotenuse is $-\frac{4}{5}$, or -4 to 5, because the hypotenuse is always positive. This means that drawn on the unit circle, and completing the 3-4-5 triangle, angle θ looks like this:

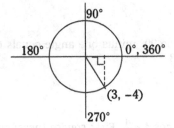

To find $\cos\theta$, place the adjacent (x-value) over the hypotenuse for $\frac{3}{5}$, which matches Choice (B).

To convert from π radians to degrees, remove the π and multiply by 180:

$$\pi = 180°$$
$$3\pi = 520°$$

And, to convert from degrees to π radians, do the opposite: Divide by 180 and place the π:

$$360° = 2\pi$$
$$90° = \frac{\pi}{2}$$

Use that to answer this question:

PLAY

If an engine rotates 1,800 degrees per second, what is its rotation per second in π radians?

(A) 8π

(B) 10π

(C) 12π

(D) 14π

Convert the 1,800 degrees to π radians by dividing by 180 and placing π:

$1,800° \div 180° = 10 \rightarrow 10\pi$ for Choice (B).

Solving trigonometric equations

You see many more of these equations in Algebra II and Trig, but there are only a few that you need on the SAT. Try these on this right triangle:

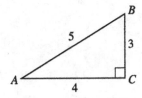

1. $\frac{\sin x}{\cos x} = \tan x$

Take angle A, for example. Using SOH CAH TOA, you know that $\sin A = \frac{3}{5}$, $\cos A = \frac{4}{5}$, and $\tan A = \frac{3}{4}$. Now prove this equation by placing these values:

$$\frac{\sin x}{\cos x} = \tan x$$

$$\frac{\frac{3}{5}}{\frac{4}{5}} = \frac{3}{5} \times \frac{5}{4} = \frac{3}{4}$$

2. $\sin x = \cos(90-x)$ or $\sin A = \cos B$

Remember, the two non-right angles total 90°, so 90° minus one angle equals the other angle. With the triangle above, $\sin A = \frac{3}{5}$ equals $\cos B = \frac{3}{5}$.

3. $\sin^2 x + \cos^2 x = 1$

Back to the 3-4-5 triangle above. $\sin A = \frac{3}{5}$ and $\cos A = \frac{4}{5}$. First square these: $\sin^2 A = \left(\frac{3}{5}\right)^2 = \frac{9}{25}$ and $\cos^2 A = \left(\frac{4}{5}\right)^2 = \frac{16}{25}$. Now add them: $\frac{9}{25} + \frac{16}{25} = \frac{25}{25} = 1$.

The SAT asks these in a conceptual form. If you understand these three equations, and more importantly, *recognize* them in the question, you save yourself a lot of math and give yourself a lot of laughter as you answer the question in well under a minute. Try this one:

PLAY

If $\cos a° = n$, which of the following must be true for all values of a?

(A) $\sin^2 a = n$

(B) $\cos(90-a)° = n$

(C) $\sin(90-a)° = n$

(D) $\tan(90-a)° = n$

Knowing that $\sin x = \cos(90-x)$, because you just read it a second ago, you know that $\cos a° = \sin(90-a)°$. Because these each equal n, the answer is Choice (C).

See? Almost no math. Practice these concepts and learn to recognize them *quickly*.

Chapter **10**

Measuring Statistics and Probability

The topic of statistics and probability builds upon numbers and operations covered in Chapter 7. Like every other topic in SAT math, the numeric part is always simple, and knowing how to set up the solution is key. This chapter reviews SAT-style questions on sets-of-number topics that include averages (also known as arithmetic mean), median, mode, and range, along with probability and reading graphs.

Measuring the Mean, Median, and Mode

Of all the methods to quantify or measure a set of numbers or data, the most common — and what you see on the SAT — involves the *mean, median,* and *mode.* Your job is to look past the tricky way that the SAT sets up the question and find the simple underlying concept.

Measuring the mean

Sometimes the SAT gives you a group of numbers and asks for the *average* (also called the *mean* or *arithmetic mean*). To find the average, divide the total by the count of numbers. For example, to find the average of 2, 4, and 9, add those numbers and divide by 3, because there are three numbers. It looks like this:

$$a = \frac{2+4+9}{3}$$
$$= \frac{15}{3}$$
$$= 5$$

If you have the average and *some* of the numbers, set up the equation with x as the missing number. If the average of 3, 6, 14, and some unknown number is 7, use x as the unknown number:

$$7 = \frac{3+6+14+x}{4}$$
$$7 = \frac{23+x}{4}$$
$$28 = 23 + x$$
$$x = 5$$

This type of question usually looks like this:

PLAY

Aisha has taken three tests, with an average (arithmetic mean) of 88. What grade must she receive on her next test for an overall average of 90 to get her A?

(A) 90

(B) 94

(C) 96

(D) 98

Set up the equation with x as the upcoming test. You don't know the other three test scores, but you do know they average 88, so use 88 for each one:

$$90 = \frac{88+88+88+x}{4}$$
$$90 = \frac{264+x}{4}$$
$$360 = 264 + x$$
$$x = 96$$

Aisha needs 96 on this next test for that A. She'll get it. The correct answer is Choice (C).

One variation of the averages question is average driving speed. To solve this, place the total distance in miles over the total time in hours. For example, if you drive the 140 miles from Phoenix to Flagstaff in 2 hours, divide 140 by 2 for your average speed of 70 miles per hour.

PLAY

If Sally drove the 120 miles from San Diego to Long Beach in 1.75 hours, and then drove back to San Diego in 2.25 hours, what was her average speed, in miles per hour?

(A) 50 miles per hour

(B) 60 miles per hour

(C) 70 miles per hour

(D) 80 miles per hour

Sally drove 120 miles there and 120 miles back, for a total distance of 240 miles. Her first trip was 1.75 hours and the second was 2.25 hours, for a total time of 4 hours. Divide 240 by 4 for her average speed:

$$\frac{240 \text{ miles}}{4 \text{ hours}} = \frac{60 \text{ miles}}{1 \text{ hour}}$$

She drove 60 miles per hour, so the answer is Choice (B).

Measuring the median and mode

The *median* is the middle number in a list, when the list is in numerical order. Say you have the numbers 5, 3, 8, 7, 2 and need the median. Put the numbers in order, 2, 3, 5, 7, 8, and the middle number, or median, is 5.

If there are two middle numbers (say with 2, 4, 5, 7, 8, 10), average the two middle numbers. In this example, the two middle numbers are 5 and 7, so the median is 6.

Finally there's the *mode*. In a mixed bag of numbers, the *mode* is the number or numbers that pop up most frequently. So with the numbers 3, 4, 4, 5, 8, 8, 9, there are two modes, 4 and 8. You can also have a set with no mode at all if everything shows up the same number of times, as with 3, 4, 5, 6.

A certain set of numbers has a mean of 18, a median of 20, and a mode of 21. Which number *must* be in the data set?

PLAY

(A) 18

(B) 20

(C) 21

(D) 22

The *mean* and *median* aren't always in the set of numbers. The mean is calculated, and the median *could* be calculated if the two middle numbers are, say, 19 and 21, for a median of 20. But the mode *has* to be in the set, because it's the most commonly occurring number. So the correct answer is Choice (C).

Mode questions are rare, but median questions are more common:

Andrew has a median score of 83 on five tests. If he scores 97 and 62 on his next two tests, his median score will

PLAY

(A) increase to 90

(B) decrease to 82

(C) decrease to 79.5

(D) remain the same

The median is the score in the middle. If 83 is in the middle, placing 97 on one side and 62 on the other doesn't change the middle number. The correct answer is Choice (D).

Once again, the SAT takes a topic you know fairly well and introduces variations that may throw you the first time you see them.

Measuring the range

The *range* is the distance between the lowest and highest numbers. For example, if your lowest exam score is 82 and your highest is 110, because you got those bonus questions, the range is the difference between those scores: $110 - 82 = 28$.

The SAT doesn't make it that simple, but this book makes it that easy. On the SAT, the range represents something like sales tax, units per box, or something that you somehow have to calculate. So all you do is calculate it, and the answer is there.

For example, if each volleyball team has either 4 or 6 players, and there are 12 teams at the tournament, what are the *lowest* and *highest* possible numbers of players? For the lowest number, use 4 players per each of the 12 teams: $4 \times 12 = 48$. For the highest number, use 6 per team: $6 \times 12 = 72$.

PLAY

Try this one:

Mariama places between $\frac{1}{5}$ and $\frac{1}{4}$, inclusive, of her weekly paycheck into a savings account. If she placed $150 into her savings account last week, then how much, in dollars, *could* last week's paycheck have been? Disregard the dollar sign when writing your answer.

First, find the amount of her paycheck with $150 as $\frac{1}{4}$ of it:

$$\frac{1}{4}x = \$150$$
$$x = \$600$$

Then find the amount of her paycheck with $150 as $\frac{1}{5}$ of it:

$$\frac{1}{5}x = \$150$$
$$x = \$750$$

So her paycheck was between $600 and $750. Don't worry about the dollar sign, so any number you place between 600 and 750 (including those numbers because the question states *inclusive*) is considered correct.

Measuring Probability

The *probability* of an event means how likely it is to occur. A 50 percent chance of rain means that the probability of rain is $\frac{1}{2}$. A probability can be defined as a fraction, percent, or decimal. Here's the equation for the probability of an event, represented by the letter *e*.

$$\text{probability } (p_e) = \frac{\text{the number you want}}{\text{the number possible}}$$

Say that you have a jar of 18 marbles where 7 are blue. The probability of reaching in and grabbing a blue marble is $\frac{7}{18}$, because there are 7 that you want and 18 possible.

Probability is always between 0 and 1. If something will *definitely* happen, the probability is 1, or 100 percent. The probability that the sun will rise tomorrow is 100 percent. If something will definitely *not* happen, the probability is 0. The probability that Elvis will sing again is 0.

The probabilities of different outcomes where only one can happen always add up to 1. Say you take a history exam. Say also the probability of you getting an A is 60 percent, a B is 20 percent, a C is 10 percent, a D is 5 percent, and an F is 5 percent. There's only one possible outcome — you can't get two grades on one exam — and all the probabilities add up to 100 percent.

If there are two events, and you want the probability of one *or* the other, add the probabilities. For that history exam, your probability of earning an A *or* a B is 80 percent, which comes from adding the 60 percent probability of an A to the 20 percent probability of a B.

If there are two *separate* events, and you want the probability of *both* happening, multiply the probabilities. Here's an example:

PLAY

Jenny arranges interviews with three potential employers. If each employer has a 50 percent probability of offering her a job, what's the probability that she gets offered all three?

(A) 10%

(B) 12.5%

(C) 75%

(D) 100%

These are three separate events, each with a probability of 50 percent. The probability of Jenny being offered all three jobs is $50\% \times 50\% \times 50\%$, or $\frac{1}{2} \times \frac{1}{2} \times \frac{1}{2} = \frac{1}{8}$, which calculates to 12.5% for Choice (B).

TIP

Probability questions are lower on the list of common SAT Math questions, but they do appear, and they're simple enough if you've worked a few.

Measuring Graph Data

Here are the three most common types of graphs you're likely to see on the SAT:

» Bar graph

» Circle or pie graph

» Two-axes line graph

Measuring bar graphs

A *bar graph* has vertical or horizontal bars.

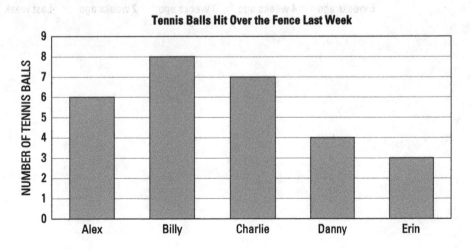

Measuring circle or pie charts

A *circle* or *pie chart* represents the total, or 100 percent.

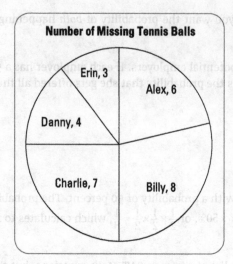

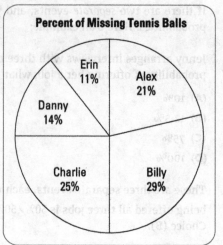

Measuring line graphs

A typical *line graph* has a bottom and a side axis.

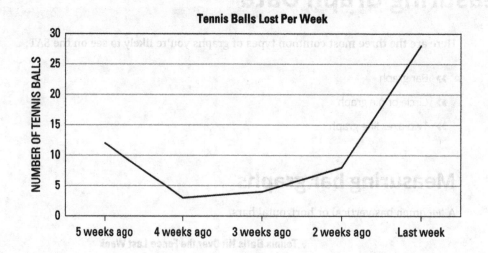

Measuring scatter plots

A special kind of two-axes graph is the *scatter plot*. A scatter plot contains a bunch of dots scattered in a pattern, like this:

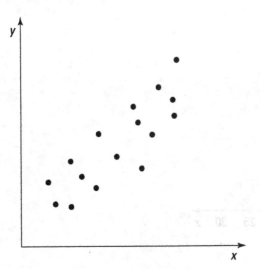

Notice how the points in this example seem to follow a certain flow, going up and to the right. When you see this, you can draw a line that captures the flow. This line is known as a *trend line* or *correlation*. On the test, you may be given a scatter plot and have to estimate where the points are going based on the trend line, like this:

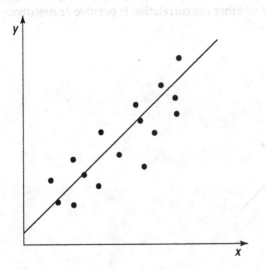

On the SAT, a correlation is typically *linear*. Going left to right, if the correlation goes *up*, it's positive, and if it goes *down*, it's negative, just like the slope of a graphed line.

PLAY

Which of the following best describes the data set?

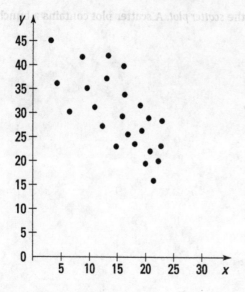

(A) A positive correlation

(B) A negative correlation

(C) An exponential correlation

(D) No correlation

There is clearly a correlation, which is rarely exponential (on the SAT), so out go Choices (C) and (D). Add the trend line to see whether the correlation is positive or negative:

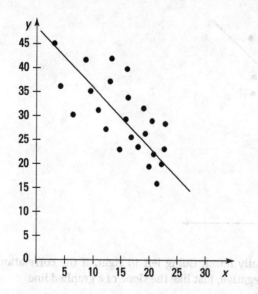

The trend line goes down, so the correlation is negative. Choice (B) it is.

Measuring multiple graphs

Sometimes the SAT places two graphs of related data with two or three related questions on these graphs. In this example, the first graph is a bar graph going from 0 to 100 percent. Read the graph by subtracting to find the appropriate percentage. For example, in 2016, "Grandparents won't donate a building" begins at 20 percent and goes to 50 percent, a difference of 30 percent. You've fallen into a trap if you say that "Grandparents won't donate a building" was 50 percent. In 2019, "Just felt like it" goes from 80 percent to 100 percent, which means it was actually 20 percent.

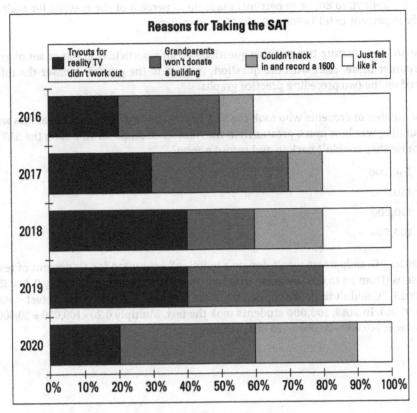

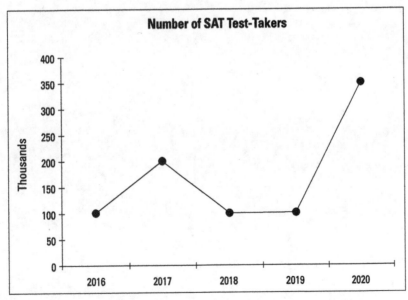

The second graph gives you the number of SAT test-takers in thousands. (By the way, these aren't real numbers.) Be sure to look at the labels of the axes. For example, *Thousands* along the side axis tells you that in 2020, there weren't 350 test-takers but 350,000. Using the two graphs together, you can find out the number of test-takers who took the SAT for a particular reason. For example, in 2017, 200,000 students took the test. Also in 2017, "Couldn't hack in and record a 1600" (from 70 to 80, or 10 percent) made up 10 percent of the reasons for taking the SAT. Multiply 10 percent or $0.10 \times 200,000 = 20,000$ test-takers.

The SAT may feature two or three questions about a particular graph or set of graphs. When you encounter these, start with the question, then go to the graphs. Answer the following question based on the two preceding practice graphs:

PLAY

The number of students who took the SAT in 2020 because their grandparents wouldn't donate a building was how much greater than the number of students who took the SAT in 2018 because they couldn't hack in and record a 1600?

(A) 250,000

(B) 140,000

(C) 120,000

(D) 100,000

In 2020, "Grandparents won't donate a building" accounted for 40 percent of test-taking reasons (from 20 to 60). Because 2020 had 350,000 test-takers, multiply $0.40 \times 350,000 = 140,000$. In 2018, "Couldn't hack in and record a 1600" counted for 20 percent of test-taking reasons (60 to 80). In 2018, 100,000 students took the test. Multiply $0.20 \times 100,000 = 20,000$. The correct answer is $140,000 - 20,000 = 120,000$, or Choice (C).

4

It's All You: Acing the SAT Practice Exams

Checking your readiness with full-length SAT practice tests

Improving your performance by reviewing answer explanations

Calculating your approximate SAT score

Chapter **11**
Practice Exam 1

You're now ready to take a practice SAT. Like the actual SAT, the following practice exam consists of 54 Reading and Writing questions (split into two 27-question modules) along with 44 Math questions (split into two 22-question modules), for 98 questions total.

Note that the paper-based practice exams provided by CollegeBoard.org have 66 Reading and Writing questions (in two 33-question modules) and 54 Math questions (in two 27-question modules), for 120 questions total. Because you're taking the SAT on a computer, not on paper, the practice exams in this book reflect the online experience of only 98 questions. You're welcome.

You get 32 minutes for each Reading and Writing module and 35 minutes for each Math module. Those plus the 10-minute break bring the exam to just under two and a half hours. Also, there is no answer sheet, so circle your answer selection right here in this book.

Take this practice test under normal exam conditions and approach it as you would the real SAT:

>> **Work where you won't be interrupted.** Leave your cell phone in another room, and ask anyone living with you (parents, siblings, dog) not to disturb you for the next few hours. (Good luck with that.)

>> **Practice with someone else who is taking the SAT.** This allows you to get used to the feeling of working with another person in the room; plus, this person can keep you focused and provide a sense of competition.

>> **Answer as many questions as time allows.** Consider answering all the easier questions within each section first and then going back to the harder questions. Because you're not penalized for guessing, go ahead and guess on the remaining questions before time expires.

>> **Set a timer for each section.** If you have time left at the end, go ahead and review your answers (within the section), continue and finish your test early, or pause and catch your mental breath before moving on to the next section.

>> **Take breaks between sections.** Take one minute after each module and ten minutes after the second Reading and Writing module.

>> **Work through the entire exam.** Get used to the experience of going through the entire exam in one sitting. It's not easy the first time, but you'll build the strength to stay focused through the entire marathon session.

>> **Circle any question that you weren't sure of or that took too long.** If you took longer than a minute on any one question, or had to take a guess, you should brush up on that topic or strategy. After the exam, you naturally review the explanations for wrong answers, but this way you review the explanations for right answers that you had guessed on or could've found faster.

After completing this practice test, go to Chapter 12 to check your answers. You could review the explanations for *each* question, not just the ones you miss, but at least review the questions you missed along with those that you circled. The answer explanations provide insight and a review of everything from the previous chapters.

Ready? Grab a pencil, some scratch paper, a calculator, and a timer. Sit back, relax, and enjoy your trip through Practice Exam 1. Remember, you got this.

Section 1: Reading and Writing
Module 1

TIME: 32 minutes for 27 questions.

DIRECTIONS: Read these passages and answer the questions that follow based on what is stated or implied in the passages and accompanying diagrams, charts, or graphs. Each question has one best answer.

1. *First Woman* tells the tale of Callie Rodriguez, the first woman to explore the Moon. While Callie is a fictional character, the first female astronaut and person of color will soon set foot on the Moon — an historic milestone and part of upcoming NASA Artemis missions. Through a series of graphic novels and digital platforms, *First Woman* aims to _____ audiences and inspire the next generation of explorers who will return to the Moon.

   Which choice completes the text with the most logical and precise word or phrase?

   (A) anticipate

   (B) captivate

   (C) decimate

   (D) peruse

2. Modern communication has evolved to the point that door-to-door mail delivery is practically _____; that is, as out-of-date as having your mail delivered today by a mailman in a horse-drawn cart.

   Which choice completes the text with the most logical and precise word or phrase?

   (A) practical

   (B) unexpected

   (C) obsolete

   (D) insular

3. Poets use the beauty of nature and its quickly changing seasons to make a statement about the futility of protesting change. They compare human lives to the evanescence of spring, _____ their brief existences with the permanence of the giant boulders that dot the vast landscape.

   Which choice completes the text with the most logical and precise word or phrase?

   (A) opposing

   (B) contrasting

   (C) relating

   (D) observing

4. Loss of forested areas poses an increasing threat to the integrity of the nation's natural resources. As these areas are fragmented and disappear, so do the benefits they provide. By providing economic incentives to landowners to keep their forests as forests, we can _____ sustainable forest management and support strong markets for forest products.

   Which choice completes the text with the most logical and precise word or phrase?

   (A) access

   (B) determine

   (C) enrich

   (D) encourage

5. American bison once numbered 60 million in North America, with the population anchored in what is now the central United States. Many Indigenous cultures, especially in areas where the species was most abundant, developed strong ties with bison and relied upon them for sustenance, shelter, and cultural and religious practices. In the 19th century, bison were nearly driven to extinction through uncontrolled hunting and a U.S. policy of eradication tied to intentional harm against and control of Tribes. By 1889, only a few hundred wild bison remained. The _____ of bison contributed to the decline of healthy grassland ecosystems and, eventually, to the Dust Bowl in the 1930s.

Which choice completes the text with the most logical and precise word or phrase?

(A) persecution

(B) enhancement

(C) identification

(D) persistence

6. The following text is an excerpt from *Labour Policy — False and True* by Lynden Macassey (1922).

Our great industrial difficulty, under modern conditions, is to combine human development with human work, and persuade people to be industrious. Formerly, people worked to benefit themselves; now, they are apt to refrain from working for fear they may benefit others. The injury to employers from such a course is evident; but the detriment to the workers themselves is less obvious, and the _____ effect on the community is seldom realized.

Which choice completes the text with the most logical and precise word or phrase?

(A) beneficial

(B) common

(C) inconclusive

(D) calamitous

7. The following text is an excerpt from *Daughter of the Sky: The Story of Amelia Earhart* by Paul L. Briand Jr. (1960). In this scene, Amelia Earhart, formerly a social worker, is being interviewed to be the first woman to fly across the Atlantic.

The demure Boston social worker survived the examination. Recalling the experience, Amelia said later: "I found myself in a curious situation. If they did not like me at all or found me wanting in too many respects, I would be deprived of the trip. If they liked me too well, they might be loath to drown me. It was, therefore, necessary for me to maintain an attitude of impenetrable mediocrity. Apparently I did, because I was chosen."

To what quality does Amelia Earhart attribute her success in the interview?

(A) her blazing courage

(B) her innate curiosity

(C) her opaque ordinariness

(D) her demure respectfulness

8. Honey bees are not native to the New World; they were brought here from Europe in the 1500s and 1600s by colonists. But many of our crops also came from the Old World and evolved in the same places as honey bees. Native pollinators exist in the United States, but honey bees are more prolific and easier to manage, especially on a commercial level for pollination of a wide variety of crops. Almonds, for example, are almost completely dependent on honey bees for pollination. In California, the almond industry makes use of almost three-quarters of all managed honey-bee colonies in the United States brought from all over the country during one short window of time in January and February each year.

Which of the following best describes the function of the underlined sentence in the text as a whole?

(A) It makes an assertion that the next sentence develops.

(B) It provides a specific detail that supports the writer's central claim.

(C) It identifies a crop that is native to Southern California.

(D) It provides an example of a crop that is not dependent on pollination by honey bees.

9. The following excerpt contains the concluding lines from Sonnet 73 by William Shakespeare. The speaker of the poem directly addresses someone he loves.

In me thou see'st the glowing of such fire,
That on the ashes of his youth doth lie
As the deathbed whereon it must expire,
Consumed with that which it was nourished by.
This thou perceivest, which makes thy love more strong.
To love that well which thou must leave ere long.

Which of the following best expresses the speaker's claim about his lover's reaction to his words?

(A) You see that I will soon die, and that understanding makes you love me more.

(B) You will be quickly consumed by the fires of passion and will cease to love me.

(C) Your love for me will fade away and die when I am no longer in your presence.

(D) Your youth prevents you from understanding the significance of true love and you will leave me.

10. Carbon is the basic building block of forests. Trees naturally absorb carbon dioxide (CO_2) through the process of photosynthesis and store it as carbon. That carbon gets locked in the trunks, roots, and leaves of trees and is deposited in surrounding soils for long periods of time. Carbon dioxide (CO_2) is the most pervasive greenhouse gas (GHG) driving rising global temperatures, so forests play a critical role in moderating CO_2 and reducing the impact of climate change.

Which of the following would provide the strongest counterargument to the claim in this passage?

(A) At several points in history, global average temperatures have been warmer than those currently observed.

(B) Atmospheric CO_2 levels positively correlate to average global temperatures and are currently at the highest levels ever recorded.

(C) Climate is always changing, and the changes in the past century are not any more dramatic than those in previous centuries.

(D) Climate changes like rising sea levels are unrelated to greenhouse gas emissions.

11. Secretary of the Interior Deb Haaland made history by becoming the first Native American to serve as a U.S. cabinet secretary. Her life story is a legacy of firsts. After running for New Mexico Lieutenant Governor in 2014, Secretary Haaland became the first Native American woman to be elected to lead a state party. She is one of the first Native American women to serve in Congress and her family has a history of public service: Her father served as a 30-year combat Marine, and her mother is a Navy veteran who served as a federal employee for 25 years at the Bureau of Indian Affairs.

Which choice concludes the paragraph most effectively?

(A) At the age of 28, Haaland enrolled at the University of New Mexico (UNM) where she earned a Bachelor's degree in English and later earned her J.D. from UNM Law School.

(B) Secretary Haaland grew up in a military family; her father was a 30-year combat Marine, and, as a military child, she attended 13 public schools before graduating from Highland High School in Albuquerque.

(C) Secretary Haaland ran her own small business producing and canning Pueblo Salsa, served as a tribal administrator at San Felipe Pueblo, and became the first woman elected to the Laguna Development Corporation Board of Directors.

(D) As a 35th-generation New Mexican and member of the Pueblo of Laguna, Secretary Haaland has broken barriers and her achievements have opened the doors of opportunity for future generations.

GO ON TO NEXT PAGE

12. While phosphorus is a naturally occurring and essential nutrient for plants and animals, too much of it can cause explosive growth of aquatic plants and algae. This can lead to a variety of water quality problems, including low dissolved oxygen concentrations, which can cause fish kills and harm other aquatic life. A major concern with phosphorus in lakes is a toxic blue-green algae bloom that can cause the lake to be closed to recreation and private landowners.

Which of the following statements by conservation or health experts best support the claim in the passage?

(A) "Habitat loss, fragmentation, and degradation are some of the primary factors in the decline of native species."

(B) "This project seeks to preserve and restore the ecosystems through partnerships between government and private sources. Let's get it started."

(C) "High levels of phosphorus are detrimental to both people and wildlife — just a couple licks of contaminated water can be lethal for pets; it's pretty bad stuff."

(D) "Phosphorus plays key roles in regulation of gene transcription, activation of enzymes, maintenance of normal pH in extracellular fluid, and intracellular energy storage."

14.

13. The following excerpt is from *O Pioneers!* by Willa Cather (1913).

Of all the bewildering things about a new country, the absence of human landmarks is one of the most depressing and disheartening. The houses were small and were usually tucked away in low places; you did not see them until you came directly upon them. Most of them were built of the sod itself, and were only the inescapable ground in another form. The roads were but faint tracks in the grass, and the fields were scarcely noticeable. The record of the plow was insignificant, like the feeble scratches on stone left by prehistoric races, so indeterminate that they may, after all, be only the markings of glaciers, and not a record of human strivings.

The comparison between the plowed fields and "the feeble scratches on stone left by prehistoric races" serves which of the following functions in the text?

(A) To introduce the idea of human weakness

(B) To show that this settlement has a long history

(C) To describe the effects of glaciers

(D) To emphasize the primitive quality of the farming

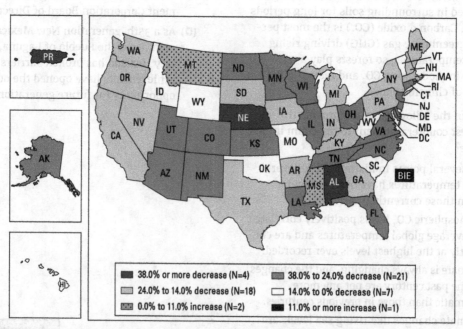

38.0% or more decrease (N=4)
24.0% to 14.0% decrease (N=18)
0.0% to 11.0% increase (N=2)
38.0% to 24.0% decrease (N=21)
14.0% to 0% decrease (N=7)
11.0% or more increase (N=1)

Source: Adapted from U.S. Department of Education

The map represents the change in the number of students who experienced homelessness in school years 2018–2019 and 2020–2021. However, various factors impact data on students who experienced homelessness, making it important to consider recent decreases within the context of longer-term trends. For example, states that experience major natural disasters such as hurricanes and flooding typically identify a larger number of students as homeless in the school year when the disaster occurs.

Based on the information in the text and in the map, which of the following might account for the decrease in homeless students in certain states in the years immediately after a natural disaster like a hurricane?

(A) During a natural disaster, many students move from their home state to another state and remain homeless in their new location.

(B) In certain states that are subject to frequent hurricanes, many students are unable to return to homes that were destroyed and cannot be rebuilt.

(C) During the year the disaster occurs, many students find themselves homeless and the number of homeless students rises; within the next year, however, many of these students obtain housing.

(D) A factor that impacted student homelessness was a decrease in student enrollment overall during the COVID-19 pandemic.

15. The following passage is an excerpt from *Biology For Dummies, 2nd Edition*, by Rene Kratz and Donna Siegfried (Wiley).

Some species, called keystone species, are so connected with other organisms in their environment that their extinction changes the entire composition of species in the area. As biodiversity decreases, keystone species may die out, causing a ripple effect that leads to the loss of many more species. If biodiversity gets too low, then the future of life itself becomes threatened. An example of a keystone species is the purple sea star, which lives on the northwest Pacific coast of the United States. Purple sea stars prey on mussels in the intertidal zone. When the sea stars are present, they keep the mussel population in check, allowing a great diversity of other marine animals to live in the intertidal zone. If the sea stars are removed from the intertidal zone, however, the mussels take over, and many species of marine animals disappear from the environment.

The text implies which of the following about large populations of mussels?

(A) They become keystone species in their environment.

(B) They may displace other species.

(C) They do not compete for food with purple sea stars.

(D) They are a major cause of extinctions.

GO ON TO NEXT PAGE ➤

16. About a century ago, in August 1914, what participants called "The Great War" and, ironically, "The War to End All Wars," _____. We know this conflict as World War I, one of the bloodiest periods in human history. When it ended in 1918, about 9 million soldiers were dead and the health of 7 million more was permanently disabled.

Which choice completes the text so that it conforms to the conventions of Standard English?

(A) begun

(B) had began

(C) has begun

(D) had begun

17. After working on the construction of his dream go-kart for seven months, David decided to test it out. He took it to the top of the hill in his neighborhood park. Turning around to greet his friends as they arrived for the inaugural run, he momentarily let go of the tethers. The runaway go-kart sped down the _____ momentum as it careened out of control.

Which choice completes the text so that it conforms to the conventions of Standard English?

(A) hill; gaining

(B) hill. Gaining

(C) hill, gaining

(D) hill gaining

18. In 1859, Thomas Austin, an Australian who enjoyed hunting, released 24 rabbits on his land. The hunter stated that "introduction of a few rabbits could do little harm" and "might provide a touch of home." He liked to hunt. Before this time, _____ some domestic rabbits in Australia, mostly in cages or other enclosures. With a moderate climate, the wild rabbits bred all year round. Soon Australia had a rabbit problem with more than 200 million rabbits overrunning the land.

Which choice completes the text so that it conforms to the conventions of Standard English?

(A) there were

(B) there was

(C) their were

(D) they're was

19. Named in honor of the _____ Hubble Space Telescope is a large, space-based observatory, which has revolutionized astronomy since its launch and deployment by the space shuttle Discovery in 1990. Far above rain clouds, light pollution, and atmospheric distortions, Hubble has a crystal-clear view of the universe. Scientists have used Hubble to observe some of the most distant stars and galaxies yet seen, as well as the other planets in our solar system.

Which choice completes the text so that it conforms to the conventions of Standard English?

(A) trailblazing astronomer, Edwin Hubble, the

(B) trailblazing, astronomer Edwin Hubble, the

(C) trailblazing astronomer Edwin Hubble, the

(D) trailblazing, astronomer, Edwin Hubble the

20. The following text is adapted from *Crime: Its Causes and Treatment* by Clarence Darrow (1922).

Strictly speaking, a crime is an act forbidden by the law of the land, and one which is considered sufficiently serious to warrant providing penalties for its commission. It does not necessarily follow that this act is either good _____ punishment follows for the violation of the law and not necessarily for any moral transgression.

Which choice completes the text so that it conforms to the conventions of Standard English?

(A) or bad; the

(B) or bad, the

(C) nor bad when

(D) nor bad because the

21. The view from the top of the mountain was _____ 30-mile drive to the base of the mountains and then the two-hour trek up the path left us too exhausted to appreciate the sight.

Which of the following completes the text with the most logical transition?

(A) spectacular; however, the

(B) spectacular. Consequently, the

(C) spectacular. For example, the

(D) spectacular; furthermore, the

22. The NASA Juno mission, launched in August of 2011, was expected to arrive at its destination in July of 2016. The mission had a far-seeking _____ to the planet Jupiter to uncover the secrets of its origin and to search for evidence of water and ammonia.

Which choice completes the text so that it conforms to the conventions of Standard English?

(A) goal: to travel

(B) goal, to travel

(C) goal; to travel

(D) goal. To travel

23. Architect I. M. Pei is celebrated for his brilliant designs that have become attractions in cities around the world. He has designed such famous buildings as the John F. Kennedy Library in Boston, the Bank of China Tower in Hong Kong, and the Museum of Islamic Art in Qatar. His design for the main entrance to the Louvre, with _____ iconic glass and steel pyramid, has become a Parisian landmark.

Which choice completes the text so that it conforms to the conventions of Standard English?

(A) their

(B) it's

(C) its'

(D) its

GO ON TO NEXT PAGE

24. The great Persian Empire extended from the shores of the Mediterranean to the east, far beyond the knowledge of the Greeks. _____ knowledge of the interior of Asia was very imperfect, and Alexander's expedition was rather that of an explorer than of a conqueror. How he overthrew the Persians and subdued an area as large as Europe in the space of twelve years reads like a romance rather than fact.

Which of the following completes the text with the most logical transition?

(A) However, their

(B) Indeed, their

(C) In contrast, their

(D) On the other hand, their

25. The value of Paramhansa Yogananda's *Autobiography of a Yogi* is greatly enhanced by the fact that it is one of the few books in English about the wise men of India which _____, not by a journalist or foreigner, but by one of their own race and training — in short, a book *about* yogis *by* a yogi. As an eyewitness recountal of the extraordinary lives and powers of modern Hindu saints, the book has importance both timely and timeless.

Which choice completes the text so that it conforms to the conventions of Standard English?

(A) was wrote

(B) had been written

(C) has been written

(D) written

26. While researching a topic, a student has taken the following notes:

- Women have traditionally been caregivers but were prohibited from professionally practicing medicine until recent times.

- In Medieval times, women had limited roles as healers; Hildegard of Bingen was the most notable of Medieval healers.

- In 1849, Elizabeth Blackwell was the first woman to receive a medical degree from a U.S. university after being rejected from every medical school in the country except Geneva Medical College in New York.

- While the male students first thought Blackwell's application was a joke, they ultimately were impressed by her fierce dedication and supported her inclusion in their class.

- Blackwell founded the New York Infirmary for Indigent Women and Children, where she trained other women to become nurses and doctors.

The student wants to emphasize the distinguishing qualities of Elizabeth Blackwell. Which choice most effectively accomplishes this goal?

(A) Although she lived in Medieval times, Hildegard of Bingen was a trailblazer who created a path for Elizabeth Blackwell to follow.

(B) Without the intervention of the males in her medical school class at Geneva Medical College, Elizabeth Blackwell would never have become the first female physician in the U.S.

(C) Following a path first blazed by Hildegard of Bingen, Elizabeth Blackwell overcame gender discrimination with courage and determination and established the place of women as professional healthcare providers.

(D) By admitting Elizabeth Blackwell, Geneva Medical College took the first steps toward establishing a place for women in the practice of medicine.

27. While researching a topic, a student has taken the following notes:

- An enormous crash near Johannesburg, South Africa, created the Vredefort crater, presently about 9 miles in diameter.

- Based on physical evidence, scientists postulate that what was likely an asteroid crashed into Earth about 2 billion years ago.

- Scientists speculate that the crater was originally much larger and that erosion has made it difficult to estimate its original size.

- Scientists study the crater to gain new insights into the environments of early Earth because it provides invaluable information about the past.

- Scientists try to simulate the impacts of such events on Earth to determine their effects in the past and the future.

The student wants to create a statement of the significance of the findings obtained from the study of the Vredefort crater. Which choice most effectively accomplishes the student's goal?

(A) The discovery of the Vredefort crater was a great boon to scientists because it happened about 2 billion years ago.

(B) The Vredefort crater is important to scientists in that it preserves an almost continuous record of Earth's history.

(C) Because of their work on the Vredefort crater, scientists can simulate impact events on Earth and other planets.

(D) The team studying the crater has used a modern approach to obtain new insights into the environment of early Earth.

Check Your Work.

Continue to the next module when you're ready to move on.

Module 2

TIME: 32 minutes for 27 questions.

DIRECTIONS: Read these passages and answer the questions that follow based on what is stated or implied in the passages and accompanying diagrams, charts, or graphs. Each question has one best answer.

1. Fungus beetles thrive in moist conditions where they feed on the mold that forms in these environments. Because their food is readily available and easily accessed, they are quite _____ and seldom move more than a foot or two in any direction.

   Which choice completes the text with the most logical and precise word?

   (A) sociable

   (B) fragile

   (C) sedentary

   (D) scarce

2. Biodiversity increases the chance that at least some living things will survive in the face of large changes in the environment, which is why protecting it is _____. The combined effect of various human actions in Earth's ecosystems is reducing the planet's biodiversity. In fact, the rate of extinctions is increasing along with the size of the human population. No one knows for certain how extensive the loss of species due to human impacts will ultimately be, but there's no question that human practices such as hunting and farming have already caused numerous species to become extinct.

   Which choice completes the text with the most logical and precise word?

   (A) crucial

   (B) unimportant

   (C) reliable

   (D) inadequate

3. In their various industries, the Egyptians made use of gold, silver, bronze, metallic iron, and copper, and their oxides, manganese, cobalt, alum, cinnabar, indigo, madder, brass, white lead, and lampblack. There is clear evidence that they smelted iron ore as early as 3400 B.C.E., maintaining a blast by means of leather tread-bellows. They also _____ temper the metal, and to make helmets, swords, lance-points, ploughs, tools, and other implements of iron.

   Which choice completes the text with the most logical and precise word?

   (A) refused to

   (B) were reluctant to

   (C) contrived to

   (D) grew to

4. Clouds are an important area of research on Mars (and on Earth, too) because of their feed-back on the climate — they can reflect incoming sunlight, which has a cooling effect, and _____ the planet's outgoing infra-red radiation, which has a warming effect. In fact, clouds may have played a crucial role in sustaining a warm atmosphere on early Mars, enabling liquid water to flow and carve out channels we see in the geology today.

   Which choice completes the text with the most logical and precise word?

   (A) monitor

   (B) absorb

   (C) characterize

   (D) interpret

5. The Streamflow Monitoring Using Computer Vision Machine Learning project will develop a lower-cost method to quantify streamflow that can be used by states, tribes, and other organizations. This approach can supplement the current methods — that is, deployment of hydrological measurement equipment (stream gauges) that is costly and _____ specialized expertise. This user-friendly alternative relies on continuous photo imagery and machine learning to estimate streamflow.

Which choice completes the text with the most logical and precise word?

(A) requires

(B) prefers

(C) portrays

(D) predicts

6. In 1884, a conference in Washington, D.C., agreed to establish a single "prime" meridian (0° longitude), passing through Greenwich. This was for both longitude and timekeeping. This 0° meridian divides the Eastern from the Western Hemisphere. Today, one can visit the Royal Observatory and straddle this 0° meridian with one foot in each hemisphere. The location of this prime meridian is _____, meaning it could be chosen to be anywhere.

Which choice completes the text with the most logical and precise word?

(A) specific

(B) dynamic

(C) dubious

(D) arbitrary

7. The following is an except from Charles Darwin's *On the Origin of Species* (1859).

A struggle for existence inevitably follows from the high rate at which all organic beings tend to increase. Every being, which during its natural lifetime produces several eggs or seeds, must suffer destruction during some period of its life, and during some season or occasional year; otherwise, on the principle of geometrical increase, its numbers would quickly become so inordinately great that no country could support the product. Hence, as more individuals are produced than can possibly survive, there must in every case be a struggle for existence, either one individual with another of the same species, or with the individuals of distinct species, or with the physical conditions of life.

Which choice best describes the function of the underlined portion in the text as a whole?

(A) It gives a specific example to support the generalization in the first sentence.

(B) It posits a new idea to counter a previously accepted conclusion.

(C) It provides further details about the particular species referred to earlier in the text.

(D) It draws a logical conclusion from the information in the previous sentences.

GO ON TO NEXT PAGE

8. Non-native species are plants and animals living in areas where they do not naturally exist. "Non-native species" and "invasive species" cannot be used interchangeably. <u>Many commonly grown fruits and vegetables are not native to the U.S.</u> For example, tomatoes and hot peppers originated from South America, while lettuce was first grown by the Egyptians. Domestic cows are non-native to North America and were introduced as a food source and considered to be a beneficial organism in an agricultural setting.

Which choice best describes the function of the underlined portion in the text as a whole?

(A) It clarifies by elaborating on terms used in the previous sentence.

(B) It offers a specific example of a fruit and vegetable to support the generalization in the previous sentence.

(C) It notes an exception to the terms used in the previous sentence.

(D) It presents a counterclaim to the assertion in the first sentence.

9. The following text is adapted from *Bohemians of the Latin Quarter* by Henri Murger (1888).

The dinner took place at a Provencal restaurant in the Rue Dauphine, celebrated for its literary waiters and its "Ayoli" [a sauce similar to mayonnaise]. As it was necessary to leave room for the supper, they ate and drank in moderation. The acquaintance, begun the evening before between Colline and Schaunard and later on with Marcel, became more intimate; each of the young fellows hoisted the flag of his artistic opinions, and all four recognized that they had like courage and similar hopes. Talking and arguing they perceived that their sympathies were akin, that they had all the same knack in that chaff which amuses without hurting, and that the virtues of youth had not left a vacant spot in their heart, easily stirred by the sight of the narration of anything noble.

According to the text, what is true of the "young fellows?"

(A) They each arrived in Paris from a different country.

(B) They expressed very diverse opinions about art and their own aspirations.

(C) They shared similar views on life, and their natures were very much alike.

(D) They argued and disagreed strongly about the virtues of youth and nobility.

10. The following excerpt is from the U.S. Fish & Wildlife Services online article, "Leave it to Beaver: Partners Collaborate on Beaver Dam Analog Project."

Historically, Thompson Creek meandered through the lower watershed; but over a century ago, it was straightened to accommodate for agriculture, helping to reduce flooding for farmers. While the straightened channel was beneficial to the farmers, it had less desirable impacts on watershed health. The straighter, less natural flow path increased the speed of the water, led to the erosion of the bank, and transported more sediment and pollutants downstream into Newman Lake. This incision of the creek has also caused a disconnection between the creek and its surrounding floodplains, which has allowed for the dominance of reed canary grass in the area, a non-native species that outcompetes more diverse and beneficial vegetation.

Which choice best states the main purpose of the text?

(A) To summarize the results of a study of erosion in Newman Lake.

(B) To present a specific example of the positive impact of straightening Thompson Creek.

(C) To explain an unintended but undesirable effect of human intervention.

(D) To speculate on the effects of competition between native grasses and non-native species.

11.

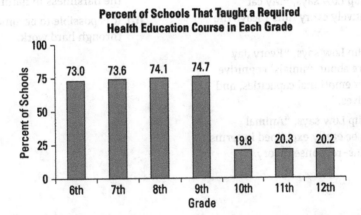

Percent of Schools That Taught a Required
Health Education Course in Each Grade

Concerned about lack of awareness of certain health issues among students in the school system, the City School Superintendent decided to track the number of schools that provided health education in each grade of secondary school. Based on the data in the graph above, he concluded that most schools in the district were consistently providing a health education course in all grades of secondary school.

Which choice describes data that weakens the Superintendent's conclusion?

(A) All schools offered students some health education in every grade from 6 through 12.

(B) Fewer schools offered students in grades 10 through 12 a health education course than they offered students in grades 6 through 9.

(C) More schools offered students a health education course in grade 9 than in grade 6.

(D) No schools offered a health education course to students in grades 1 through 5.

GO ON TO NEXT PAGE ▶

12. Veterinarians who study animal behavior have entered a relatively new area of study. In earlier times, what was going on inside an animal's mind was not a concern. The Greek philosopher Aristotle (384–322 B.C.E.) said that animals couldn't think. French philosopher Rene Descartes (1596–1650 C.E.) compared the cry of an animal to the squeak of a clock spring, a mechanical reaction. Even in the modern era, animal behaviorists are reluctant to commit to the existence of complex emotions in animals for fear of being accused of anthropomorphism, ascribing human traits to nonhuman beings, and are belittled for being "unscientific" when they refer to an animal's inner life.

Which of the following quotes most logically supports the claim in the last sentence of the text?

(A) Scientist Philip Low says, "If you ask my colleagues whether animals have emotions and thoughts, many will drop their voices or change the subject."

(B) Scientist Philip Low says, "My cat meows plaintively every time I leave the house."

(C) Scientist Philip Low says, "Every day we learn more about animals' cognitive abilities, their emotional capacities, and their moral lives."

(D) Scientist Philip Low says, "Animal behavior can be easily explained in terms of the stimulus-response theory."

13. The following text is an excerpt from "Sound and Sense," a poem by Alexander Pope (1688–1744).

True ease in writing comes from art, not chance,
As those move easiest who have learned to dance.
'Tis not enough no harshness gives offense,
The sound must seem an echo to the sense;
Soft is the strain when Zephyr* gently blows,
And the smooth stream in smoother numbers flows;

* God of the west wind

Which choice makes a statement with which the poet would most likely agree?

(A) Writing, like dance, arises from natural talent.

(B) Writing should be focused on content rather than sound.

(C) A writer must listen to and respond to the harshness in nature.

(D) It is possible to become a skilled writer through hard work.

14. Charles Dickens's novel *Great Expectations* tells the story of Pip, a poor orphan in mid-19th century England. An unexpected encounter with a convict results in a dramatic change in Pip's life. He becomes wealthy, deserts his old friends, and ultimately learns that he has lost more than he has gained.

Which quotation from *Great Expectations* most effectively illustrates the claim?

(A) "The broken heart. You think you will die, but you just keep living, day after day after terrible day."

(B) "Pause you who read this, and think for a moment of the long chain of iron or gold, of thorns or flowers, that would never have bound you, but for the formation of the first link on one memorable day."

(C) "There was a long hard time when I kept far from me, the remembrance, of what I had thrown away when I was quite ignorant of its worth. But, since my duty has not been incompatible with the admission of that remembrance, I have given it a place in my heart."

(D) "I looked at the stars, and considered how awful it would be for a man to turn his face up to them as he froze to death, and see no help or pity in all the glittering multitude."

15. The following excerpt is from the 2022 Study Update from the Agricultural Health Study (AHS).

In some previous studies, agricultural work and occupational pesticide use have been associated with increased rates of renal cell carcinoma (RCC), the most common form of kidney cancer. However, few of those studies had investigated links to specific pesticides. Researchers evaluated associations with 38 pesticides, including one labeled 2,4,5-T, that were relatively commonly used at enrollment among pesticide applicators in the Agricultural Health Study, 308 individuals who developed RCC during follow-up until 2015. They hypothesized that certain pesticides, including and other agricultural exposure might influence the development of kidney disease and kidney cancer.

Which of the findings, if true, would directly support the researchers' hypothesis?

(A) Farmers and agricultural workers face health risks from work-related injuries at a rate of 18 deaths per 100,00 workers.

(B) Farmers and agricultural workers face stress from environmental factors, such as droughts, floods, wildfires, pests, and diseases affecting crops and livestock, as well as from working long hours, financial concerns, and feelings of isolation and frustration.

(C) Farmers and agricultural workers who use methods of organic food production (avoiding artificial fertilizers and pesticides and using crop rotation and other forms of husbandry to maintain soil fertility, control weeds and diseases) were less likely to report incidences of cancer.

(D) Farmers and agricultural workers who use the herbicide 2,4,5-T were three times more likely to develop RCC compared with those who never used this product.

GO ON TO NEXT PAGE

16. A branch of the Nez Percé tribe from the Pacific Northwest refused to be relocated to a reservation and attempted to flee to Canada. The U.S. Cavalry pursued them and forced them to return. In 1877, Chief Joseph of the Nez Percé tribe surrendered to General Oliver O. Howard. The following text is an excerpt from his speech.

"If the white man wants to live in peace with the Indian he can live in peace. There need be no trouble. Treat all men alike. Give them all an even chance to live and grow. All men were made by the same Great Spirit Chief. They are all brothers. The earth is the mother of all people, and all people should have equal rights upon it. You might as well expect all rivers to run backward as that any man who was born a free man should be contented penned up and denied liberty to go where he pleases."

Which choice best expresses the main idea of Chief Joseph's speech?

(A) The Native American people had settled this land long before the arrival of the Europeans and deserve to have their land returned to them.

(B) Freedom is the natural state of every man, and every man deserves the right to live his life fairly and equally.

(C) Freedom should be available to all men and women, as long as they obey the laws that govern their society.

(D) Although they have lost this battle, the Native Americans will continue to fight for control of their land and their rivers.

17.

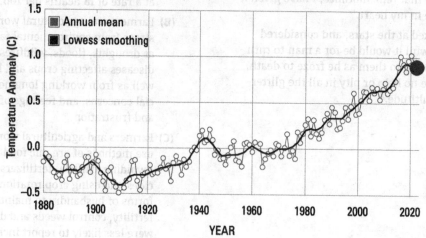

GLOBAL LAND-OCEAN TEMPERATURE INDEX

Source: climate.NASA.gov

Lowess smoothing (Locally Weighted Scatter-plot Smoothing) is a tool used in data analysis that creates a smooth line through a time plot or scatter plot to help you to see a relationship between variables and predict trends.

Among environmental scientists, there is a strong consensus that global surface temperatures have increased in recent decades and that the trend is caused by human-induced emissions of greenhouse gases. The extra energy that results from human activities has warmed the atmosphere, ocean, and land, and widespread and rapid changes in the atmosphere, ocean, cryosphere, and biosphere have occurred. The actual warming of temperatures is something they say they can document. In fact, according to an intergovernmental panel on climate change, the scientific evidence that points to climate change is undeniable.

Which of the following findings, if true, would appear to weaken the conclusion of the intergovernmental panel?

(A) The global mean sea levels have doubled compared to the 20th-century trend of 1.6 mm per year, and this is accelerating slightly every year. The global sea levels rose about 8 inches in the last century.

(B) The increased heat in the atmosphere from greenhouse gas emissions has been absorbed by the oceans, with the top 700 meters (about 2,300 feet) of ocean showing warming of more than 0.4 degree Fahrenheit since 1969.

(C) Core measures of the Arctic ice show that it has increased in volume since 2012 — by 50 percent in 2012 alone.

(D) Tracking global atmospheric temperatures since the 1800s, scientists point to a steady rise with a stronger period in the 1970s, a lull in the 1990s, and a return to the rising pattern in the 2000s.

18. Habitat protection afforded by the Endangered Species Act, the federal government's banning of the insecticide DDT, and conservation actions taken by the American public have helped bald eagles make a remarkable recovery. Bald eagle sightings are now a common occurrence in many parts of the country. When America adopted the bald eagle as the national symbol in 1782, anecdotal accounts stated that the country may have had as many as 100,000 nesting eagles. The first major decline of the species probably began in the mid to late 1800s, coinciding with the decline of waterfowl, shorebirds, and other prey. Although they primarily eat fish and carrion, bald eagles used to be considered marauders that preyed on chickens, lambs, and domestic livestock. _____ large raptors were shot in an effort to eliminate a perceived threat. Coupled with the loss of nesting habitat, bald eagle populations declined. In 1940, noting that the species was threatened with extinction, Congress passed the Bald Eagle Protection Act, which prohibited killing, selling, or possessing the species. A 1962 amendment added the golden eagle, and the law became the Bald and Golden Eagle Protection Act.

Which of the following completes the text with the most logical transition?

(A) Consequently, the

(B) Nonetheless, the

(C) For instance, the

(D) In addition, the

GO ON TO NEXT PAGE

19. A tornado is a narrow, violently rotating column of air _____ from a thunderstorm to the ground. Because wind is invisible, it is hard to see a tornado unless it forms a condensation funnel made up of water droplets, dust, and debris. Tornadoes can be among the most violent phenomena of all atmospheric storms we experience.

Which of the following completes the text so that it conforms to the conventions of Standard English?

(A) that extend

(B) by which it extends

(C) that extends

(D) in which it extends

20. Many behavioral studies about the role of play in developing a cat's predatory skills conclude that play is not necessary for the cat to be a successful hunter. The evidence for this conclusion lies in studies of cats that are reared in isolation; _____ they have no opportunity to engage in playful activities with other cats.

Which of the following completes the text with the most logical transition?

(A) thus,

(B) similarly

(C) although

(D) in reality,

21. Some sugars used by manufacturers in foods and drinks that you buy may be different from what you traditionally think of as sugar, like sucrose or table sugar. These sugars meet the chemical definition of a _____ metabolized, or used by your body, differently than traditional sugars like sucrose.

Which of the following completes the text so that it conforms to the conventions of Standard English?

(A) sugar, which they are

(B) sugar, so it is

(C) sugar, and it is

(D) sugar, but they are

22. When I was growing up, my family always went to a lake in the Adirondack Mountains for a week of camping. My brothers and _____ would spend hours fishing, swimming, and searching for tadpoles in the lake.

Which of the following completes the text so that it conforms to the conventions of Standard English?

(A) we

(B) me

(C) I

(D) them

23. The faculty committee investigating the accident in the chemistry lab was less concerned about why the experiment was conducted than in whether _____ conducted with all safety precautions in place.

Which of the following completes the text so that it conforms to the conventions of Standard English?

(A) they were

(B) they was

(C) it were

(D) it was

24. The first edition of the *Green Book*, a listing of lodgings, restaurants, and businesses that were safe for Black travelers, was published by postal employee Victor Green and his wife in 1936. Timing is important to understanding its _____ started the publication within an established context of protest and social action by African Americans eager to push back against discrimination.

Which of the following completes the text so that it conforms to the conventions of Standard English?

(A) success; Green

(B) success, for which Green

(C) success was: Green

(D) success. The reason was because Green

25. Our planet Earth is composed of several layers. Each layer has a unique density (density = mass/volume). Scientists believe that all planets formed on the basis of _____ the layering of Earth is a result of gravitational pull. The densest layer (inner core) is at the center and the least dense layer (crust) is the outermost layer. The atmosphere, composed of gases, can technically be considered a layer as well and is obviously lighter than the crust.

Which of the following completes the text with the most logical transition?

(A) gravity; therefore,

(B) gravity; however,

(C) gravity, but

(D) gravity; instead,

26. While researching a topic, a student has taken the following notes:

- The density of Jupiter is $1.326g/cm^3$.
- Jupiter is larger than any other planet in the solar system.
- The stripes and swirls on the surface of Jupiter are cold, windy clouds of ammonia and water.
- The density of Saturn is $0.687g/cm^3$.
- Saturn has the most complicated rings — primarily chunks of ice — of any planet.
- Saturn is a massive ball made mostly of hydrogen and helium.

The student wants to compare the size of the two planets. Which choice most effectively uses relevant information from the notes to accomplish this goal?

(A) Some of the planets in the solar system like Jupiter and Saturn are mostly composed of gases.

(B) Both Saturn and Jupiter have distinctive surface features which have been captured in images taken by NASA spacecraft.

(C) Although both Saturn and Jupiter are composed of similar gases, Jupiter is bigger and denser than Saturn.

(D) Saturn's rings are composed mostly of chunks of ice while Jupiter's distinctive stripes and swirls are clouds.

GO ON TO NEXT PAGE

27. While researching a topic, a student has taken the following notes:

- Robert Frost wrote the poem, "Nothing Gold Can Stay" (1923), about how quickly things in nature fade.

- Frost often wrote about scenes from rural life in New England.

- The poem, "Nothing Gold Can Stay," was published in a collection called *New Hampshire* the same year (1923), which would later win the 1924 Pulitzer Prize.

- In "Nothing Gold Can Stay," Frost applies the images of nature to the larger themes such as the passage of time.

- Frost draws a parallel from nature to the short-lived quality of beauty, youth, and life in "Nothing Gold Can Stay."

The student wants to create a statement that will introduce the poet and his major themes to an audience unfamiliar with Robert Frost. Which choice most effectively uses information from the notes to accomplish this task?

(A) Pulitzer Prize–winning poet Robert Frost often uses nature images from rural New England to express themes about nature and human existence.

(B) Robert Frost wrote "Nothing Gold Can Stay" in 1923, and the collection of poems that it was published in won a Pulitzer Prize.

(C) "Nothing Gold Can Stay," written by Robert Frost in 1923, is about the fleeting quality of nature, youth, and time.

(D) Robert Frost, who wrote many poems, is famous for his poems about life and nature.

Check your work.

Continue to the next module when you're ready to move on.

Section 2: Math

Module 1

TIME: 35 minutes for 22 questions.

DIRECTIONS: For multiple-choice questions, choose only one answer for each question. For fill-in questions, write only one answer, even if you find more than one correct answer. Don't include symbols such as a percent sign, comma, or dollar sign.

NOTES:

- All numbers used in this exam are real numbers.

- All figures lie in a plane.

- All figures may be assumed to be to scale unless the problem specifically indicates otherwise.

- The domain of a given function f is the set of all real numbers x for which $f(x)$ is a real number, unless the problem specifically indicates otherwise.

- You may use a calculator.

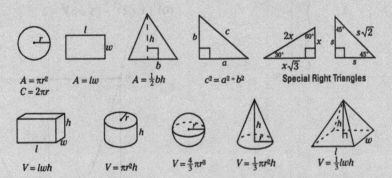

- The number of degrees in a circle is 360.

- The number of radians in a circle is 2π.

- The sum of the measures of the angles of a triangle is 180.

GO ON TO NEXT PAGE

1. In the *xy*-coordinate plane, what is the area of the rectangle with opposite vertices at $(-3,-1)$ and $(3,1)$?

   (A) 3

   (B) 6

   (C) 9

   (D) 12

2. The following Venn diagram shows the ice-cream flavor choice of 36 children at an ice-cream party. Each child could choose vanilla ice cream, chocolate ice cream, both, or neither. What percent of the children had chocolate ice cream only?

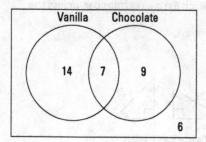

   (A) 10%

   (B) 25%

   (C) 50%

   (D) 75%

3. If $\frac{4}{5}$ of a number is 24, what is $\frac{1}{5}$ of the number?

   (A) 5

   (B) 6

   (C) 8

   (D) 18

4. The formula below is used in finance to compute A, the payment Amount per period, where P is the initial Principal, or loan amount, r is the interest rate per period, and n is the total number of payments per period.

   $$A = P\frac{r(1+r)^n}{(1+r)^n-1}$$

   Which of the following correctly gives P in terms of A, n, and r?

   (A) $P = A\dfrac{r(1+r)^n}{(1+r)^n-1}$

   (B) $P = A\dfrac{(1+r)^n-1}{r(1+r)^n}$

   (C) $P = A\dfrac{r(1+r)^n-1}{(1+r)^n}$

   (D) $P = A\dfrac{(1+r)^n}{r(1+r)^n-1}$

5. A circle in the *xy*-coordinate plane has a center of $(2,5)$ and a radius of 3. Which of the following is an equation of the circle?

   (A) $(x-2)^2+(y-5)^2=9$

   (B) $(x-2)^2+(y-5)^2=3$

   (C) $(x+2)^2-(y+5)^2=9$

   (D) $(x+2)^2-(y+5)^2=3$

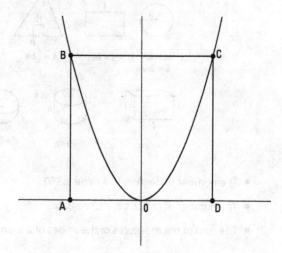

6. In the figure above, $ABCD$ is a square and points B, C, and O lie on the graph of $y = \dfrac{x^2}{k}$, where k is a constant. If the area of the square is 36, what is the value of k?

   (A) 1.5

   (B) 3

   (C) 4.5

   (D) 6

7. How much greater than $t-5$ is $t+2$?

   (A) 2

   (B) 4

   (C) 5

   (D) 7

8. $f(x) = x^3 - 4x$

$g(x) = x^2 + x - 2$

Which of the following expressions is equivalent to $\dfrac{f(x)}{g(x)}$, for $x > 2$?

(A) $\dfrac{x-2}{x(x-1)}$

(B) $\dfrac{x-1}{x(x-2)}$

(C) $\dfrac{x(x-1)}{x-2}$

(D) $\dfrac{x(x-2)}{x-1}$

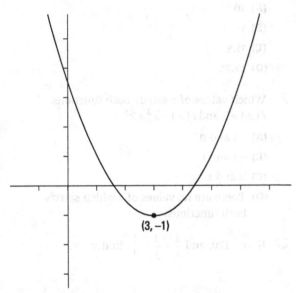

(3, −1)

9. In the parabola above, the vertex is at $(3, -1)$. Which of the following are x-coordinates of two points on this parabola whose y-coordinates are equal?

(A) 1 and 5

(B) 1 and 6

(C) 2 and 5

(D) 2 and 6

10. The price of a television was first decreased by 10 percent and then increased by 20 percent. The final price was what percent of the initial price?

(A) 88%

(B) 90%

(C) 98%

(D) 108%

11. In the xy-plane, the center of a circle has coordinates $(-2, 4)$. If one endpoint of a diameter of the circle is $(-2, 1)$, what are the coordinates of the other endpoint of this diameter?

(A) $(-5, 4)$

(B) $(-2, 6)$

(C) $(-2, 7)$

(D) $(1, 4)$

12. If $\dfrac{3n}{2p} = \dfrac{4}{3}$, what is the value of $\dfrac{n}{p}$?

(A) 2

(B) 1

(C) $\dfrac{9}{8}$

(D) $\dfrac{8}{9}$

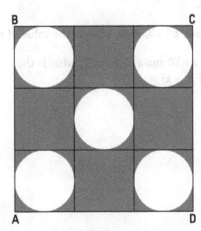

13. Square $ABCD$ is divided into nine equal squares, five of which have circles inscribed in them. If $AB = 6$, what is the total shaded area?

(A) $24 - 10\pi$

(B) $24 - 5\pi$

(C) $36 - 10\pi$

(D) $36 - 5\pi$

14. In the xy-plane, line l passes through $(-1, 3)$ and is parallel to the line $4x + 2y = k$. If line l passes through the point $(p, -p)$, what is the value of p?

(A) -2

(B) -1

(C) 1

(D) 2

GO ON TO NEXT PAGE

15. $y = x^2 - 2x + 3$
$y = -3x + 5$

How many solutions are there to the system of equations above?

(A) The answer cannot be determined with the information given.

(B) There are no solutions.

(C) There is exactly one solution.

(D) There are exactly two solutions.

16. Find the smallest even number divisible by 3, 5, and 7.

17. A certain fraction is equivalent to $\frac{2}{3}$. If the fraction's denominator is 12 less than twice its numerator, find the denominator of the fraction.

18. If $p > 0$ and $p^2 = 3p + 40$, what is the value of p?

19. If $x^2 - 3x = 50$ and $x^2 + 5x = 12$, what is the value of $x^2 + x$?

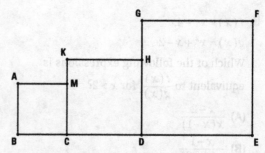

20. In the preceding figure, each shape is a square, BC has length 4, and CD has length 7. Points A, K, and G all lie in the same line. Find the length of DE.

(A) 10

(B) 11

(C) 11.5

(D) 12.25

21. Which values of x satisfy both functions $f(x) = 3$ and $f(x) = x^2 + 2$?

(A) −1 and 0

(B) −1 and 1

(C) 0 and 1

(D) There are no values of x which satisfy both functions.

22. If $xy = 120$, and $\frac{1}{x} + \frac{1}{y} = \frac{1}{4}$, find $x + y$.

Check your work.

Continue to the next module when you're ready to move on.

Module 2

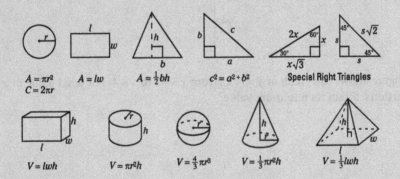
GO ON TO NEXT PAGE

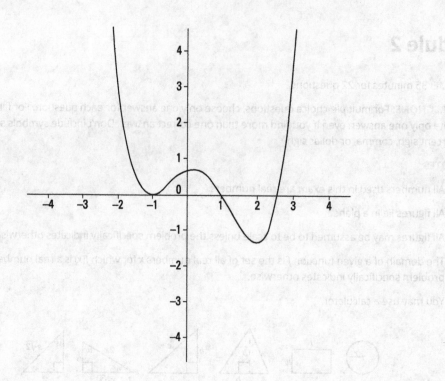

1. The preceding figure shows the graph of $y = f(x)$ from $x = -3$ to $x = 4$. For what value of x in this interval does the function f attain its minimum value?

    (A) 2

    (B) 1

    (C) 0

    (D) −2

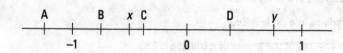

2. Which point on the preceding number line best represents the product of x and y?

    (A) A

    (B) B

    (C) C

    (D) D

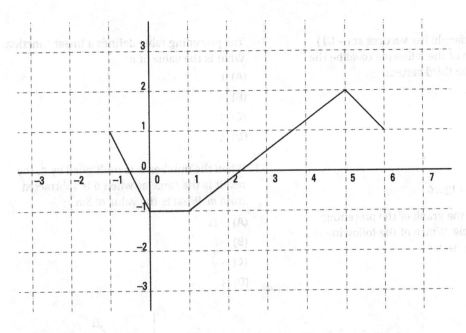

3. The graph of $y = f(x)$ is shown above. If $f(3) = k$, which of the following is the value of $f(k)$?

(A) -1

(B) $-\dfrac{1}{2}$

(C) 0

(D) $\dfrac{1}{2}$

4. If $-1 < x < 0$, which of the following statements must be true?

  I. $x > \dfrac{x}{2}$

  II. $x^2 > x$

  III. $x^3 > x^2$

(A) I only

(B) II only

(C) I and II only

(D) II and III only

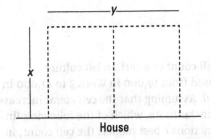

House

5. A gardener is building a fence to enclose their garden and divide it in half, as shown in the preceding figure. The fourth side of the garden is adjacent to their house, so it does not require fencing. The total area of the garden is 2,400 square feet. In terms of x, how many feet of fencing does the gardener require?

(A) $2,400 - 3x$

(B) $x + \dfrac{2,400}{x}$

(C) $3x + \dfrac{2,400}{x}$

(D) $3x + \dfrac{1,200}{x}$

GO ON TO NEXT PAGE

6. An equilateral triangle has vertices at $(-1,1)$ and $(5,1)$. Which of the following *could* be the coordinates of the third vertex?

(A) $(2,-5)$

(B) $(2,1-3\sqrt{3})$

(C) $(2,3\sqrt{3})$

(D) $(3\sqrt{3},1)$

7. $x^2+y^2-4x-6y+12=0$

In the *xy*-plane, the graph of the preceding equation is a circle. Which of the following is the radius of the circle?

(A) 4

(B) 3

(C) 2

(D) 1

8. The office supply store offers pens in two different boxes: one containing 6 pens and the other containing 12 pens. If Maria orders 28 boxes for a total of 204 pens, how many boxes of 12 pens are in the order?

(A) 6

(B) 8

(C) 10

(D) 12

9. The cell count of a certain lab culture increased from 19,000 in Week 3 to 41,000 in Week 6. Assuming that the cell count increased at a constant rate, which of the following linear functions *f* best models the cell count, in thousands of cells, *t* weeks after Week 3?

(A) $f(t)=\dfrac{3}{22}t-19$

(B) $f(t)=\dfrac{22}{3}t-19$

(C) $f(t)=\dfrac{3}{22}t+19$

(D) $f(t)=\dfrac{22}{3}t+19$

k	1	2	3	4	5	6
f(k)	15	11	7	n	−1	−5

10. The preceding table defines a linear function. What is the value of *n*?

(A) 1

(B) 2

(C) 3

(D) 4

11. When the number *m* is multiplied by 5, the result is the same as when 6 is subtracted from *m*. What is the value of $8m$?

(A) −12

(B) −6

(C) $-\dfrac{3}{2}$

(D) 3

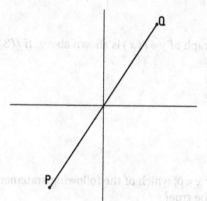

12. The coordinates of point *P* in the preceding figure are (a,b), where $|b|>|a|$. Which of the following could be the slope of *PQ*?

(A) −3

(B) $-\dfrac{1}{2}$

(C) $\dfrac{1}{2}$

(D) $\dfrac{3}{2}$

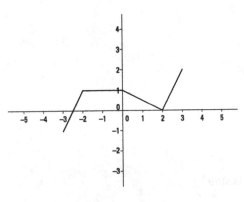

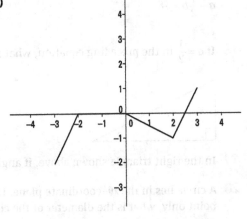

13. The graph of $y = g(x)$ is shown above. Which of the following could be the graph of $y = g(x-1)$?

(A)

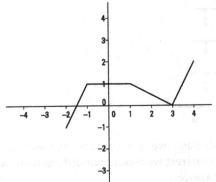

14. In the xy-plane, lines p and q are perpendicular. If line p contains the points $(-2, 2)$ and $(2, 1)$, and line q contains the points $(-2, 4)$ and $(k, 0)$, what is the value of k?

(A) −3

(B) −2

(C) −1

(D) 0

15. If $x^2 - y^2 = 39$ and $x - y = 3$, what is the value of y?

(B)

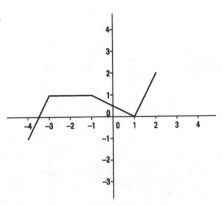

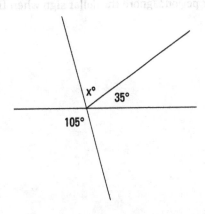

16. What is the value of x in the preceding figure?

17. Six times a number is the same as the number added to 6. What is the number?

(C)

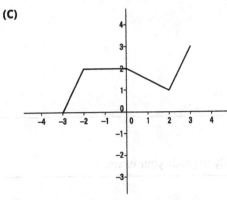

GO ON TO NEXT PAGE

$$a - \frac{1}{2}b = -8$$

18. If $a = \frac{1}{2}$ in the preceding equation, what is the value of b?

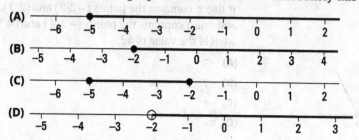

19. In the right triangle shown above, if angle $\theta = 30°$, what is $\sin\theta$?

20. A circle lies in the xy-coordinate plane. If the circle is centered at $(-3, 17)$ and touches the y-axis at one point only, what is the diameter of the circle?

21. Which of the following represents all values of x that satisfy this inequality: $7 \geq -2x + 3$?

(A)

(B)

(C)

(D)

22. If \$1,000 invested at i percent simple annual interest yields \$200 over a 2-year period, how much interest would the \$1,000 investment yield if the i percent interest were compounded annually over the 2-year period? Ignore the dollar sign when filling in your answer.

Check your work.

Continue to Chapter 12 when you're ready to grade your exam.

Chapter 12

Practice Exam 1: Answers and Explanations

fter you finish the practice test sections in Chapter 11, take some time to go through the answers and explanations in this chapter to find out which questions you missed and why. Even if you answered the question correctly, the explanation may offer a useful strategy that speeds up your performance on the next round. There is also additional information that'll be useful on the real SAT. If you're short on time, turn to the end of this chapter to find an abbreviated answer key.

Section 1: Reading and Writing

Module 1

1. **B.** The text states that the book *First Woman* is intended to inspire the next generation of space explorers. To inspire readers, the book will need to **captivate** (attract and hold the interest of) their attention. Choice B is the best answer.

2. **C.** A mailman delivering your mail in a horse-drawn cart would be out of date, no longer in use, or **obsolete**. Choice C is the best answer.

3. **B.** The sentence sets up a contrast between evanescence (existing only briefly) and permanence (lasting a long time). Thus, Choice B, **contrasting**, best expresses the relationship between the two ideas.

4. **D.** The text suggests that to counter the threat to natural resources, incentives will **encourage** landowners to use sustainable management. While Choice C is tempting because it is a positive word, you should take the time to put the words into the sentence and reread it to find the **best** choice. The context clue *incentive* should lead you to choose **encourage**. Choice D is the best answer for the context.

5. A. The text states that "bison were nearly driven to extinction through uncontrolled hunting and a U.S. policy of eradication." This context clue should lead you to Choice A, **persecution** (hostility and ill treatment).

6. D. The text sets up an increasing series of negative effects of modern working conditions. First injury to employers, then detriment to workers, and finally a **calamitous** (disastrous) effect on the community. Choice D is the best answer for the context.

7. C. The passage states that Amelia Earhart "maintained an attitude of impenetrable mediocrity," and that's what got her the job. That phrase should lead you to select Choice C, opaque (impenetrable) and ordinariness (averageness or mediocrity). Don't allow words in the text like "curious," "demure," and "respectful" to tempt you to choose the incorrect answer Choices B or D. While those choices are used in the text to describe Earhart, they are not the qualities that got her the job.

8. B. The function of the underlined sentence in the text is to provide the reader with a specific example of a crop that relies extensively on the honey bee for pollination. Notice that the sentence says, "Almonds, for example . . ." This use of a specific example that supports the claim honey bees are valuable pollinators should lead you to select Choice B.

9. A. In these lines, the speaker in the poem claims that "you" (the person being addressed) see in "me" (the speaker) someone nearing the end of his life ("on the ashes of his youth doth lie"). You see this ("This thou perceivest") and that makes you love me more ("makes thy love more strong"). Thus, the knowledge that the speaker will soon die drives the partner to love him even more. No evidence in the poem supports the other choices. Choice A is the best answer.

10. C. The claim in the text is that rising amounts of greenhouse gases contribute to global warming, yet if the warming trend is part of the fluctuating nature of climate and is well within "normal" temperature ranges, then the claim is weakened. Choice C is the best answer.

11. D. The sentence that best concludes the text is one that sums up the brief biography of Deb Haaland. Choices A, B, and C offer more details about Secretary Haaland's life. Only Choice D offers a summary of Secretary Haaland's life and her accomplishments thus far.

12. C. Choice C is the best answer because this statement by a conservation expert supports the claim in the text that high levels of phosphorus are dangerous to animals and humans. None of the other choices offer a direct link between phosphorus and its potentially harmful effects on people and animals.

13. D. The "insignificant" marks left by the plow indicate that it is a primitive implement that leaves a trail similar to the "feeble" marks left by prehistoric people. This comparison with prehistoric people creates a picture of a very early and somewhat ineffectual form of farming. Choice D is the best statement of the purpose of this line in the text.

14. C. The most logical choice to explain the decrease in homelessness among young people within a year after a disaster is Choice C. There is an increase in homelessness during and immediately after a disaster as homes are destroyed. Then, as homes are rebuilt the following year, homelessness decreases as young students find new housing. None of the other choices offer a logical explanation of the decrease in homelessness after a disaster.

15. **B.** The text states that when "mussels take over," other marine animals "disappear from the environment." In other words, the mussels *displace* or remove other species — as Choice (B) states. Choice (D) may have tempted you, but that answer is too extreme. You know only that the other species "disappear," not that they become extinct. They could be thriving in another spot! Choice (B) is the best answer.

16. **D.** The past perfect form of the verb is needed to show action that occurred in the past over a period of time. Choice A is incorrect because *begun* can only be used as a verb in conjunction with a form of the verb *to have*. Choice B is incorrect because the correct form of the verb to use with *had* is the past participle *begun*. Choice C is incorrect because *has begun* is the present perfect tense, and the war took place in the past.

17. **C.** The choice that conforms to the conventions of Standard English has a comma followed by the participial phrase *gaining momentum*. Choice A incorrectly uses the semicolon: *gaining momentum as it careened out of control* is not an independent clause. Choice B incorrectly uses a period for the same reason. Choice D is incorrect because it is missing the necessary comma between *hill* and *gaining*.

18. **A.** Choice A uses the correctly spelled *there* and the correct plural form of the verb *were* to agree with the plural noun *rabbits*. Choice B incorrectly uses the singular form of the verb *was*. Choice C uses the incorrect word *their*. Choice D incorrectly uses *they're*, the contraction of *they are*.

19. **C.** Choice C correctly punctuates the participial phrase *Named in honor of the trailblazing astronomer* by putting a comma after it and by omitting the unnecessary comma between *trailblazing* and *astronomer* and between *astronomer* and *Edwin Hubble*. The other choices are incorrectly punctuated.

20. **A.** Choice A uses the correct correlative conjunction *or* (remember the pairs: *either-or*, *neither-nor*) and the correct mark of punctuation, the semicolon, to join two independent clauses. Choice B has the dreaded comma splice error! Never use a comma to connect two independent clauses. Choices C and D incorrectly use *nor* rather than *or*.

21. **A.** The best transitional word to use between the first clause and the second is *however* because the information in the second clause contrasts with the information in the first clause: The view was great, but we were too exhausted to appreciate it! The punctuation (semicolon before and comma after) is correct when *however* is used to connect two independent clauses. Choice B is incorrect because the second sentence is not a consequence or a result of the first sentence. Choice C, *For example*, is incorrect because the second clause is not an example of the first clause. Choice D is incorrect because *furthermore* does not reflect the contrast between the content of the first clause and the content of the second clause.

22. **A.** Choice A correctly uses the colon after a main clause before information that clarifies the main clause. The other choices are incorrectly punctuated.

23. **D.** Choice D correctly uses the singular possessive pronoun *its* to refer to his design for the entrance to the Louvre. Choice A incorrectly uses the plural pronoun *their*. Choice B incorrectly uses *it's*, the contraction of *it is*. Choice C incorrectly adds an apostrophe to the possessive pronoun *its*. (A possessive pronoun never has an apostrophe because it is already possessive.)

24. **B.** Choice B correctly uses the transitional word *Indeed* to add emphasis to the point of the second sentence, which agrees with and extends the idea of the lack of knowledge of the Greeks. Choices A, C, and D incorrectly use contrast words.

25. **C.** Choice C correctly uses the present perfect tense *has been written* about an action which has taken place over a period of time that began in the past and continues into the present. (*Tip:* Look at the other verbs in the passage and notice that they are written in the present tense.) Choice A is grammatically incorrect — you can never say *was wrote.* Choice B incorrectly uses the past perfect tense *had been written.* Choice D incorrectly uses the past participle *written* without a helping verb.

26. **C.** Choice C is the best answer because it highlights the distinguishing character qualities of Elizabeth Blackwell, which is what the prompt asks you to consider when selecting a choice. While Choices A, B, and D are true, they do not emphasize Blackwell's distinguishing qualities.

27. **B.** Choice B is the best answer to accomplish the student's goal of stating the significance of the findings obtained from the study of the Vredefort crater. Choices A, C, and D are true statements that don't effectively focus on the significance of the findings.

Module 2

1. **C.** Choice C is the best word to complete the text. The context clue "seldom move more than a foot or two in any direction" should lead you to **sedentary**, which means inactive or not moving.

2. **A.** Choice A is the best word to fill in the blank because biodiversity is very important or **crucial** to the survival of living things.

3. **C.** Choice C, **contrived to**, is the best choice to fit into the context of the sentence. The Egyptians **contrived** (created or managed to do something) a method of tempering iron ore so that they could shape it into tools and weapons. Choices A and B suggest the Egyptians didn't want to make tools and weapons, which is illogical based on the text. Choice D doesn't make logical sense.

4. **B.** Logically, to retain heat to create a warming effect, the clouds **absorb** outgoing infrared radiation. None of the other choices would create a warming effect.

5. **A.** The logic of the context suggests that the new, lower-cost method is preferable to the current method, which is costly and **requires** the help of experts (which would add to the cost and make it less user-friendly). None of the other choices are logical in the context of the sentences.

6. **D.** Choice D is the most logical word to fill in the blank. The meaning of **arbitrary**, based on whim or random choice, is included in the second half of the last sentence: "it could be chosen to be anywhere." None of the other choices complete the sentence logically.

7. **D.** Choice D is the best choice because, beginning with the word *Hence* (which means *for this reason*), it presents a statement of what will happen as a result of the previously described situation. The underlined text draws a logical conclusion from the information in the previous sentences. It isn't a specific example (Choice A) or a new idea (Choice B) that counters a previously accepted conclusion. It doesn't provide further detail about any particular species (Choice C).

8. **A.** Choice A is the best choice because the underlined sentence clarifies the meaning of *non-native*. It doesn't offer a specific example, so Choice B is incorrect. Choice C is incorrect because it doesn't offer an exception. Choice D is incorrect because there is no counterclaim.

9. **C.** Choice C is true of the "young fellows." According to the text, "they perceived that their sympathies were akin [alike]" and "they had like courage and similar hopes." Don't let Choice D fool you into thinking that because they were "talking and arguing," they disagreed strongly; the passage suggests they agreed on most topics. Choice A can be eliminated because you don't know if they arrived from different countries. Choice B is the opposite of what the text suggests.

10. **C.** The main purpose of the text is to explain how human intervention (straightening the creek) had an unintended, but harmful, effect (more erosion and pollutants) on the land. The text doesn't summarize the results of a study (Choice A), present a positive impact of straightening (Choice B), or speculate on the effect of plant competition (Choice D).

11. **B.** The City School Superintendent concluded that most schools in the district were consistently providing a health education course in all grades of secondary school. However, according to the data, less than 25 percent of the schools offered students in grades 10 through 12 a health education course as compared to close to 75 percent of the schools in grades 6 through 9. This data clearly weakens the Superintendent's conclusion. Nothing in the data supports the other choices.

12. **A.** According to the text, most animal behaviorists are unwilling to admit that animals have thoughts and feelings. (Dog and cat lovers among us know differently!) Choice A most accurately reflects the current thinking about attributing emotions and thoughts to animals. Choice B is off topic. Choice C, while it may be true, isn't supported by the text. Choice D is also somewhat off topic.

13. **D.** A careful reading of the poem reveals Pope's belief that good writing, like good dancing, comes from practicing one's craft, not just chance (or natural talent); Choice A says the opposite of what Pope says. Pope would also disagree with Choice B; he makes a point that "The sound must seem an echo to the sense." Nothing in the poem supports the conclusion in Choice C.

14. **C.** The quotation in Choice C reveals that Pip remembers what he had "thrown away" when he was "ignorant of its worth," but he has given "his duty" a "place in his heart." This illustrates the claim that he ultimately learns that he has lost more than he gained. The quotations in Choices A, B, and D don't effectively illustrate the claim as well as Choice C does.

15. **D.** The evidence that farmers who use a herbicide are three times more likely to develop renal cell carcinoma supports the conclusion that certain pesticides (including the herbicide 2,4,5-T) lead to the development of kidney disease and kidney cancer. Choice A is too general to support the claim. Choice B is off topic. Choice C is also off topic.

16. **B.** The main idea of Chief Joseph's speech is that everyone deserves freedom, and we are all brothers and should have equal rights. Choice B best states the main idea. Choice A is not relevant to the main idea of the speech. Choice C brings in the unrelated topic of laws. Choice D is not a topic that Chief Joseph addresses in this speech.

17. C. If it is true that Arctic ice increased in volume by 50 percent in 2012 alone, this statistic would appear to weaken the conclusion that the evidence pointing to climate change is undeniable. A decrease in the Artic ice core is often used as a measurement of global warming. Choices A, B, and D all support, not weaken the conclusion of the panel.

18. A. The most logical transition to complete the text is *consequently*, Choice A. *Consequently* means as a result (or consequence); this fits the evidence in the text that as a consequence of the perception of bald eagles as predators who ate livestock, they were shot. Choice B, *nonetheless*, means *in spite of that*, which doesn't make sense in the context. Choice C is incorrect because shooting the eagles is not an *instance* of the first half of the sentence. Choice D is incorrect because it doesn't logically follow as an *addition* to their being perceived as predators; it is a result, not simply an additional piece of information.

19. C. Choice C completes the text with the most concise and grammatically correct phrase *that extends*. The subject of the verb *extends* is a singular noun, *tornado*, which agrees with the singular form of the verb *extends*. Choice A is incorrect because it uses the plural form of the verb *extend*, which doesn't agree with the singular subject *tornado*. Choice B is both wordy and inaccurate; the air is not the method *by which* the tornado extends. The tornado is the air. Choice D is also wordy and inaccurate: The tornado doesn't extend *in* the air; it is the air.

20. A. Choice A, *thus*, is the most logical transitional word for this context because it expresses a cause-and-effect relationship: Some cats are reared in isolation (cause), and they have no opportunity to engage in play activities (effect or result). Choice B is incorrect because the two ideas are not similar. Choice C is incorrect because *although* suggests that the cats' inability to engage in play activities contrasts with their being reared in isolation rather than being a result of the isolation. Choice D doesn't make logical sense because it doesn't indicate the cause-and-effect relationship.

21. D. Choice D is the most logical and grammatically correct choice to complete the sentence. First, Choice D uses the correct plural pronoun *they* to refer to the plural subject *sugars*. Choices B and C incorrectly use the singular pronoun *it* to refer to the plural subject *sugars*. Choice A uses the correct pronoun *they*, but it uses the ungrammatical and illogical wording *which they are metabolized* instead of the conjunction *but* + *they are* to show the contrast between the ways these sugars are metabolized.

22. C. This is an example of tricky pronoun case. *I* is a subject pronoun and *me* is an object pronoun; they are never interchangeable. If the pronoun is a doer (as in *I* would spend hours fishing. . .), then you always use the subject pronoun. If the pronoun receives the action (my brother handed *me* the rod), then you always use the object pronoun. . .not so tricky now, right? The only correct pronoun in this case is Choice C.

23. D. Take these choices two at time. First, ask yourself: Is the sentence about one experiment or many experiments? The sentence states "the experiment," so just one. That eliminates Choices A and B because both have the plural pronoun, *they*. Now you must decide whether you need the singular verb *was* or the plural verb *were*. You've already established that the subject is singular, so eliminate Choice C, and you're good.

24. A. Choice A offers the clearest and most concise correctly punctuated choice, effectively using the semicolon to connect two independent clauses. All the other choices are unnecessarily wordy or awkward.

25. **A.** The logical relationship between the first half of the sentence and the second half is cause-and-effect. The best word to indicate that the layering is a result of gravity is *therefore*. Gravity (the cause) creates layering (the result). Choices B, C, and D, *however, but,* and *instead*, all indicate a contrast, which does not conform to the logic of the sentence.

26. **C.** In this question, your careful reading of the prompt is very important. (Actually, it always is!) Your task is to choose relevant information from the notes to compare the sizes of the planets, so all the other information in the notes is not relevant to your choice. Choice C is the best choice because it uses relevant information (not all the information) to make a comparison between the sizes of Saturn and Jupiter. All the other choices contain true — but irrelevant — information.

27. **A.** Choice A most effectively introduces the poet and his major themes to an audience unfamiliar with Robert Frost. (Hard to imagine!) None of the other choices include all the important information, and none are written as effectively as Choice A.

Section 2: Math

Module 1

1. **D.** Sketch out this problem to help you solve it:

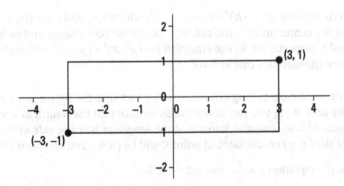

The length of the rectangle is 6, and the height is 2. The area of a rectangle is *length* times *width*, so the area of this rectangle is $(6)(2) = 12$.

2. **B.** Because you're interested in the children who had only chocolate ice cream, you want to look in the chocolate circle where it doesn't overlap with the vanilla circle; the number in that section is 9. That means 9 kids had only chocolate ice cream, out of the 36 kids at the party. To find the percent of children who had chocolate ice cream, simply divide the part that you're interested in (9) by the whole (36):

$$\frac{9}{36} = \frac{1}{4} = 25\%$$

3. B. Set up the equation with x as the number and solve for x.

$$\frac{4}{5}x = 24$$
$$4x = 120$$
$$x = 30$$

Now find $\frac{1}{5}$ of 30, which is 6.

4. B. Don't let this one drive you mad. To transfer the clunky fraction from P to A, simply multiply both sides by the reciprocal and cancel.

$$A = P\frac{r(1+r)^n}{(1+r)^n - 1}$$

$$\left(\frac{(1+r)^n - 1}{r(1+r)^n}\right)A = P\frac{r(1+r)^n}{(1+r)^n - 1}\left(\frac{(1+r)^n - 1}{r(1+r)^n}\right)$$

$$\left(\frac{(1+r)^n - 1}{r(1+r)^n}\right)A = P\frac{\cancel{r(1+r)^n}}{\cancel{(1+r)^n - 1}}\left(\frac{\cancel{(1+r)^n - 1}}{\cancel{r(1+r)^n}}\right)$$

$$\left(\frac{(1+r)^n - 1}{r(1+r)^n}\right)A = P$$

$$P = A\frac{(1+r)^n - 1}{r(1+r)^n}$$

5. A. The equation for a circle is $(x-h)^2 + (y-k)^2 = r^2$, where h, k, and r are the x- and y-coordinates of the center and r is the radius. Place these coordinates and radius 2, 5, and 3 for h, k, and r, respectively, in the equation for $(x-2)^2 + (y-5)^2 = 3^2$ and square the 3 on the end. Choice (A) matches this answer.

6. A. The key to this problem is paying attention to the fact that the figure is a square. Knowing that the area is 36, you can immediately deduce that the length of a side of the square is 6 because $6^2 = 36$. You also know that the length of half the side of the square is 3. That means that the (x, y) coordinates of point C will be $(3, 6)$. You can then plug those coordinates into the equation $y = \frac{x^2}{k}$ and solve for k:

$$6 = \frac{3^2}{k}$$
$$6 = \frac{9}{k}$$
$$6k = 9$$
$$k = \frac{3}{2} \text{ or } 1.5$$

7. D. Get rid of the t, and the question becomes, "How much greater than -5 is 2?" Well, that would be 7, so Choice (D) is the right answer.

8. D. If $f(x) = x^3 - 4x$ and $g(x) = x^2 + x - 2$, simply place $x^3 - 4x$ over $x^2 + x - 2$, factor the expressions, and cancel what you can:

$$\frac{x^3 - 4x}{x^2 + x - 2}$$

$$\frac{x(x-2)\cancel{(x+2)}}{(x-1)\cancel{(x+2)}}$$

$$\frac{x(x-2)}{x-1}$$

9. A. The key to this problem is remembering that parabolas are symmetrical along the line that passes vertically through the vertex (known as the *axis of symmetry*). That means that if you were to fold the parabola along that line, both sides would line up. For the purpose of this problem, it means that x-values with the same y-coordinates must be the same distance from the axis of symmetry, which is at $x = 3$ in this case. Both values in Choice (A) are two away from 3, so that looks like a great option. In Choice (B), 1 is two away from 3, but 6 is three away, so that option doesn't work. For Choice (C), 2 is one away from 3, but 5 is two away; again they're not the same distance from the axis of symmetry. Choice (D) keeps 2, which is still one away from 3, and moves the other point farther away, to 6. Choice (A) it is!

10. D. Whenever you're working on percentage problems, start with $100. So if the TV cost $100, and then the price was decreased by 10 percent ($10), the reduced price is $90. You add 20 percent on to 90 by finding 20 percent of 90 and adding it to $90: $0.20(90) = 18$; $90 + \$18 = \$108$. It's easy to see that $108 is 108 percent of $100: $\frac{\$108}{\$100} = 1.08 = 108\%$.

11. C. It's always a great idea to sketch problems where you're told the coordinates but not given a picture.

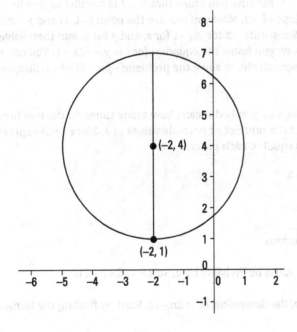

Looking at your picture, it's easy to see that the other endpoint of the diameter is also going to have –2 as its x-coordinate. Now all you need to do is determine the radius of the circle so you can figure out the y-coordinate. Looking at the two points that were given in the problem, you can see that the radius is 3 $(4 - 1 = 3)$. That means that the y-coordinate of the other endpoint will be 3 away from the center: $(-2, 4 + 3) = (-2, 7)$.

12. **D.** To isolate $\frac{n}{p}$, multiply both sides by the reciprocal of the coefficient, or $\frac{2}{3}$:

$$\frac{3n}{2p} = \frac{4}{3}$$

$$\left(\frac{\cancel{2}}{\cancel{3}}\right)\frac{3n}{2p} = \frac{4}{3}\left(\frac{\cancel{2}}{\cancel{3}}\right)$$

$$\frac{n}{p} = \frac{8}{9}$$

13. **D.** The first step is to find the area of square *ABCD*. You know the length of one of the sides, so you know that the area is that length squared: $6^2 = 36$. Now you just need to subtract off the area of the five circles. You can see that each of the nine smaller squares has a side length equal to one-third of the length of the big square: $\frac{1}{3}(6) = 2$. This means that each circle has a diameter of 2 and a radius of 1. The area of a circle is $A = \pi r^2$, so the area of each circle is $A = \pi (1)^2 = \pi$. Now you can find the area of the shaded part of the diagram. The area will be the total square area minus the area of five circles: $36 - 5\pi$, or Choice (D).

14. **C.** The first step is to find the slope of the given line by solving for y:

$$2y = -4x + k$$

$$y = -2x + \frac{k}{2}$$

The slope of this line is –2. Because you know that line *l* is parallel to this line, you now know that line *l* has a slope of –2. Now you can use the point $(-1, 3)$ and $y = mx + b$ to determine the equation of *l*. Substitute –2 for *m*, –1 for *x*, and 3 for *y*, and then solve for *b*: $3 = -2(-1) + b$, so $b = 1$. Now you know the equation for *l* is $y = -2x + 1$. You can substitute *p* and –*p* in for *x* and *y*, respectively, to solve the problem: $-p = -2(p) + 1$. Simplifying, $-p = -2p + 1$, or $p = 1$.

15. **D.** The number of solutions as graphed means how many times do the two functions cross, but in algebra it refers to the number of possible values of *x*. Since each expression is equal to *y*, set the expressions equal to each other:

$$x^2 - 2x + 3 = -3x + 5$$

$$x^2 + x - 2 = 0$$

$$(x + 2)(x - 1) = 0$$

Looks like *x* has two solutions.

16. **210.** Every even number must be divisible by 2, so $2 \times 3 \times 5 \times 7 = 210$.

17. **36.** If the numerator is *n*, the denominator is $2n - 12$. Start by finding the numerator:

$$\frac{2}{3} = \frac{n}{2n - 12}$$

$$2(2n - 12) = 3n$$

$$4n - 24 = 3n$$

$$n = 24$$

Hold on, though — n is the *numerator*, but you need the *denominator*. You know that the fraction is equivalent to $\frac{2}{3}$, so set up the equation with d as the denominator:

$$\frac{2}{3} = \frac{24}{d}$$
$$2d = 72$$
$$d = 36$$

18. **8.** Although you could use trial and error, without answer choices to try, it may be better to factor it. To factor a *quadratic equation* (that is, an equation with something "squared" in it), first set the equation equal to 0 with the squared term positive:

$$p^2 = 3p + 40$$
$$p^2 - 3p - 40 = 0$$
$$(p - 8)(p + 5) = 0$$
$$p = -5, 8$$

Because $p > 0$, $p = 8$.

19. **31.** Don't math it out. You *could* solve for x and place the value into $x^2 + x$, but because this is the SAT, you know there's an easier way. First add the equations:

$$x^2 - 3x = 50$$
$$+\left(x^2 + 5x = 12\right)$$
$$\overline{2x^2 + 2x = 62}$$

Divide both sides by 2, and $x^2 + x = 31$.

20. **D.** This is a tricky one. The key is that points A, K, and G are on the same line, because it tells you that the side-length ratio of the medium-to-small squares is the same as the side-length ratio of the large-to-medium squares. Look at this drawing to see the pattern:

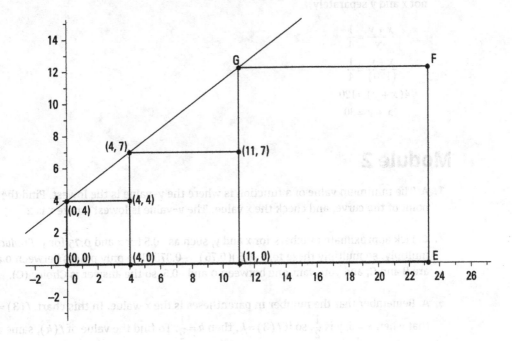

You know from the question that the medium-square side length is 7 and the small-square side length is 4, making the ratio 7 to 4. Multiply this ratio by the medium-square side length to find the large-square side length:

$$7\left(\frac{7}{4}\right) = \frac{49}{4} = 12.25$$

21. B. You know that $f(x)$ equals both 3 and $x^2 + 2$, so set those expressions equal to each other and solve for x:

$$3 = x^2 + 2$$
$$1 = x^2$$
$$x = 1, -1$$

And this matches answer Choice (B).

22. 30. This question is all about working with fractions. Consider the following:

$$\frac{1}{x} + \frac{1}{y} = \frac{1}{4}$$

When you're working with fractions, getting a common denominator on each side is a good idea. Here's how it works out:

$$\left(\frac{y}{y}\right)\frac{1}{x} + \left(\frac{x}{x}\right)\frac{1}{y} = \frac{1}{4}$$

$$\frac{y}{xy} + \frac{x}{xy} = \frac{1}{4}$$

$$\frac{x+y}{xy} = \frac{1}{4}$$

You know that $xy = 120$, so plug that in and solve for $x + y$ as a single unit (in other words, not x and y separately).

$$\frac{x+y}{xy} = \frac{1}{4}$$

$$\frac{x+y}{(120)} = \frac{1}{4}$$

$$4(x+y) = 120$$

$$x+y = 30$$

Module 2

1. A. The minimum value of a function is where the y-value is the lowest. Find the lowest point of the curve, and check the x value: The y-value is lowest where x is 2.

2. C. Pick approximate numbers for x and y, such as -0.5 for x and 0.75 for y. *Product* means multiply, so multiply these for $(-0.5)(0.75) = -0.375$. The only points between 0 and -1 are B and C, and you want one between 0 and -0.5, so the answer is Choice (C).

3. A. Remember that the number in parentheses is the x-value. In this chart, $f(3) = k$ tells you that when $x = 3$, y is $\frac{1}{2}$, so if $f(3) = k$, then $k = \frac{1}{2}$. To find the value of $f(k)$, same as $f\left(\frac{1}{2}\right)$, go to where $x = \frac{1}{2}$, and $y = -1$.

4. B. This problem is easier if you pick a number for x, such as -0.5 or $-\frac{1}{2}$, and try out each statement. Try the first statement:

$$-0.5 > \frac{-0.5}{2}$$
$$-0.5 > -0.25$$

This is false, so eliminate Choices (A) and (C). Choices (B) and (D) both claim that Statement II is true, but try it just to be sure:

$$(-0.5)^2 > -0.5$$
$$0.25 > -0.5$$

This is true, so now check Statement III for the tiebreaker:

$$(-0.5)^3 > (-0.5)^2$$
$$-0.125 > 0.25$$

And it's not true. Choice (B) is the answer.

5. C. The fence that the gardener needs is equal to $3x + y$, so what you really need to do is figure out a way to represent y in terms of x. Because the area of the garden is 2,400 square feet, you can use your knowledge of the area of a rectangle to see that $2,400 = xy$. Divide both sides by x to solve for y for $y = \frac{2,400}{x}$, and then place that back in to the original expression for the total fencing needed: $3x + y = 3x + \frac{2,400}{x}$, Choice (C).

6. B. To help solve this problem, sketch a picture. Keep in mind that the triangle can point upward or downward.

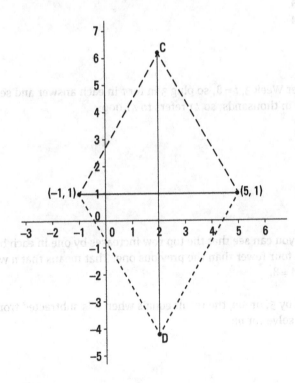

The third vertex of the triangle will lie along the line that cuts through the midpoint between the two given vertices. You can find the coordinates of that midpoint by finding the average of the x's and the average of the y's: $\left(\frac{-1+5}{2}, \frac{1+1}{2}\right) = (2,1)$. So the x-coordinate of the third vertex will be 2, which eliminates Choice (D). Because equilateral triangles have 60-degree angles in them, you can drop an altitude from the unknown vertex to make a 30-60-90 triangle. You know that the leg connecting a vertex to the 90-degree angle is going to be 3 units long, and from there, you can use your knowledge of common right triangles to see that the unknown altitude is $3\sqrt{3}$. That means that the unknown vertex is $3\sqrt{3}$ away from 1, so it's either at $\left(2, 1+3\sqrt{3}\right)$ or $\left(2, 1-3\sqrt{3}\right)$. Choice (B) is the only choice that fits.

7. **D.** Convert the equation of the circle to the center-radius form, where the center is (h,k) and the radius is r: $(x-h)^2 + (y-k)^2 = r^2$.

$$x^2 + y^2 - 4x - 6y + 12 = 0$$
$$x^2 + y^2 - 4x - 6y = -12$$
$$\left[x^2 - 4x\right] + \left[y^2 - 6y\right] = -12$$
$$\left[(x-2)^2 - 4\right] + \left[(y-3)^2 - 9\right] = -12$$
$$(x-2)^2 + (y-3)^2 = 1$$

Because $r^2 = 1$, $r = 1$ and the answer is Choice (D).

8. **A.** If x boxes each hold 12 pens, then that group has $12x$ pens. If there are 28 boxes total, then $28 - x$ boxes each hold 6 pens, and that group has $6(28-x)$ pens. Set up the equation for the total of 204 pens:

$$12x + 6(28-x) = 204$$
$$12x + (168 - 6x) = 204$$
$$6x = 36$$
$$x = 6$$

9. **D.** In the third week after Week 3, $t = 3$, so plug 3 in for t in each answer and see which one yields 41. The answer is in thousands, so 41 refers to 41,000:

$$f(t) = \frac{22}{3}t + 19$$
$$f(3) = \frac{22}{3}(3) + 19$$
$$= 22 + 19$$
$$= 41$$

10. **C.** Looking at the chart, you can see that the top row increases by one in each box. In the bottom row, each box is four fewer than the previous one. That means that n will be four fewer than 7, or n is $7 - 4 = 3$.

11. **A.** When m is multiplied by 5, or $5m$, the result equals when 6 is subtracted from m, or $m - 6$. Set up the equation and solve for m:

$$5m = m - 6$$
$$4m = -6$$
$$m = -\frac{6}{4}$$
$$= -\frac{3}{2}$$

Now multiply this result by 8 for $8m$:

$$-\frac{3}{2} \times 8 = -12$$

12. D. Looking at the picture, you can see that the line has a positive slope (as you read left to right, the line goes up). Already you can eliminate Choices (A) and (B). To find the slope of the line, use the points (a, b) and $(0, 0)$:

$$m = \frac{b-0}{a-0} = \frac{b}{a}$$

You know from $|b| > |a|$ that the fraction will be larger than 1, making Choice (D) the only viable choice.

13. A. When you change the x-value in a function, the graph changes horizontally. In this case, you're subtracting 1 from x before plugging it into the function g, so the graph shifts either left or right. Knowing this narrows your choices down to Choices (A) and (B). You can look at the original graph and see that $g(2) = 0$. To get $y = g(x-1)$ to equal 0, you need $x-1$ to equal 2: $x-1 = 2$, $x = 3$. That means that $(3, 0)$ will be a point on the transformed graph. Choice (A) is the only graph with that point on it.

14. A. Your first step is to find the slope of line p.

$$m = \frac{2-1}{-2-2} = \frac{1}{-4} = -\frac{1}{4}$$

Because perpendicular lines have opposite (negative) reciprocal slopes, the slope of line q must be 4. So far, you know that line q has a slope of 4 and passes through the point $(-2, 4)$. You can use the equation $y = 4x + b$ and substitute in the point to figure out what b is: $4 = 4(-2) + b$ becomes $b = 12$ when you solve it. Now you have the equation of line q: $y = 4x + 12$. Substitute in the point $(k, 0)$ and solve for k: $0 = 4k + 12$, $-12 = 4k$, and $k = -3$.

15. 5. For this problem, you need to factor a difference of perfect squares: $x^2 - y^2 = (x-y)(x+y)$. Substitute in the numbers that you know, $39 = (3)(x+y)$, and then divide both sides by 3 to get $x + y = 13$. Because you know both $x + y$ and $x - y$, you can add the two together: $(x+y) + (x-y) = 2x = 13 + 3 = 16$. Now you know that x is 8. If x is 8 and $x + y = 13$, then y is 5.

16. 70. The trick is to see that $105°$ is a vertical angle to $35° + x°$. Because vertical angles are equal, you know that $105 = 35 + x$.

17. 1.2 or $\frac{6}{5}$. Call the number x. Translating the words into math: "Six times x is the same as x added to 6" becomes $6x = 6 + x$. Now solve for x:

$$6x = 6 + x$$
$$5x = 6$$
$$x = 1.2$$

18. 17. Place $\frac{1}{2}$ for a and solve for b:

$$a - \frac{1}{2}b = -8$$

$$\left(\frac{1}{2}\right) - \frac{1}{2}b = -8$$

$$-\frac{1}{2}b = -8\frac{1}{2}$$

$$b = 17$$

19. $\frac{1}{2}$ **or 0.5.** If one angle is 90° and angle $\theta = 30°$, then the third angle is 60°, making this a 30-60-90 triangle with a side ratio of $1 : \sqrt{3} : 2$. The sine of an angle is the angle's opposite side, which in this case is the triangle's smallest side, over the triangle's hypotenuse. From the ratio, you know that the smallest side is half the length of the hypotenuse, for an answer of $\frac{1}{2}$ or 0.5. When you type in your answer, either $\frac{1}{2}$ or 0.5 is considered correct.

20. 6. Sketch out the problem to help you solve:

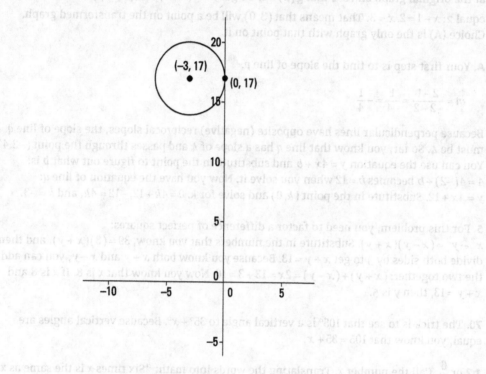

For the circle to touch the y-axis in only one place, it must touch the y-axis at (0,17). That point is three units away from the center of the circle, meaning that the radius of the circle is 3 and the diameter is 6.

21. **B.** Simplify the expression. Just remember that when you divide both sides by a negative (in this case, −2), you switch the inequality sign. Then you swap the x and the value, meaning you switch the inequality sign again:

$$7 \geq -2x + 3$$
$$4 \geq -2x$$
$$-2 \leq x$$
$$x \geq -2$$

Both Choices (B) and (D) include numbers greater than −2, but Choice (B) has the circle at −2 filled in, meaning that −2 is included in the solution set, which is exactly what you want because you're looking for all numbers greater than or *equal to* −2.

22. **210.** If \$1,000 invested at *i* percent simple annual interest yields \$200 over a two-year period, you can deduce that it earns \$100 over one year. To find *i*, the interest rate, yielding \$100 simple annual interest on \$1,000, divide the amount of interest by the amount of the investment:

$$\frac{100}{1,000} = 0.1 = 10\%$$

Now you know that $i = 10$, for an interest rate of 10 percent.

To calculate compound interest, you can use the compound interest formula. However, for only two cycles, you can find the answer without the formula. Simply calculate the simple interest twice: once for the first year, and once for the second year. Start with the original \$1,000 investment, and increase it 10 percent:

$$\$1,000 + (10\% \times \$1,000) = \$1,000 + \$100 = \$1,100$$

The investment is worth \$1,100 at the end of the first year. To find its value at the end of the second year, increase \$1,100 by 10 percent:

$$\$1,100 + (10\% \times \$1,100) = \$1,100 + \$110 = \$1,210$$

The question asks for the amount of interest yielded, not the final value. To find the amount of interest, subtract the original value from the final value:

$$\$1,210 - \$1,000 = \$210$$

Answer Key

Section 1: Reading and Writing, Module 1

1.	B	8.	B	15.	B	22.	A
2.	C	9.	A	16.	D	23.	D
3.	B	10.	C	17.	C	24.	B
4.	D	11.	D	18.	A	25.	C
5.	D	12.	C	19.	C	26.	C
6.	D	13.	D	20.	A	27.	B
7.	C	14.	C	21.	A		

Section 2: Reading and Writing, Module 2

1.	C	8.	A	15.	D	22.	C
2.	A	9.	C	16.	B	23.	D
3.	C	10.	C	17.	C	24.	A
4.	B	11.	B	18.	A	25.	A
5.	A	12.	C	19.	C	26.	C
6.	D	13.	D	20.	A	27.	A
7.	D	14.	C	21.	A		

Section 3: Math, Module 1

1.	D	7.	D	13.	D	19.	31
2.	B	8.	D	14.	C	20.	D
3.	B	9.	A	15.	D	21.	B
4.	B	10.	D	16.	210	22.	30
5.	A	11.	C	17.	36		
6.	A	12.	D	18.	8		

Section 4: Math, Module 2

1.	A	7.	D	13.	A	19.	.5 or $\frac{1}{2}$
2.	C	8.	A	14.	A	20.	6
3.	A	9.	D	15.	5	21.	B
4.	B	10.	C	16.	70	22.	210
5.	C	11.	A	17.	1.2 or $\frac{6}{5}$		
6.	B	12.	D	18.	17		

Chapter 13

Practice Exam 2

N ow for another. Like the actual SAT — and the other practice exam in Chapter 11 — the following practice exam consists of 54 Reading and Writing questions (split into two 27-question modules) along with 44 Math questions (split into two 22-question modules), for 98 questions total.

Remember that the paper-based practice exams provided by CollegeBoard.org have 66 Reading and Writing questions (in two 33-question modules) and 54 Math questions (in two 27-question modules), for 120 questions total. Because you're taking the SAT on a computer, not on paper, the practice exams in this book reflect the online experience of only 98 questions. You'll thank me later.

You get 32 minutes for each Reading and Writing module and 35 minutes for each Math module. Those plus the 10-minute break bring the exam to just under two and a half hours. Also, with no answer sheet, circle your answer selection right here in this book.

Take this practice test under normal exam conditions and approach it as you would the real SAT:

» **Work where you won't be interrupted.** Leave your cell phone in another room, and ask anyone living with you (parents, siblings, dog) not to disturb you for the next few hours. (Good luck with that.)

» **Practice with someone else who is taking the SAT.** This allows you to get used to the feeling of working with another person in the room; plus, this person can keep you focused and provide a sense of competition.

» **Answer as many questions as time allows.** Consider answering all the easier questions within each section first and then going back to the harder questions. Because you're not penalized for guessing, go ahead and guess on the remaining questions before time expires.

» **Set a timer for each section.** If you have time left at the end, go ahead and review your answers (within the section), continue and finish your test early, or pause and catch your mental breath before moving on to the next section.

» **Take breaks between sections.** Take one minute after each module and ten minutes after the second Reading and Writing module.

>> **Work through the entire exam.** Get used to the experience of going through the entire exam in one sitting. It's not easy the first time, but you'll build the strength to stay focused through the entire marathon session.

>> **Circle any question that you weren't sure of or that took too long.** If you took longer than a minute on any one question, or had to take a guess, you should brush up on that topic or strategy. After the exam, you naturally review the explanations for wrong answers, but this way you review the explanations for right answers that you had guessed on or could've found faster.

After completing this practice test, go to Chapter 14 to check your answers. You could review the explanations for *each* question, not just the ones you miss, but at least review the questions you missed along with those that you circled. The answer explanations provide insight and a review of everything from the previous chapters.

Ready? Grab a pencil, some scratch paper, a calculator, and a timer. Sit back, relax, and enjoy your trip through Practice Exam 2. You got this.

Section 1: Reading and Writing
Module 1

TIME: 32 minutes for 27 questions.

DIRECTIONS: Read these passages and answer the questions that follow based on what is stated or implied in the passages and accompanying diagrams, charts, or graphs. Each question has one best answer.

1. Threatened species are plants and animals that are _____ become endangered within the foreseeable future throughout all or a significant portion of its range. According to the former Attorney General Loretta Lynch, "We all have a responsibility to protect endangered species, both for their sake and for the sake of our own future generations."

   Which choice completes the text with the most logical and precise word or phrase?

   (A) definitely going to
   (B) inevitably bound to
   (C) probably able to
   (D) likely to

2. It is important for clinical trials to have participants of _____ ages, sexes, races, and ethnicities. When research involves a group of people who are similar, the findings may not apply to or benefit everyone.

   (A) consistent
   (B) different
   (C) similar
   (D) conflicting

3. Hurricanes Irma and Maria highlighted the challenges for Federal agencies that rely on residential addresses to supply services in Puerto Rico. Relief efforts during the 2017 hurricane season were _____ by the absence of an island-wide system of addressing and the lack of physical addresses for approximately one-third of the island.

   Which choice completes the text with the most logical and precise word?

   (A) hampered
   (B) assisted
   (C) enhanced
   (D) enlightened

4. The following excerpt is adapted from *A Short History of the World* by H. G. Wells (1922).

   The telescope reveals to us in various parts of the heavens luminous spiral clouds of matter, the spiral nebula, which appear to be in rotation about a center. It is _____ by many astronomers that the Sun and its planets were once such a spiral, and that their matter has undergone concentration into its present form.

   Which choice completes the text with the most logical and precise word?

   (A) ordered
   (B) supposed
   (C) undermined
   (D) required

5. The rapidly rising river was another element of danger. It was a fearful sight to see the _____ flood plunging by, bearing great trees and logs of driftwood on its muddy surface many feet above the ground.

   Which choice completes the text with the most logical and precise word?

   (A) deceitful
   (B) placid
   (C) sluggish
   (D) relentless

GO ON TO NEXT PAGE

6. The Box Tree Moth is an invasive pest that can significantly damage and potentially kill boxwood (*Buxus* species) plants if left unchecked. The insect is native to East Asia and has become a serious invasive pest in Europe, where it continues to spread. The caterpillars feed mostly on boxwood, and heavy infestations can _____ host plants. Once the leaves are gone, larvae consume the bark, leading to plant death.

Which choice completes the text with the most logical and precise word?

(A) defoliate

(B) embark

(C) empower

(D) engender

7. Non-chronological storytelling is not new to modern novels and films; in the *Odyssey*, for example, Homer uses flashbacks to _____ earlier scenes in Odysseus' adventures.

Which choice completes the text with the most logical and precise word?

(A) recount

(B) reuse

(C) reinstate

(D) rescind

8. The following passage is adapted from an article on the USGS Volcano Hazards Program website.

USGS scientists monitor over 160 active and potentially active volcanoes in the United States. Most of these volcanoes are located in Alaska, a state where eruptions occur almost every year. The rest of the volcanoes are located throughout the American West, and in Hawaii. Since there are on average between 50 and 60 volcanoes that erupt each year somewhere on Earth (about one every week), some of Earth's volcanoes may actually erupt within a few days or hours of each other, possibly suggesting a cause-and-effect relationship between eruptions. Upon closer inspection, however, the eruptions are almost always preceded by very different build-up periods in terms of time (days to weeks to months to years) and type of activity (earthquakes, ground deformation, gas emissions, and small eruptions).

Which choice best describes the function of the last sentence in the overall structure of the text?

(A) It states a hypothesis that is contradicted by evidence provided earlier in the text.

(B) It presents a generalization that is exemplified by the discussion of the volcanoes in Hawaii.

(C) It offers an alternative explanation to a speculative relationship referred to earlier in the text.

(D) It provides context that clarifies why volcanoes are preceded by different build-up periods.

9. The following is an excerpt from a National Institutes of Health article titled "Genetics."

All living things evolved from a common ancestor. Therefore, humans, animals, and other organisms share many of the same genes, and the molecules made from them function in similar ways.

Scientists have found many genes that have been preserved through millions of years of evolution and are present in a range of organisms living today. They can study these preserved genes and compare the genomes of different species to uncover similarities and differences that improve their understanding of how human genes function and are controlled. This knowledge helps researchers develop new strategies to treat and prevent human disease. Scientists also study the genes of bacteria, viruses, and fungi for solutions to prevent or treat infection. Increasingly, these studies are offering insight into how microbes on and in the body affect our health, sometimes in beneficial ways.

Which choice poses a question that can be answered by the information in the text?

(A) Why do scientists study the genes of organisms other than human beings?

(B) What genes do humans share with bacteria, fungi, and viruses?

(C) How do genes function to treat and prevent human disease?

(D) How do researchers preserve the genes of organisms that no longer exist today?

10. To get a grasp of the complex interactions between living things, we can start by looking at a simple linear food chain: sun, dandelion, rabbit, and hawk. Sunlight is converted into chemical energy by green plants. Part of that energy is captured by herbivorous insects and vertebrates when they eat the plants. Carnivores then eat herbivores. In reality, however, the flow of energy through an ecosystem is more like a web. Species share energy back and forth in subtle ways. If we consider other relationships (for example, plants that provide cover and nesting habitats to animals; insects, birds, and bats that pollinate flowers; rodents that disperse seeds; animals that require shade created by plants; and so on), our web approaches a symbol of what nature is really like.

Which choice best explains the difference between a linear and a web-like representation of the food chain?

(A) A linear representation expresses a more complex relationship while a web representation expresses a simpler relationship.

(B) A linear representation expresses an inorganic relationship while a web representation expresses an organic relationship.

(C) A linear representation expresses a non-human relationship while a web representation expresses a human-to-human relationship.

(D) A linear representation expresses a relationship in a straight line while a web representation expresses a multi-directional relationship.

GO ON TO NEXT PAGE

11. The gender pay gap is greater for women in certain sectors. For example, in the following graph, among workers who were self-employed, women earned an estimated 69 cents for every dollar earned by men. In private, for-profit companies, women earned an estimated 78 cents for every dollar earned by men. In government agencies and non-profit organizations, women earned an estimated 85 cents for every dollar earned by men. The gender pay gap also varied by level of education. For example, among workers — including both full-time and part-time workers — with less than a high school diploma, women earned an estimated 66 cents for every dollar earned by men. Among workers with a bachelor's degree, women earned an estimated 70 cents for every dollar earned by men.

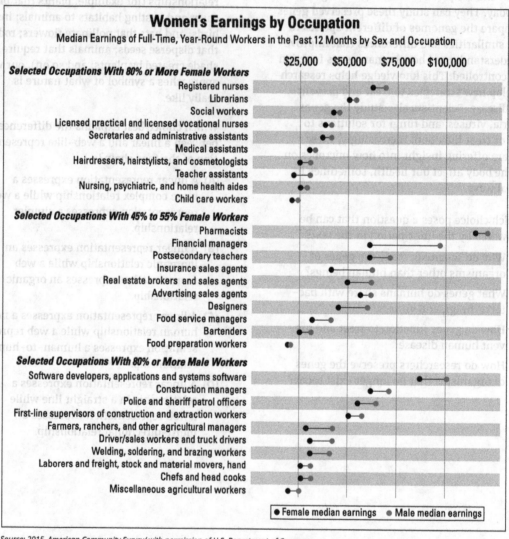

Women's Earnings by Occupation
Median Earnings of Full-Time, Year-Round Workers in the Past 12 Months by Sex and Occupation

Source: 2015, American Community Survey/ with permission of U.S. Department of Commerce.

Which choice most effectively uses data from the chart that supports information in the text?

(A) Postsecondary female teachers had a higher median income than that of male chefs and head cooks.

(B) Male truck drivers had a higher median income than that of female child care workers.

(C) Except in the field of education, females earned less than males in every occupation listed on the graph.

(D) The smallest salary gap between males and females was in financial management occupations.

12. Table 1.1   Time taken to add each billion to the world population, 1800–2046 (projection)

Date	Estimated world population (billions)	Years to add 1 billion people
1800	1	2,000,000
1930	2	130
1960	3	30
1974	4	14
1987	5	13
1999	6	12
2011	7	12
2024 (projected)	8	13
2046 (projected)	9	22

Source: Adapted from Population Division

Which choice most effectively uses data from the chart to complete the sentence?

According to the data on the chart, as the estimated world population increases, the number of years estimated to add 1 billion people _____.

(A) decreases sharply

(B) decreases and then increases slightly

(C) increases sharply

(D) increases and then decreases slightly

13. The following excerpt is adapted from *The Wiley-Blackwell Companion to Sociology*, edited by George Ritzer (Wiley-Blackwell).

Ritzer (2009) has recently argued that the focus on either production or consumption has always been misplaced and that all acts always involve both. That is, all acts of production and consumption are fundamentally acts of "prosumption." The assembly-line worker is always consuming all sorts of things (parts, energy, tools) in the process of production, and conversely the consumer in, for example, a fast-food restaurant is always producing (garnishes for a sandwich, soft drinks from the self-serve dispenser, the disposal of debris derived from the meal). This suggests a dramatic reorientation of theorizing about the economy away from production or consumption and in the direction of "prosumption."

According to the text, what does Ritzer argue is the difference between production and consumption?

(A) Production is creating, and consumption is using.

(B) Production is recent, and consumption is historical.

(C) Production is permanent, and consumption is temporary.

(D) They are opposite sides of the same spectrum.

14. The following poem was written by American poet Walt Whitman (1868).

A noiseless patient spider,
I mark'd where on a little promontory it stood isolated,
Mark'd how to explore the vacant vast surrounding,
It launch'd forth filament, filament, filament, out of itself,
Ever unreeling them, ever tirelessly speeding them.

And you O my soul where you stand,
Surrounded, detached, in measureless oceans of space,
Ceaselessly musing, venturing, throwing, seeking the spheres to connect them,
Till the bridge you will need be form'd, till the ductile anchor hold,
Till the gossamer thread you fling catch somewhere, O my soul.

Which of the following best describes the structure of the poem?

(A) The first stanza is metaphorical, and the second stanza is literal.

(B) The first stanza admires the spider, and the second stanza reviles the spider.

(C) The first stanza is literal, and the second stanza is philosophical.

(D) The first stanza presents the spider as repulsive, and the second stanza personifies the spider.

15. The following passage is adapted from the *Library of the Best American Literature*, by William W. Birdsall and Rufus M. Jones (1897).

In his personality, his wide range of themes, his learning, and his wonderful power of telling stories in song, Henry Wadsworth Longfellow stood in his day and still stands easily in front of all other poets who have enriched American literature. Admitting that he was not rugged and elemental like Bryant and did not possess the latter's feelings for the colossal features of wild scenery, that he was not profoundly thoughtful and transcendental like Emerson, that he was not so earnestly and passionately sympathetic as Whittier, nevertheless he was our first artist in poetry. Bryant, Emerson, and Whittier commanded but a few stops of the grand instrument upon which they played; Longfellow understood perfectly all its capabilities.

Which choice best describes the function of the underlined sentence in the text as a whole?

(A) It anticipates a possible criticism of Longfellow and answers it with a bold declaration.

(B) It affirms qualities that dismiss Longfellow from the ranks of great American poets.

(C) It provides specific examples to illustrate Longfellow's superiority to Bryant in depicting wild scenery.

(D) It illustrates a unique transcendent quality of Longfellow's poetry.

16. The following passage is an excerpt from *GRE For Dummies*, 8th edition, by Ron Woldoff and Joe Kraynak (Wiley).

A key study has shown that the organic matter content of a soil can be altered to a depth of 10 cm or more by intense campfire heat. As much as 90 percent of the original organic matter may be oxidized in the top 1.3 cm of soil. In the surface 10 cm, the loss of organic matter may reach 50 percent if the soil is dry and the temperature exceeds 250 degrees. The loss of organic matter reduces soil fertility and water-holding capacity and renders the soil more susceptible to compaction and erosion.

Which of the following best describes the function of the underlined sentence in the text as a whole?

(A) It elaborates on an example of organic matter as a measure of soil fertility.

(B) It explains the methodology used to determine soil fertility and water-holding capacity.

(C) It calls attention to the harmful effects of a common occurrence in campgrounds.

(D) It offers a solution to an unfortunate result of the increase in the popularity of camping.

17.

YEARLY CYCLE of Western Washington Beavers

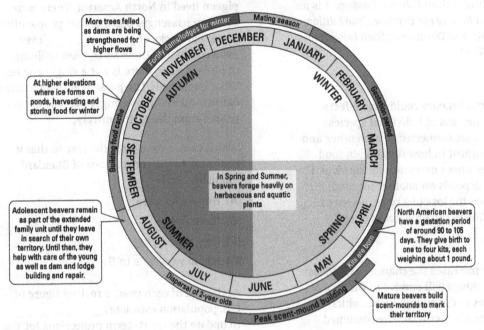

Source: King County / Public Domain

The following excerpt was adapted from *Planning for Beavers Manual: Anticipating Beavers when Designing Restoration Projects*, King County, Washington.

Land managers throughout the Puget Sound region are investing large sums of money and other resources to improve salmon habitat in streams and rivers. In the last 15 years, King County ecologists and land managers have seen a pattern of beavers colonizing these restoration sites anywhere from immediately to within 2 to 5 years of finishing a restoration project. Frequently, the beavers extensively browse newly planted vegetation. They have also built dams at some sites that flooded adjacent properties. Beaver colonization is now expected following construction of restoration projects along streams and rivers in King County, where restoration sites are usually also close to roads, culverts, farms, orchards, lawns, and houses. At the end of the summer, _____.

Which choice most effectively uses information from the graphic and the text to complete the sentence?

(A) beavers begin their mating season and mark their territory in preparation for giving birth.

(B) beavers build scent-mounds around the perimeter of their territory to indicate that a certain location is spoken for.

(C) properties located near beaver colonies will experience an increase in flooding as adolescent beavers join dam-building efforts.

(D) newly planted vegetation will flourish as beavers enter a period of hibernation and consume less food than usual.

GO ON TO NEXT PAGE

18. Passage 1 is an excerpt from *Novel Plant Bioresources* by Gurib Fakim (Wiley). Passage 2 is an excerpt from *Biology For Dummies, 2nd Edition,* by Rene Kratz and Donna Siegfried (also published by Wiley).

Text 1

The loss in biodiversity could have effects beyond just the loss of individual species. Living things are connected to each other and their environment in how they obtain food and other resources necessary for survival. If one species depends on another for food, for example, then the loss of a prey species can cause a decline in the predator species.

Text 2

Biodiversity increases the chance that at least some living things will survive in the face of large changes in the environment, which is why protecting it is crucial. The combined effect of various human actions in Earth's ecosystems is reducing the planet's biodiversity. In fact, the rate of extinctions is increasing along with the size of the human population. No one knows for certain how extensive the loss of species due to human impacts will ultimately be, but there's no question that human practices such as hunting and farming have already caused numerous species to become extinct.

With which of the following statements would both the writer of Text 1 and the writer of Text 2 agree?

(A) Reliance on a small number of food sources is a problem now and may become more severe in the future.

(B) Extinction of species is a naturally occurring process and is independent of human intervention.

(C) The key to maintaining an adequate food supply is reducing the planet's biodiversity.

(D) Reducing the number of predator species is crucial to protecting human food supplies.

19. A century ago, a bird called the passenger pigeon lived in North America. There were so many passenger pigeons that people often saw great flocks of _____ overhead containing thousands, even millions, of birds. Today, there is not a single one left. What happened? The passenger pigeon became extinct. All living passenger pigeons disappeared from the earth entirely.

Which choice completes the text so that it conforms to the conventions of Standard English?

(A) those who were

(B) them flying

(C) they were flying

(D) whom were able to fly

20. At the end of each year, a revised figure of U.S. population estimates _____ to update the short-term projections for the population clock. Once the updated series of monthly projections is completed, the daily population clock values are derived by interpolation. Within each calendar month, the daily numerical population change is assumed to be constant, subject to negligible differences caused by rounding.

Which choice completes the text so that it conforms to the conventions of Standard English?

(A) are used

(B) is used

(C) are being used

(D) used

21. English Gothic architecture has been usually subdivided into three periods or stages of _____ early stage, occupying the 13th century, is known as Early English.

Which choice completes the text so that it conforms to the conventions of Standard English?

(A) advancement, the

(B) advancement; in the

(C) advancement in the

(D) advancement: The

22. Polar bears' seasonal movements are driven by regional ice dynamics and can be quite extensive. Most polar bears remain with the pack ice as it recedes north during the summer melting season; _____ along Alaska's Beaufort Sea coast, some polar bears also come on land to rest until shore-fast ice begins to develop along the coast in late fall and the pack ice advances south, once again providing them with a suitable platform for hunting seals.

Which choice completes the text with the most logical transition?

(A) however,

(B) similarly,

(C) consequently,

(D) moreover,

23. Charlie hated driving home in a snowstorm. He was afraid his vision was impaired by the blowing snow and the wildly waving windshield wipers. Then, his worst fears were realized. While taking a few seconds to clean his glasses, _____ skidded off the highway.

Which choice completes the text so that it conforms to the conventions of Standard English?

(A) his car suddenly lurched to the left and

(B) Charlie's car suddenly swerved and

(C) his heart pounded wildly as he

(D) Charlie had to clutch the wheel quickly as his car

24. The rivalry between tennis great Monica Seles and Steffi Graf began at the French Open Tournament in 1989. Their match in the semifinals _____ eagerly watched by fans all over the world. Monica Seles was only 16 years old; Steffi Graf had the advantage in years and experience, and her wins in their first few matches established her strength. It was in their fourth encounter that Seles finally defeated the more established Graf.

Which choice completes the text so that it conforms to the conventions of Standard English?

(A) were

(B) is

(C) was

(D) are

25. The Nez Percé National Historic Trail ranges from the _____ incised Columbia River Plateau, across the Continental Divide and a succession of ranges, canyons, and valleys, through forests and plains, across thermal areas and major rivers. The Trail winds through some of the most rugged and spectacular scenery in western America. It traverses some of the largest undisturbed tracts of sagebrush steppe habitat, and a tremendous variety of wildlife and plant species thrive across the varied habitats of the Trail corridor.

Which choice completes the text so that it conforms to the conventions of Standard English?

(A) deeply

(B) deep

(C) deeper

(D) deepest

GO ON TO NEXT PAGE

26. While researching a topic, a student has taken the following notes:

- An organism's complete set of DNA is called its genome. Virtually every single cell in the body contains a complete copy of the approximately 3 billion DNA base pairs, or letters, that make up the human genome.

- With its four-letter language, DNA contains the information needed to build the entire human body. A gene traditionally refers to the unit of DNA that carries the instructions for making a specific protein or set of proteins.

- The human genome is a complete set of nucleic acid sequences for humans, encoded as DNA within the 23 chromosome pairs in cell nuclei and in a small DNA molecule found within individual mitochondria.

- Unlocking the genetic code allows scientists to assess an individual's genetic susceptibility to specific diseases, to diagnose genetic disorders, and to formulate new drugs.

- Proteins make up body structures like organs and tissue, as well as control chemical reactions and carry signals between cells. If a cell's DNA is mutated, an abnormal protein may be produced, which can disrupt the body's usual processes and lead to a disease such as cancer.

The student wants to emphasize the aim of the research study. Which choice most effectively uses relevant information from the notes to accomplish this goal?

(A) Each of the estimated 20,000 to 25,000 genes in the human genome codes for an average of three proteins.

(B) Understanding the structure and function of DNA and unlocking an individual's genetic code has helped scientists revolutionize the investigation of disease pathways.

(C) Abnormal proteins caused by mutated DNA can be the source of life-threatening diseases such as cancer.

(D) By mapping the human genome, scientists can obtain a complete set of nucleic acid sequences.

27. While researching a topic, a student has taken the following notes:

River Name	Countries	Outlet	Length in Miles
Amazon	Peru, Brazil	Atlantic Ocean	3,900
Congo	Zaire, Congo, Angola	Atlantic Ocean	3,900
Missouri-Mississippi	U.S.	Gulf of Mexico	3,990
Nile	Uganda, Sudan, Egypt	Mediterranean Sea	4,160
Huang He (Yellow R.)	China	Gulf of Bohai	2,800

The student wants to compare the lengths of the two longest rivers. Which choice most effectively uses relevant information from the notes to accomplish this goal?

(A) While the Nile River in Egypt, Uganda, and Sudan is the longest river in the world, the Huang He River empties into the Gulf of Bohai.

(B) The five longest rivers in the world are the Amazon, the Congo, the Missouri-Mississippi, the Nile, and the Huang He.

(C) Of the five longest rivers in the world, two have their outlets in the Atlantic Ocean, while three others have their outlets in smaller bodies of water.

(D) At 4,160 miles, the longest river in the world is the Nile River, while the Missouri-Mississippi in the U.S. is the second longest at 3,990 miles long.

Check Your Work.

Continue to the next module when you're ready to move on.

Module 2

TIME: 32 minutes for 27 questions.

DIRECTIONS: Read these passages and answer the questions that follow based on what is stated or implied in the passages and accompanying diagrams, charts, or graphs. Each question has one best answer.

1. The paintings of Salvador Dali, the renowned surrealist artist, are immediately recognizable for their bizarre images and technical precision. He created highly personal paintings that broke with tradition and _____ optical illusions.

   Which choice completes the text with the most logical and precise word?

   (A) featured

   (B) overwhelmed

   (C) discredited

   (D) renewed

2. Two particularly useful _____ of the timing of spring events are the first leaf dates and the first bloom dates of two flowering plants: lilacs and honeysuckles. These plants have an easily monitored flowering season, a relatively high survival rate, and a large geographic distribution.

   Which choice completes the text with the most logical and precise word?

   (A) effects

   (B) varieties

   (C) species

   (D) indicators

3. Eighteenth-century stories of the strange appearance and behavior of an unidentified creature left naturalists _____ as to what could fit its seemingly catch-all characteristics. The strange animal captured the imagination of scientists who did not know how to classify the duck-billed platypus. We now know that the platypus is a monotreme, an ancient type of mammal that lays eggs.

   Which choice completes the text with the most logical and precise word?

   (A) mystified

   (B) delighted

   (C) settled

   (D) confident

4. Comparative genomics is directly related to evolution because all living things share a common ancestor. By using computer tools to examine genes that have remained the same in many organisms over millions of years, researchers can _____ signals that control how genes work.

   Which choice completes the text with the most logical and precise word?

   (A) disrupt

   (B) locate

   (C) question

   (D) influence

GO ON TO NEXT PAGE

5. The Antiquities Act of 1906 was inspired by the need to _____ ancient American Indian ruins in the southwestern United States during the 19th-century push to open the country's western frontier. One hundred years after its enactment, the Antiquities Act remains one of the nation's most important conservation laws.

Which choice completes the text with the most logical and precise word?

(A) raze

(B) reconfigure

(C) safeguard

(D) complete

6. The rather pedestrian plot of the film was elevated by its _____ cinematography; the magnificent panoramas of the African veldt were photographed in stunning clarity and breathtaking beauty.

Which choice completes the text with the most logical and precise word?

(A) ordinary

(B) abundant

(C) exquisite

(D) banal

7. The following excerpt is adapted from *Punch*: Volume 118, Nos. 3052–3077.

"Assuredly," I said. "We don't take enough advice, in my opinion — just as we don't take enough exercise or wholesome food. It is too much the fashion to ask advice and not take it. But if we modelled our lives on the disinterested opinion of other people, and availed ourselves of the combined judgment of our fellows, the world would be both happier and wiser in many directions. And if men knew when they were invited to express an opinion that it was no mere conventional piece of civility or empty compliment which prompted us to ask their criticism, consider how they would put their best powers forward."

Which of the following best expresses the primary claim of the speaker in the passage?

(A) It is far healthier to follow one's personal inclination than to accept the opinions of others.

(B) The primary qualities that allow society to function are civility and good judgment in interpersonal interactions.

(C) Advice that is not requested should never be offered.

(D) Our lives would be improved if we were to seek and heed the objective opinions of others.

8. The following excerpt is from *Bedouins* by James Huneker (1920).

Some years ago in Paris I saw and heard Mary Garden sing *La Traviata*. The singing was superlative; she then boasted a coloratura style that would surprise those who now only know her vocalization. It was, however, the conception and acting that intrigued me. Originality stamped both. The death scene was of unusual poignancy; evidently the young American had been spying upon Bernhardt and Duse.*

*Sarah Bernhardt and Eleonora Giulia Amalia Duse were famous actresses of the late 19th century.

Which choice best states the function of the underlined sentence in the overall structure of the text?

(A) To offer a criticism of the singer's performance

(B) To provide objectivity to an analysis of the singer's acting ability

(C) To indicate the qualities that fascinated the writer

(D) To praise the coloratura style of the singer

9. The following text is adapted from *Democracy in America* by Alexis de Tocqueville (1835).

The settlers who established themselves on the shores of New England all belonged to the more independent, knowledgeable, and skilled classes of their native country. Their union on the soil of America at once presented the singular phenomenon of a society containing neither lords nor common people, neither rich nor poor. These men possessed, in proportion to their number, a greater mass of intelligence than is to be found in any European nation of our own time. All, without a single exception, _____.

Which choice most logically completes the text?

(A) had received a good education, and many of them were known in Europe for their talents and their acquirements.

(B) belonged to the aristocracy and thus had been provided with the best tutors and instructors.

(C) had been either indentured servants in Europe or had been poor, so the New World offered them the opportunity to escape a life of servitude.

(D) had a natural affinity for the menial jobs required by the new settlements and put their physical prowess to good use as they attempted to carve a home out of the wilderness.

10. The following text is an excerpt from *A Brief History of the Olympic Games* by David C. Young (Wiley).

"Victory by speed of foot is honored above all." Those are the words of Xenophanes, a 6th century B.C.E. philosopher who objected to athletes and their popularity. The phrase "speed of foot" may recall the words expressed in Homer's *Odyssey* stressing the glory which an athlete may win "with his hands or with his feet." The shortest foot race, the stade, was one length of the stadium track, the practical equivalent of our 200-meter dash (actually, only 192.27 meters at Olympia, the site of the original Olympic games). Greek tradition held that this 200-meter race was the first and only event held at the first Olympiad in 776 B.C.E.

Which of the following best states the purpose of the quotations in the text?

(A) To offer conflicting opinions

(B) To establish an authoritative tone

(C) To invite the reader to conduct further research

(D) To give a sense of Greek literary style

11. The following passage is adapted from the *Library of the Best American Literature*, by William W. Birdsall and Rufus M. Jones (1897).

As a poet Poe ranks among the most original in the world. He is preeminently a poet of the imagination. He brings into his poetry all the weirdness, subtlety, artistic detail and facility in coloring which give the charm to his prose stories, and to these he adds a musical flow of language which has never been equalled. To him poetry was music, and there was no poetry that was not musical. For poetic harmony he has had no equal certainly in America, if, indeed, in the world. Admirers of his poems are almost sure to read them over and over again, each time finding new forms of beauty or charm in them, and the reader abandons himself to a current of melodious fancy that soothes and charms like distant music at night, or the rippling of a nearby, but unseen, brook. As one of his biographers has written, _____

Which of the following quotations most logically and effectively completes the text?

(A) "I never heard a voice so musical as his. It was full of the sweetest melody. No one who heard his recitation of the 'Raven' will ever forget the beauty and pathos with which this recitation was rendered."

(B) "The images which he creates are vague and illusive."

(C) "The artful ingenuity with which he works up the details of his plot, and minute attention to the smallest illustrative particular, give his tales a vivid interest from which no reader can escape."

(D) "The scenes of gloom and terror which he loves to depict, the forms of horror to which he gives almost actual life, render his mastery over the reader most exciting and absorbing."

GO ON TO NEXT PAGE

12. The following passage is adapted from *A Practical Guide to Scientific Data Analysis* by David J. Livingstone (Wiley-Blackwell).

Statistics is often concerned with the treatment of a small number of samples which have been drawn from a much larger population. Each of these samples may be described by one or more variables which have been measured or calculated for that sample. For each variable there exists a population of samples. It is the properties of populations of variables that allow the assignment of probabilities, for example, _____.

Which choice completes the text with the most logical example?

(A) all the characteristics of the sample that remain constant throughout the population.

(B) the total number of a population from which the samples have been chosen.

(C) the likelihood that the variable will fall into a particular range and the assessment of significance.

(D) the exact number of all the occurrences of a particular set of circumstances within a population.

13. Mr. Burns, concerned about the growth of his tomato plants in his garden, decides to conduct an experiment to test several recommended fertilizers to determine which one, if any, he should use to protect his plants from infestation. He uses three different fertilizers on his plants and measures them after four weeks to determine the most effective fertilizer. At the end of four weeks, Mr. Burns is pleased with the growth of Plant 5 but is puzzled by the results for Plant 3.

Fertilizers:

A, Potassium

B, Nitrogen + Potassium

C, Nitrogen + Phosphorous

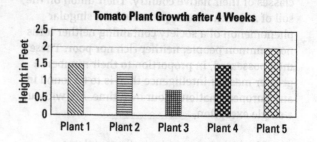
Tomato Plant Growth after 4 Weeks

Plant Number	Fertilizer Used
Plant 1	B
Plant 2	A
Plant 3	C
Plant 4	B
Plant 5	C

Which of the following would explain the discrepancy in the results of Mr. Burns' experiment?

(A) Mr. Burns used an automatic watering system that ensured the tomato plants received water at 5:00 a.m. and 5:00 p.m. each day.

(B) Mr. Burns planted the tomatoes in five different areas of his yard to protect them from overcrowding.

(C) Mr. Burns purchased tomato plants identical in size and type of tomato at the beginning of his experiment.

(D) Mr. Burns applied the fertilizer once a week in equal quantities.

14. The following passage is an excerpt from *Biology For Dummies, 2nd Edition*, by Rene Fester Kratz, PhD, and Donna Rae Siegfried (Wiley).

The cuticle is a layer of cells found on the top surfaces of a plant's leaves. It lets light pass into the leaf but protects the leaf from losing water. Many plants have cuticles that contain waxes that resist the movement of water into and out of a leaf, <u>much like wax on your car keeps water off the paint</u>. Guard cells are found on the bottom of a plant's leaves, near a stomate, a tiny opening that you can't see with your naked eye. (An individual opening is called a stomate, or stoma; several openings are called stomates, or stomata.)

Which of the choices describes the function of the underlined portion of the text?

(A) It clarifies a function by using an analogy.

(B) It refutes an assertion in the first part of the sentence.

(C) It provides an example that is expanded upon in the next sentence.

(D) It indicates another function of the cuticle layer of cells in a plant.

15. The following passage is adapted from *Dendroclimatic Studies: Tree Growth and Climate Change in Northern Forests*, by Rosanne D'Arrigo, Nicole Davi, Gordon Jacoby, Rob Wilson, and Greg Wiles (Wiley-Blackwell).

The science of dendroclimatology evolved from the need to understand past and present climate variability as well as the factors impacting tree growth and climate response on a range of spatial and vascular scales. Determination of how climate has varied in the past is also critically important for evaluating the sensitivity of the Earth's climate system to both natural and anthropogenic forces. <u>Yet instrumental observations are limited in length and spatial coverage, particularly in many remote, far-northern regions, where station records may only span a few decades.</u> Overcoming these limitations requires high-resolution, precisely dated proxy data archives, like tree rings, so that we may derive a long-term perspective for conditions during the recent anthropogenic era, during which profound and rapid changes are now taking place.

Which of the choices describes the function of the underlined portion of the text?

(A) It summarizes the results of a study.

(B) It offers an example of how observations can assist by providing eyewitness evidence.

(C) It describes a shortcoming of a method of scientific investigation.

(D) It presents a central finding in the science of dendroclimatology.

16. The following is an excerpt from *Life on the Mississippi* by Mark Twain (1883). The writer is recalling the time he spent as an assistant pilot on a steamboat.

Now when I had mastered the language of this water and had come to know every trifling feature that bordered the great river as familiarly as I knew the letters of the alphabet, I had made a valuable acquisition. But I had lost something, too. I had lost something which could never be restored to me while I lived. All the grace, the beauty, the poetry had gone out of the majestic river! I still keep in mind a certain wonderful sunset which I witnessed when steamboating was new to me. A broad expanse of the river was turned to blood; in the middle distance the red hue brightened into gold, through which a solitary log came floating, black and conspicuous; in one place a long, slanting mark lay sparkling upon the water; in another the surface was broken by boiling, tumbling rings, that were as many-tinted as an opal . . .

Which choice best states the main idea of the text?

(A) The writer is training to become a pilot because he wants to spend his days simply appreciating nature.

(B) The writer has gained technical knowledge of the river as a pilot but has lost an appreciation of its beauty.

(C) The beauty of the river hides a danger that an unsuspecting pilot might miss.

(D) Now that he has spent more time on the river, the writer is inspired to create a poem about his steamboat travels.

17. An automobile starts from rest and travels along a straight road. Point A is the starting point; Point E is the stopping point.

Points	Time Elapsed in Minutes	Distance Traveled in Feet
A Start	2	20
B	4	50
C	5	70
D	6	90
E Stop	9	100

Which of the following choices is true based on the information in the chart?

(A) During Interval B – C, the automobile is traveling at a constant speed.

(B) The automobile travels the farthest during Interval C – D.

(C) At the end of Interval D – E, the automobile is both stationary and farthest from the starting point.

(D) The automobile travels at the greatest speed during Interval A – B.

18. A conservation botanist studied the plants growing in an abandoned field. Once a year for 3 years, they checked the number of plants of each variety. Their results are indicated in the chart below.

Number of Plants per Acre

Year	Winter Bentgrass	Purple Lovegrass	Little Bluestem	Path Rush	Canada Goldenrod
1	2,600	3,980	450	395	2
2	1,100	1,890	1,970	990	805
3	698	127	2,380	1,100	1,750

Which choice is supported by the information in the chart?

(A) Little Bluestem and Canada Goldenrod compete with one another for resources.

(B) All the plants are negatively impacted by climate change.

(C) Little Bluestem and Path Rush have similar life spans.

(D) Plant populations are replacing one another.

19. Listening to _____ about flight delays, inaccurate train schedules, poorly maintained rental cars, and unsafe pedestrian pathways, it is rather tempting to stay home and cuddle up on the couch with a good book.

Which of the following completes the text so that it conforms to the conventions of Standard English?

(A) traveler's stories'

(B) travelers' stories

(C) travelers stories

(D) travelers' story's

20. *Inherit the Wind*, a play by Jerome Lawrence and Robert E. Lee, is a fictionalized account of the Scopes "Monkey" trial in which the famous _____ "what happened in a schoolroom of your town has unloosed a wicked attack from the big cities of the North!"

Which of the following completes the text so that it conforms to the conventions of Standard English?

(A) attorney, Matthew Brady, claims to have come because,

(B) attorney Matthew Brady claims to have come because

(C) attorney, Matthew Brady, claims to have come because

(D) attorney, Matthew Brady claims to have come, because

21. The following passage is adapted from *The Life of Ludwig van Beethoven* by Alexander Wheelock Thayer (1921).

It is a family tradition that Louis van Beethoven, owing to some financial difficulties, secretly left his father's house at an early age and never saw it again. Gifted with a good voice and well educated musically, _____ and applied for a vacant position as tenor, receiving it on November 2, 1731. A few days later the young man of 18 years was appointed substitute for three months for the singing master who had fallen ill.

Which of the following completes the text so that it conforms to the conventions of Standard English?

(A) it was the city of Louvain he first went to

(B) the city of Louvain was where he went

(C) Louvain was the destination where he went

(D) he first went to the city of Louvain

22. The following was adapted from an article titled "Women in the Civil Rights Movement Historic Context Statement and AACRN Listing Guidance" on the National Park Service website.

Septima Poinsette Clark, the daughter of a formerly enslaved father and a free-born mother, was born in 1898 and raised in Charleston, South Carolina. After graduating from the Avery Normal Institute in 1916, Clark began her career as a teacher. Black teachers were not allowed to teach in the Charleston public schools _____ found themselves teaching in rural, underfunded schools. After Clark joined the Charleston branch of the National Association for the Advancement of Colored People (NAACP), she began to get more involved in social justice issues. Clark and other schoolteachers created a campaign to protest the discrimination they faced. Their campaign was successful, and they gained the right to teach at public schools in Charleston.

Which of the following completes the text so that it conforms to the conventions of Standard English?

(A) system, though; most

(B) system, though, most

(C) system; though. Most

(D) system, though most,

23. Adult monarch butterflies are large and conspicuous, with bright orange wings surrounded by a black border and covered with black veins. The black border has a double row of white spots, present on the upper side of the wings. Adult monarchs are sexually dimorphic, with males having a narrower arrangement of veins and scent patches. The bright coloring of a monarch serves _____ to predators that eating them can be toxic.

Which of the following completes the text so that it conforms to the conventions of Standard English?

(A) to warn

(B) as a warning

(C) by warning

(D) and it is a warning

24. Consumers are eagerly leasing and purchasing electric cars because these cars cause no air pollution, make little or no noise, and _____.

Which of the following completes the text so that it conforms to the conventions of Standard English?

(A) gas is not used for fuel.

(B) they aren't using gas for fuel.

(C) use no gas.

(D) they don't use gas.

25. The birds of New Zealand had no natural _____ wings became unnecessary, and many varieties, including the kiwi and the kakapo parrot, became flightless.

Which of the following completes the text with the most logical transition?

(A) predators, when

(B) predators, but,

(C) predators; therefore,

(D) predators; nonetheless,

GO ON TO NEXT PAGE ▶

26. The following was adapted from an article titled "History & Culture" on the National Park Service website.

While researching a topic, a student has taken the following notes:

- With the support of many early conservationists, scientists, and other advocates, Everglades National Park was established in 1947 to conserve the natural landscape and prevent further degradation of its land, plants, and animals.

- The shallow, slow-moving sheet of water in South Florida covered almost 11,000 square miles, creating a mosaic of ponds, sloughs, sawgrass marshes, hardwood hammock, and forested uplands.

- From the sawgrass prairies to pine rocklands to mangrove forests to towering palms to open marine waters, Everglades is home to many diverse ecosystems, each with their own unique features and associated plants and wildlife, including a variety of threatened and endangered species.

- A long-standing wildlife monitoring program in Everglades National Park has provided information critical to the management of wading birds, eagles and ospreys, sea turtles, alligators and crocodiles, white-tailed deer, and the Cape Sable seaside sparrow.

- Many unique reptiles inhabit the park, including a variety of turtles, snakes, alligators, crocodiles, and lizards.

The student wants to explain why the Everglades National Park is such a captivating attraction to tourists, conservationists, plant enthusiasts, animal lovers, and so many others.

Which choice effectively uses relevant information to accomplish that goal?

(A) The shallow, slow-moving sheet of water in South Florida covered almost 11,000 square miles, creating a mosaic of ponds, sloughs, sawgrass marshes, hardwood hammock, and forested uplands.

(B) Much of the appeal of the Everglades in South Florida stems from its unique ecosystem, with its endless marshes, dense mangroves, towering palms, and tropical fauna like alligators, crocodiles, manatees, and lizards.

(C) Various groups and people navigated through and wrestled with the watery landscape to make it home, and even to exploit its resources.

(D) For thousands of years, this intricate system evolved into a finely balanced ecosystem that formed the biological infrastructure for the southern half of the state.

27. While researching a topic, a student has taken the following notes:

- Asthma is a disease that affects the lungs, and causes wheezing, breathlessness, chest tightness, and coughing.

- About 8 percent of white children in the U.S. suffer from asthma.

- From 2018–2020, 4.0 million non-Hispanic Blacks (adults and children) reported that they currently have asthma.

- Blacks and American Indian/Alaska Natives have the highest current asthma rates compared to other races and ethnicities. In 2018, Blacks (10.9 percent) were 42 percent more likely than Whites (7.7 percent) to still have asthma, and 14.5 percent of Black children have been diagnosed with asthma.

- The percentage of children in the U.S. with asthma doubled in the 1980s and 1990s and has been increasing steadily since then. The reason for the increase has remained mysterious, but there may be many possible factors, including exposure to secondhand smoke, obesity, and children's immune systems failing to develop properly.

- Non-Hispanic Black children were 4.5 times more likely to be admitted to the hospital for asthma, as compared to non-Hispanic White children, in 2019.

The student wants to compare the prevalence of asthma in children based on race. Which choice most effectively uses relevant information from the notes to accomplish this goal?

(A) The reasons for the increase in childhood asthma are unknown, but race is clearly a factor as almost twice as many Black children (14.5 percent compared to 8 percent of White children) report that they currently have asthma.

(B) While explanations for the increase in asthma remain inconclusive, Black children are more likely than White children to be hospitalized.

(C) The percentage of U.S. children with asthma, a disease that affects the lungs, doubled in the 1980s and 1990s and had been increasing steadily since then.

(D) Some researchers attribute the rise in childhood asthma to pollutants in the air, unhealthy diets, and poorly developed immune systems.

Check Your Work.

Continue to the next module when you're ready to move on.

Section 2: Math
Module 1

TIME: 35 minutes for 22 questions.

DIRECTIONS: For multiple-choice questions, choose only one answer for each question. For fill-in questions, write only one answer, even if you find more than one correct answer. Don't include symbols such as a percent sign, comma, or dollar sign.

NOTES:

- All numbers used in this exam are real numbers.

- All figures lie in a plane.

- All figures may be assumed to be to scale unless the problem specifically indicates otherwise.

- The domain of a given function f is the set of all real numbers x for which $f(x)$ is a real number, unless the problem specifically indicates otherwise.

- You may use a calculator.

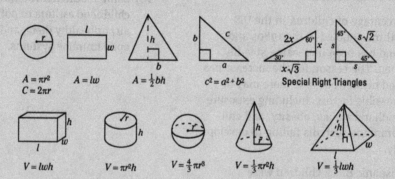

$$A = \pi r^2 \qquad A = lw \qquad A = \tfrac{1}{2}bh \qquad c^2 = a^2 + b^2 \qquad \text{Special Right Triangles}$$
$$C = 2\pi r$$

$$V = lwh \qquad V = \pi r^2 h \qquad V = \tfrac{4}{3}\pi r^3 \qquad V = \tfrac{1}{3}\pi r^2 h \qquad V = \tfrac{1}{3}lwh$$

- The number of degrees in a circle is 360.

- The number of radians in a circle is 2π.

- The sum of the measures of the angles of a triangle is 180.

---

1. If $2a + 3b = 17$ and $2a + b = 3$, then $a + b =$

(A) 1

(B) 5

(C) 7

(D) 10

2. A bicycle has a front wheel radius of 15 inches. If the bicycle wheel travels 10 revolutions, how far has a point on the outside of the wheel traveled, in inches?

(A) 10π

(B) 30π

(C) 300π

(D) 450π

3. If p and q are positive integers, then $\left(5^{-p}\right)\left(5^{q+1}\right)^{p}$ is equivalent to

(A) 5^{pq+p}

(B) 5^{pq}

(C) 5^{pq-p}

(D) 5^{q+1}

4. In a set of five positive whole numbers, the mode is 90 and the average (arithmetic mean) is 80. Which of the following statements is false?

   (A) The number 90 appears two, three, or four times in the set.

   (B) The number 240 cannot appear in the set.

   (C) The number 80 must appear exactly once in the set.

   (D) The five numbers must have a sum of 400.

5. In a triangle, the second side is 3 centimeters longer than the first side. The length of the third side is 5 centimeters less than twice the length of the first side. If the perimeter is 34 centimeters, find the length, in centimeters, of the longest side.

   (A) 3

   (B) 9

   (C) 12

   (D) 13

6. Melvin, Chris, Enoch, Dave, Carey, Mike, Dan, and Peter are choosing dorm rooms for college. Each room holds four people. They have the following requirements:

   I. Mike and Melvin refuse to live together.

   II. Enoch will live with Chris or Carey (or possibly both).

   III. If Dave and Dan live together, Peter will live with them.

   When rooms are chosen, Melvin, Carey, and Dan live together. Which of the following groups must live in the other room?

   (A) Chris, Dave, and Mike

   (B) Chris, Mike, and Peter

   (C) Dave, Enoch, and Peter

   (D) Dave, Mike, and Peter

7. If the distance from Springfield to Watertown is 13 miles and the distance from Watertown to Pleasantville is 24 miles, then the distance from Pleasantville to Springfield in miles could not be

   (A) 10

   (B) 11

   (C) 13

   (D) 24

8. In a certain game, there are only two ways to score points; one way is worth 3 points, and the other is worth 5 points. If Brandon's total score is 61, which of the following could be the number of 3-point scores that Brandon had?

   (A) 10

   (B) 11

   (C) 12

   (D) 13

9. Which of the following complex numbers is equal to $(2-3i)-(4i^2+5i)$ for $i^2=-1$?

   (A) $6+2i$

   (B) $6-2i$

   (C) $6-8i$

   (D) $6-12i$

10. If the square of x is 12 less than the product of x and 5, which of the following expressions could be used to solve for x?

    (A) $x^2=5x-12$

    (B) $x^2=12-5x$

    (C) $2x=12-5x$

    (D) $2x=5x-12$

11. If $2y-c=3c$, then $y=$

    (A) $\dfrac{c}{2}$

    (B) c

    (C) $\dfrac{3c}{2}$

    (D) $2c$

12. The solution set to the equation $|3x-1|=7$ is

    (A) $\{2\}$

    (B) $\left\{2,\dfrac{2}{3}\right\}$

    (C) $\left\{-2,\dfrac{2}{3}\right\}$

    (D) $\left\{-2,\dfrac{8}{3}\right\}$

GO ON TO NEXT PAGE

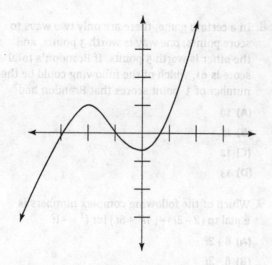

13. If this graph represents $f(x)$, then the number of solutions to the equation $f(x) = 1$ is

(A) zero

(B) one

(C) two

(D) three

14. A square with an area of 25 is changed into a rectangle with an area of 24 by increasing the width and reducing the length. If the length was reduced by 2, by how much was the width increased?

(A) 2

(B) 3

(C) 4

(D) 5

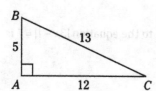

15. In triangle ABC above, if $\sin B = \frac{12}{13}$ and $\cos B = \frac{5}{13}$, what is $\tan C$?

(A) $\frac{5}{13}$

(B) $\frac{12}{13}$

(C) $\frac{5}{12}$

(D) $\frac{12}{5}$

16. Samira took four exams. Her scores on the first three were 89, 85, and 90. If her average (arithmetic mean) of all four exams was 90, what did she get on the fourth exam?

17. If $p > 0$ and the distance between the points $(4, -1)$ and $(-2, p)$ is 10, find p.

18. If $a - b = 8$ and $ab = 10$, find $a^2 + b^2$.

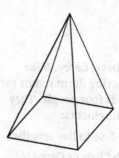

19. The preceding pyramid has a square base of length 10 centimeters and a height of 12 centimeters. Determine the total surface area of all five faces, in square centimeters.

20. If $a > 0$, which of the following statements must be true?

(A) $a^2 > a$

(B) $a > \frac{1}{a}$

(C) $2a > a$

(D) $\frac{1}{a} < 1$

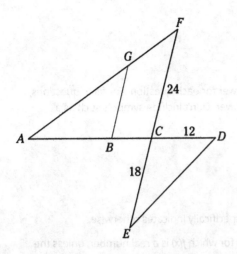

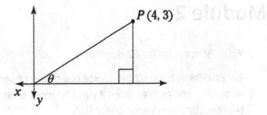

22. In the preceding drawing, what is $5(\sin\theta)$?

21. In this diagram, $AF \parallel ED$, $GB \parallel EF$, and $AG = GF$. What is the length of AB?

(*Note:* Figure not drawn to scale.)

(A) 18

(B) 16

(C) 12

(D) 8

Check Your Work.

Continue to the next module when you're ready to move on.

Module 2

TIME: 35 minutes for 22 questions.

DIRECTIONS: For multiple-choice questions, choose only one answer for each question. For fill-in questions, write only one answer, even if you find more than one correct answer. Don't include symbols such as a percent sign, comma, or dollar sign.

NOTES:

- All numbers used in this exam are real numbers.

- All figures lie in a plane.

- All figures may be assumed to be to scale unless the problem specifically indicates otherwise.

- The domain of a given function f is the set of all real numbers x for which $f(x)$ is a real number, unless the problem specifically indicates otherwise.

- You may use a calculator.

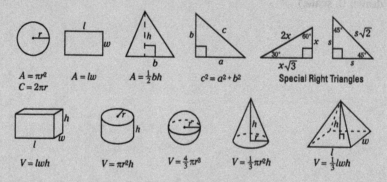

- The number of degrees in a circle is 360.

- The number of radians in a circle is 2π.

- The sum of the measures of the angles of a triangle is 180.

$$y = 20x + 25$$

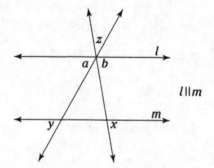

$l \parallel m$

1. In the preceding diagram, $x = 70°$ and $y = 30°$. The sum $a + b + z$ equals

(A) 90°

(B) 100°

(C) 120°

(D) 180°

2. The preceding equation models the total cost y, in dollars, that a sports shop charges a customer to rent a pair of skis for x days. The total cost consists of a flat fee plus a charge per day. When the equation is graphed in the xy-plane, what does the y-intercept of the graph represent in terms of the model?

(A) Total daily charges of $45

(B) A flat fee of $25

(C) A charge per day of $20

(D) A charge per day of $25

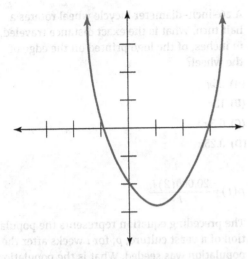

3. The above graph represents a function, $f(x)$. Which of the following graphs could represent $f(x+4)$?

(A)

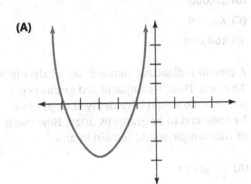

(B)

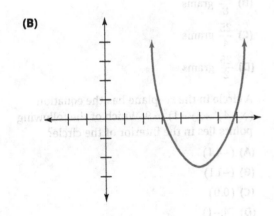

(C)

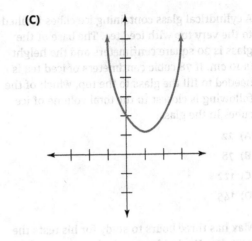

(D)

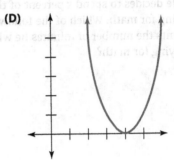

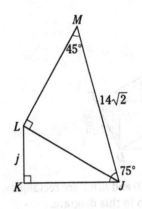

4. In the diagram above, the measure of side j is

(A) 7

(B) $7\sqrt{2}$

(C) $7\sqrt{3}$

(D) 14

GO ON TO NEXT PAGE

5. A cylindrical glass containing ice cubes is filled to the very top with iced tea. The base of the glass is 20 square centimeters and the height is 10 cm. If 78 cubic centimeters of iced tea is needed to fill the glass to the top, which of the following is closest to the total volume of ice cubes in the glass?

(A) 22

(B) 78

(C) 122

(D) 145

6. Max has three hours to study for his tests the next day. He decides to spend k percent of this time studying for math. Which of the following represents the number of minutes he will spend studying for math?

(A) $\dfrac{k}{300}$

(B) $\dfrac{3k}{100}$

(C) $\dfrac{100k}{180}$

(D) $\dfrac{180k}{100}$

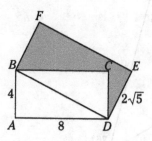

7. Given that $ABCD$ and $BDEF$ are rectangles, find the shaded area in this diagram.

(A) 24

(B) $16\sqrt{5}$

(C) 20

(D) $8\sqrt{5}$

8. A 26-inch-diameter bicycle wheel rotates a half turn. What is the exact distance traveled, in inches, of the logo printed on the edge of the wheel?

(A) 26π

(B) 13π

(C) 6.5π

(D) 3.25π

$$p(t) = \frac{20{,}000(2)^{\frac{t}{4}}}{t}$$

9. The preceding equation represents the population of a yeast culture, p, for t weeks after the population was seeded. What is the population after 8 weeks?

(A) 10,000

(B) 20,000

(C) 40,000

(D) 160,000

10. A certain radioactive element has a half-life of 20 years. Thus, a sample of 100 grams deposited in 1980 would have decayed to 50 grams by 2000 and to 25 grams by 2020. How much of this sample would remain in 2100?

(A) $\dfrac{25}{16}$ grams

(B) $\dfrac{25}{8}$ grams

(C) $\dfrac{25}{4}$ grams

(D) $\dfrac{25}{2}$ grams

11. A circle in the xy-plane has the equation $(x-4)^2 + (y-1)^2 = 9$. Which of the following points lies in the interior of the circle?

(A) $(-4, 1)$

(B) $(-1, 1)$

(C) $(0, 0)$

(D) $(4, -1)$

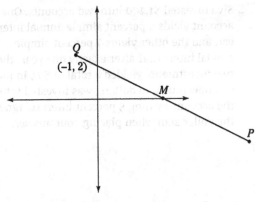

(−1, 2)

M

P

12. In this figure, the slope of line ℓ is $-\frac{1}{3}$, and M is the midpoint of the line PQ. What are the coordinates of Point P?

(A) $(8, -1)$

(B) $(9, -1)$

(C) $(10, -2)$

(D) $(11, -2)$

13. If $ab = n$, $b + c = x$, and $n \neq 0$, which of the following must equal n?

(A) $ax + c$

(B) $ax - c$

(C) $a(x - c)$

(D) $x(a - c)$

14. The number g is divisible by 3 but not by 9. Which of the following could be the remainder when $7g$ is divided by 9?

(A) 0

(B) 2

(C) 4

(D) 6

15. Darren receives \$15 an hour for his afterschool job but gets paid $1\frac{1}{2}$ times this rate for each hour he works on a weekend. If he worked 18 hours one week and received \$315, how many of these hours did he work during the weekend?

16. In a school survey, 40% of all students chose history as their favorite subject; 25% chose English; and 14 students chose some other subject as their favorite. How many students were surveyed?

17. If $\sqrt{|x + 3|} = 3$ and $x \geq 0$, what is the value of x?

18. $y = x^2 - 2x + 6$
$y = 2x + 3$

If the ordered pair (x, y) satisfies the preceding system of equations, what is one possible value of x?

19. To rent a private party room in a restaurant, there is a fixed cost plus an additional fee per person. If the cost of a party of 8 is \$270 and the cost of a party of 10 is \$320, find the cost, in dollars, of a party of 18.

20. The volume of a gas, V, in cubic centimeters (cc), is directly proportional to its temperature, T, in Kelvins (K). If a gas has a volume of 31.5 cc at 210 K, then its volume at 300 K would be

(A) 121.5 cc

(B) 49 cc

(C) 45 cc

(D) 22.05 cc

GO ON TO NEXT PAGE

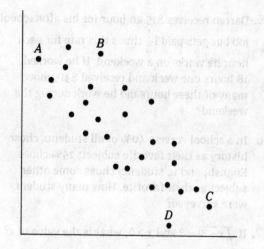

22. Siva invested $1,200 into two accounts. One account yields 5 percent simple annual interest, and the other yields 7 percent simple annual interest. If after exactly one year, the two investments yielded a total of $74 in interest, how much, in dollars, was invested into the account earning 5 percent interest? Ignore the dollar sign when placing your answer.

21. If the data in the preceding scatter plot were approximated by a linear function, the line would come closest to which pair of points?

(A) A and B

(B) A and C

(C) B and C

(D) C and D

Chapter 14

Practice Exam 2: Answers and Explanations

After you finish the practice test sections in Chapter 13, take some time to go through the answers and explanations in this chapter to find out which questions you missed and why. Even if you answered the question correctly, the explanation may offer a useful strategy that speeds up your performance on the next round. There is also additional information that'll be useful on the real SAT. If you're short on time, turn to the end of this chapter to find an abbreviated answer key.

Section 1: Reading and Writing

Module 1

1. **D.** Choice D, *likely to*, is the most logical phrase to fit in the blank in the sentence. Choices A and B are illogical because these species are threatened, which indicates that their becoming endangered isn't *definite* or *inevitable*. Choice C is incorrect because *probably able to* suggests the species have some say in the matter, which they don't.

2. **B.** The best word to fill in the blank is *different* because the sentence states that choosing people who are similar won't yield accurate or beneficial results. Choices A and C are both words that mean the opposite of what the text states. Choice D isn't logical because *conflicting* ages doesn't make sense.

3. **A.** Choice A, *hampered*, means hindered or impeded by, so it logically fits into the blank. It makes sense that the absence of a system of addressing would impede efforts to supply services. None of the other choices have the negative connotation of *hampered*.

4. **B.** Choice B, *supposed* is the best word to fill in the blank because the astronomers don't know for sure that the Sun and its planets were once in such a spiral. *Supposed* means generally assumed or believed to be the case. None of the other choices make sense in the sentence.

5. **D.** All the evidence in the sentence points to Choice D, *relentless*, which means nonstop or incessant. It is the best word to describe a river that is rapidly rising and a flood plunging by carrying trees and logs. Choices B and C are the opposite of *relentless* and Choice A, *deceitful*, is illogical.

6. **A.** The context clues in the sentence (the leaves are gone, larvae consume the bark) lead to Choice A, *defoliate*, which means to remove the leaves from a plant. The other choices, embark (to begin), empower (to give power), and engender (to give rise to), do not make sense in the context of the passage.

7. **A.** Choice A, *recount*, means to tell or give an account of something. It is the logical choice to fill in the blank in a sentence about Homer using flashbacks in his storytelling. The other choices, reuse (to use again), reinstate (to put back into a position), and rescind (to take back what was previously given) are not logical in this sentence.

8. **C.** The underlined sentence offers an alternative explanation (*eruptions are preceded by different build-up periods*) to a speculative relationship (*possibly suggesting a cause-and-effect relationship*) referred to earlier in the text. The underlined sentence doesn't state a hypothesis that is contradicted by evidence (Choice A) or present a generalization that is exemplified by the discussion of the volcanoes (Choice B). It also doesn't clarify **WHY** volcanoes are preceded by different build-up periods (Choice D).

9. **A.** Of the four questions in the choices, only Choice A, *Why do scientists study the genes of organisms other than human beings?* can be answered by the information in the text. The questions in Choices B, C, and D cannot be answered by the information in the text.

10. **D.** Choice D is the best explanation of the difference between a linear and a web-like representation of the food chain. As the text implies, the linear relationship is a straight line; for example, the sun provides energy to the dandelion; the dandelion provides food for the rabbit; the rabbit is food for the hawk. In a web-like system, energy flows in multiple directions, not simply in a straight line. Choice A is inaccurate; a linear representation is less complex than a web-like representation. Choice B is incorrect because the representations have nothing to do with inorganic versus organic relationships. Choice C is incorrect; the difference has nothing to do with human versus non-human.

11. **A.** No trick here: just a careful reading of the chart and the legend. Notice on the legend that the dark-gray dot represents *females* and the light-gray dot represents *males*. Find each occupation on the chart and locate the earnings data. The placement of the dots will reveal that postsecondary female teachers have a higher median income than that of male chefs and head cooks. None of the other choices are supported by the data on the chart.

12. **B.** Once again, use your careful reading techniques to follow the data. You will note that as the estimated world population increases from 1 to 9 billion, the number of years estimated to add 1 billion people decreases and then increases slightly at the end of the column. None of the other choices accurately interpret the data.

13. **D.** According to the text, *all acts of production and consumption are fundamentally acts of "prosumption."* This means that while the two processes are on opposite sides of the spectrum, they are on the same spectrum. None of the other choices are accurate based on the textual information.

14. **C.** In the first stanza of the poem, the speaker describes a literal spider that he watches as it spins a web. In the second stanza, the speaker uses this web-creating image to philosophize about his soul as it too tries to form connections. Choice C best describes the structure of the two stanzas. Choice A reverses the structure of the poem. Choices B and D are not accurate readings of the poem.

15. **A.** The underlined sentence anticipates and responds to a critical response to his claim that Longfellow *stands easily in front of all other poets who have enriched American literature.* The writer concedes that Longfellow is not rugged, elemental, profoundly thoughtful, transcendental, and sympathetic, but he answers this argument with the bold claim that Longfellow *was our first artist in poetry.* Choice B is incorrect because the writer doesn't dismiss Longfellow from the ranks of great American poets. Choice C is incorrect because the sentence doesn't provide specific examples to illustrate Longfellow's superiority. (It does the opposite!) Choice D is incorrect because the sentence doesn't illustrate a transcendent quality of Longfellow's poetry — in fact, it says he isn't transcendent.

16. **C.** The text presents information about the effects of campfires on the soil. In the underlined sentence, the writer calls attention to the harmful effects of a common camping activity — making a campfire. The underlined sentence doesn't elaborate on an example of organic matter as a measure of fertility (Choice A), or explain a methodology (Choice B), or offer a solution (Choice D).

17. **C.** To answer this question correctly, you must synthesize information from the text and the graphic. The graphic provides information about the seasonal life cycle of the beaver. To complete the sentence in the text, find the end of the summer on the graphic to determine what the beavers are doing. In August, as the beavers begin preparing for adulthood, they work on dam and lodge repair. The text indicates that as beavers build dams, some adjacent sites are flooded. By combining these two pieces of information, you will find that Choice C correctly uses the information from the graphic and the text as evidence that the properties near the beaver colonies will experience flooding. None of the other choices can be supported with text-based or graphic-based evidence.

18. **A.** Both Passage 1 and Passage 2 emphasize the importance of biodiversity. Passage 1 points out that the loss of biodiversity has harmful effects on living things and the environment. Passage 2 points out that biodiversity increases survival for living things. Thus, both passages agree that a loss of biodiversity or *reliance on a small number of food sources is a problem now and may become more severe in the future.* Choice B is incorrect because Passage 1 doesn't mention extinction. Choice C is incorrect because Passage 2 emphasizes that biodiversity increases food supply. Choice D is incorrect because Passage 1 explains that the interdependence of prey and predator is essential to biodiversity.

19. **B.** Choice B completes the text and conforms to the conventions of Standard English. The plural pronoun *them* (in the objective case because it is the object of the preposition *of*) is needed to refer to the plural noun *flocks.* Choice A is incorrect because it uses the wrong pronoun (*those*) and is unnecessarily wordy. Choice C is incorrect because it also uses the wrong pronoun (the subject pronoun *they*) and illogically adds a new verb phrase (*were flying*). Choice D is incorrect because it uses the pronoun *whom* to refer to flocks of birds and adds an unnecessary and wordy new verb phrase (*were able to fly*).

20. **B.** Choice B conforms to the conventions of Standard English because it uses the singular form of the verb *is used* to agree with the singular subject *figure*. Don't fall into the trap of thinking that *estimates* is the subject of the verb; *estimates* is the object of the preposition in the prepositional phrase *of U.S. population estimates*; thus, it can't be the subject. Choices A and C incorrectly use the plural form of the verb *to be*. Choice D is incorrect because it lacks the helping verb *is*.

21. **D.** This sentence provides a somewhat complicated punctuation issue, but if you analyze the clauses — and recognize the two independent clauses — you'll be fine. The first independent clause ends with the word *advancement*. This main clause is followed by additional information (also an independent clause) that explains or clarifies the main clause. The best mark of punctuation to use at the end of a main clause and before clarifying information is the colon. Choice A incorrectly uses a comma (remember to avoid the dreaded comma splice error!). Choice B uses the semicolon, which can be used to connect two independent clauses, but it adds the words *in the*, which don't make sense with the second clause that already has the verb phrase *is known*. Choice C is incorrect because it also adds the extra verb phrase without punctuation. Choice D correctly uses the colon after an independent clause and before clarifying information. (*Note:* An independent clause that follows a colon usually starts with a capital letter, but this is not a hard and fast rule.)

22. **A.** Choice A, *however*, is the most logical transitional word to express the contrast between polar bears that remain on the receding pack ice and those that come on land to rest. None of the other choices provide a word to express a contrast.

23. **D.** Choice D is the only choice to avoid a modification error by correctly beginning with the word *Charlie*. The modifying phrase that begins the sentence *While taking a few seconds to clean his glasses*, must be followed by the word being modified, *Charlie*. Logically, neither Charlie's car nor his heart is taking the time to clean his glasses (as is suggested by Choices A, B, and C).

24. **C.** The singular form of the verb *was* is needed to agree with the singular subject *match*. Again, don't be tricked by those pesky prepositional phrases (*in the semifinals*) that comes between the subject (*match*) and the verb (*was*). Be sure to also be consistent in tenses: Choices B and D incorrectly use the present tense to refer to action that took place in the past.

25. **A.** Choice A correctly uses the adverb *deeply* to modify the adjective *incised*. Choice B incorrectly uses the adjective *deep*: You need an adverb to describe how much (or to what extent) the plateau is *incised* (or carved). Choice C is incorrect because *deeper* is the comparative form of the adjective *deep*. Choice D is incorrect because *deepest* is the superlative form of the adjective *deep*.

26. **B.** The best choice to emphasize the aim of the study is Choice B: *Understanding the structure and function of DNA and unlocking an individual's genetic code has helped scientists revolutionize the investigation of disease pathways.* Choice A is a detail about the human genome rather than a statement of the aim of the research study. Choice C is also a detail about DNA, not about the aim of the study. Choice D is close, but Choice B explains why scientists are doing this research, so it is the better choice.

27. **D.** This question is another illustration of the importance of reading the prompt carefully. The prompt asks you to select the choice that best compares the lengths of the two longest rivers, so information that is **NOT** about the two longest rivers and their lengths is not relevant. Only Choice D most effectively compares the lengths of the two longest rivers.

Module 2

1. **A.** Choice A, *featured*, is the best word to fit in the blank. In the context of the sentence, *featured* means included as an important part, and Dali included optical illusions as an important part of his paintings. Choice B is incorrect because *overwhelmed* is not logical in the context of the sentence. Choice C is also incorrect because nothing in the sentence suggests Dali *discredited* optical illusions. Choice D, *renewed*, also does not fit in the logic of the sentence.

2. **D.** Choice D is the best answer because it logically completes the sentence. The two flowering plants are useful *indicators* of the timing of spring. Choices A, B, and C are illogical; the plants aren't useful *effects* or *varieties* or *species* of the timing.

3. **A.** Choice A, *mystified*, is the best word to fit in the blank. The unidentified creature *mystified* (puzzled) naturalists *who did not know how to classify* it. Choice B might have tempted you because it's possible the naturalists were *delighted* with the creature, but the context clues in the sentence (*seemingly catch-all characteristics, did not know, we now know*) suggest they were confused or *mystified*. They certainly weren't *settled* or *confident*, so Choices C and D are illogical.

4. **B.** Choice B, *locate*, is the best word to fill in the blank. The researchers are using computer tools to find or *locate* signals that control how genes work. There is no contextual evidence to suggest the researchers want to *disrupt*, *question*, or *influence* the signals, so Choices A, C, and D are incorrect.

5. **C.** Always use the logic of the sentence and the context clues to help you select the best word to fill in the blank. In this sentence, the logic suggests that a conservation law has been enacted to *safeguard* or protect ancient ruins. It certainly wouldn't attempt to *raze* (tear down) or *reconfigure* (rearrange) the ruins, so Choices A and B are incorrect. It also doesn't make sense to enact a conservation law to *complete* ancient ruins; then they wouldn't be ancient ruins! And, there is no context clue to suggest this action.

6. **C.** Choice C completes the text with the most logical and precise word because it conveys the elevation of the *pedestrian* (dull, ordinary) plot by the *exquisite* (gorgeous) cinematography of the film. Choices A, *ordinary*, and D, *banal* (dull or trite), are too close in meaning to *pedestrian* and so would not elevate the plot. Choice B, *abundant*, doesn't make sense: The whole film consists of cinematography.

7. **D.** Choice D best expresses the primary claim of the speaker. The speaker clearly states that we *don't take enough advice . . . and we should model* our lives on the disinterested opinion of other people. Based on the context, the speaker would disagree with Choices A, B, and C, none of which are stated in or implied by the text.

8. **C.** Choice C best states the function of the underlined sentence in the overall structure of the text. The text describes the singing style of Mary Garden but points out that her *conception and acting* were qualities that most *intrigued* the writer. The sentence doesn't criticize the performance (Choice A) or provide an objective analysis (Choice B) or praise the coloratura style of the singer (Choice D).

9. **A.** Choice A most logically completes the text. It follows that *the more independent, knowledgeable, and skilled classes* would have received a better education and have *talents and acquirements*. Choice B is clearly contradicted by the text: *neither lords nor common people*. Choice C is also contradicted by the text: *neither rich nor poor*. Choice D sounds like it could be true, but no evidence in the text indicates they had a *natural affinity for menial jobs* or *physical prowess*.

10. **B.** Choice B is the best choice because the quotations in the text establish an authoritative tone; they use the words of well-known Greek philosophers to support the content. Choice A is incorrect because the quotations do not conflict with the evidence. Choice C is incorrect because the text doesn't imply that more research is wanted or needed. Choice D is incorrect because the quotations are too short to give a sense of Greek literary style, and they are included to suggest that the evidence of the historical context adds authority to the informative text.

11. **A.** Choice A is the quotation that most logically and effectively completes the text. The focus of the content is Poe's *musical flow of language*. The text mentions *poetic harmony, melodious fancy*, and *distant music at night*, all descriptions of the musical quality of Poe's writing. Thus, Choice A logically follows the text. While the other choices do describe Poe's writing, only Choice A directly references the musical quality of his writing.

12. **C.** Choice C completes the text with the most logical example; the correct answer must be an example of a variable that allows the assignment of probability. Choice A is incorrect because the characteristics of the sample that remain constant are not variables. Choice B is incorrect for the same reason: The total number of a population is not a variable that allows the assignment of probability. Choice D can be eliminated for the same reason: There is no assignment of probability.

13. **B.** Choice B would explain the discrepancy in the results of Mr. Burns' experiment: if one area of the yard has better soil or more sun, for example, these factors could affect the growth of the plant. Choices A, C, and D are incorrect because none of these choices offer any variable to account for the discrepancy.

14. **A.** Choice A best describes the function of the underlined portion of text. To clarify how the waxes in the cuticle prevent water loss, the writer uses an analogy, comparing the wax in the leaf to the wax on your car that prevents water from reaching the paint. Choice B is incorrect because the underlined portion doesn't refute an assertion in the first part of the sentence. Choice C is incorrect because the underlined portion doesn't provide an example that is expanded on in the next sentence. Choice D is incorrect because the underlined portion doesn't indicate another function of the cuticle layer; it simply offers an analogy.

15. **C.** By pointing out a limitation of instrumental observations, the underlined sentence describes *a shortcoming of a method of scientific investigation* (that is, using instruments for observation). The underlined sentence doesn't summarize the results of a study (Choice A) or offer *an example of how observations can assist by providing eyewitness evidence* (Choice B) or present *a central finding in the science of dendroclimatology* (Choice D).

16. **B.** The main idea of the text is that the writer has gained technical knowledge of the river (*mastered the language of this water*) as a pilot but has lost an appreciation of its beauty (*lost something which could never be restored to me while I lived. All the grace, the beauty, the poetry had gone out of the majestic river!*). Choice A is incorrect because a pilot must watch the river carefully and analytically and cannot spend his days simply appreciating nature. Choice C may indeed be true, but it is not the main idea of the text. There is no evidence to support Choice D as the main idea of the text.

17. **C.** Based on the data in the chart, at the end of Interval D – E, the automobile is both stationary and farthest from the starting point (of course, because it is at the end of the drive). No data in the chart supports Choices A or D because speed is not included in the chart. Choice B is incorrect because it is inaccurate; the automobile travels the greatest distance during interval A – B.

18. **D.** Choice D is supported by the information in the chart: The numbers of Winter Bentgrass and Purple Lovegrass decline while those of Little Bluestem, Path Rush, and Canada Goldenrod increase. Thus, you may conclude that plant populations are replacing each other. Choice A is incorrect because both these species thrive, so you can't conclude that they compete. No evidence in the text or chart supports either Choice B or Choice C.

19. **B.** Choice B is correct; *travelers'* is the correct punctuation for a plural possessive noun, and no apostrophe is needed with *stories* — it is simply plural. Choice A incorrectly adds an apostrophe to a plural noun that is not possessive (*stories'*). Choice C omits the necessary apostrophe with *travelers*. Choice D incorrectly adds an apostrophe to make *story's* a singular possessive rather than plural (*stories*).

20. **B.** Choice B conforms to the conventions of Standard English and is correct because no commas are used with essential information; the name of the attorney is essential to the sentence. Choice A is incorrect because no commas are needed around *Matthew Brady* or after *because*. Choice C and D both have unnecessary commas.

21. **D.** Choice D conforms to the conventions of Standard English because the participial phrase *Gifted with a good voice and well educated musically* modifies *he*, so *he* must immediately follow the modifying phrase. When modification is the grammatical issue in the text, remember to put the word being modified as close as possible to the modifying phrase. Choice A incorrectly begins with *it* rather than *he*. Choice B incorrectly begins with *the city* rather than *he*. Choice C incorrectly begins with *Louvain* rather than *he*. Logically, only *he* is gifted, so only *he* can follow the modifying phrase.

22. **A.** The punctuation is a bit tricky in this text. It is important to determine whether *though* belongs to the first clause (*Black teachers were not allowed to teach in the Charleston public schools*) or the second clause (*most found themselves teaching in rural, underfunded schools*). Logically, *though* belongs with the first clause because that clause contrasts with the previous sentence that ends with *her career as a teacher*. The comma before *though* is correct: when *though* is used at the end of a sentence, it is an adverb meaning *however*. It is separated from the first part of the sentence by a comma. The semicolon after *though* is correct because it joins two main clauses. Choice B makes the dreaded comma splice error. Choice C incorrectly uses a semicolon before *though*. Choice D is incorrect because it doesn't punctuate the two main clauses correctly and uses an unnecessary comma after *most*.

23. **B.** Only Choice B completes the text so that it conforms to the conventions of Standard English: *The bright coloring of a monarch serves as a warning to predators . . . .* Choice A may tempt you, but notice the word *to* after the blank. You wouldn't write *serves to warn to predators*. Choice C uses the non-idiomatic *serves by warning to*. Choice D is awkward, wordy, and ungrammatical.

24. **C.** The conventions of Standard English require parallelism in items in a series. In Choice C, all the items in the series are parallel verb phrases: *cause no pollution, make little or no noise, use no gas*. Choices A, B, and D are all unparallel.

25. **C.** Choice C, *therefore*, is the logical transition in this sentence because the second half of the sentence is a result of the first half. *Therefore* means as a result: Because the birds had no natural enemies, they became wingless. None of the other choices indicate the *as a result* relationship.

26. B. Choice B is the best choice to explain why the Everglades National Park is such a captivating attraction to tourists, conservationists, plant enthusiasts, animal lovers, and so many others. Choice B specifically explains that the appeal of the Everglades lies in its unique ecosystem, its plant life, and its fauna (animals). Choices A, C, and D are true statements, but they offer details from the notes that do not directly answer the prompt.

27. A. Choice A answers the prompt most effectively because it specifically compares the prevalence of asthma in children based on race. Choice B compares one aspect of the prevalence of asthma by race, but it does not respond as clearly and specifically to the prompt as Choice A. Choice C is incorrect because it doesn't mention race. Choice D also doesn't mention race.

Section 2: Math

Module 1

1. B. Add the two expressions:

$$2a + 3b = 17$$
$$\underline{+(2a + b = 3)}$$
$$4a + 4b = 20$$
$$a + b = 5$$

2. C. An SAT classic. (The SAT should have its own YouTube channel. Oh wait, it does.) If the wheel has a radius of 15 inches, it has a circumference of 30π (because circumference is $2\pi r$). Ten revolutions carry a point on the outside of the wheel 10 times the circumference, for $10 \times 30\pi = 300\pi$.

3. B. Start with $\left(5^{q+1}\right)^p$. When you take a power of a power, such as $\left(5^{q+1}\right)^p$, you multiply the powers: $\left(5^{q+1}\right)^p = \left(5^{pq+p}\right)$. Next, multiply this by the other part of the question, $\left(5^{-p}\right)$. When you multiply the same numbers with exponents, you add the exponents, so leave the 5 and just add the exponents. In this case, the p and $-p$ cancel out, leaving the pq: $\left(5^{pq+p}\right)\left(5^{-p}\right) = 5^{pq}$.

4. C. Look at the statements one at a time. Choice (A) is true. The mode appears most often, so there will be two, three, or four 90s. Choice (B) requires you to remember the formula *total = number × mean*. In this case, the five numbers must add up to $5 \times 80 = 400$. Because you know there are at least two 90s, which add up to 180, the other three numbers must add up to 220. But because the numbers are all positive, and 240 is greater than 220, there is no room in the set for 240 and 2 additional values. However, for Choice (C), you can make a list that averages 80 but doesn't have 80 in it. The list *could* have 80 but doesn't *have to* have 80. Choice (D) is definitely true; you used this fact already when you checked Choice (A).

5. D. Draw the triangle with x as the first side, $x + 3$ as the second side, and $2x - 5$ as the third side. The finished triangle looks like this:

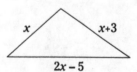

The perimeter, 34, is the sum of all the sides. Solve for x; then place that value for x to get the side lengths:

$$(x)+(x+3)+(2x-5)=34$$
$$4x-2=34$$
$$4x=36$$
$$x=9$$
$$(9)+(9+3)+(2\cdot9-5)=34$$
$$9+12+13=34$$

6. **A.** Call the room shared by Melvin, Carey, and Dan room X, and the other room Y. Because Mike and Melvin won't live together, Mike must be in room Y. Now, if Dave and Dan live together, Peter will live with them, but you can't fit two more people into room X, so Dave and Dan must live apart, which puts Dave in room Y also. Similarly, you know that Enoch will live with Chris or Carey, so Chris can't be in room X, either. That puts Chris, Dave, and Mike in room Y.

7. **A.** Make a quick drawing of the situation. (Remember, the towns don't have to be in a straight line.)

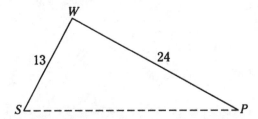

The distance you're interested in is the dotted line. Use the triangle inequality, which tells you that the sum of any two sides of a triangle must be greater than the third side. The number 10 doesn't satisfy the inequality, because $10+13=23$, which is less than 24.

8. **C.** If you multiply each of the choices by 3 points, you get 30, 33, 36, and 39. Because all the other scores are worth 5 points, you must be able to add a multiple of 5 to one of these numbers to get 61. The only one that works is 36, because $36+25=61$.

9. **C.** Distribute the negative and simplify the expression:

$$(2-3i)-\left(4i^2+5i\right)$$
$$2-3i-4i^2-5i$$
$$2-8i-4(-1)$$
$$2-8i+4$$
$$6-8i$$

10. **A.** Twelve less than something is the thing minus 12, not the other way around. So you want an expression that says "x squared equals 5 times x minus 12," and that's Choice (A).

11. **D.** To solve for y, isolate y on one side of the equation:

$$2y-c=3c$$
$$2y=4c$$
$$y=2c$$

12. **D.** Solve the equation using the positive and negative values of the expression:

$$|3x - 1| = 7$$
$$3x - 1 = 7, -7$$
$$3x = 8, -6$$
$$x = \frac{8}{3}, -2$$

13. **C.** The number of solutions to the equation $f(x) = 1$ is just the number of times that the graph has a height of 1, as shown here.

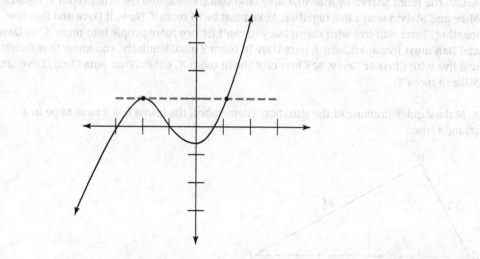

14. **B.** The length and width of the square are both 5 (because $5 \times 5 = 25$), so the new length, being narrower by 2, is 3. And 3 times the new width is 24 (the area of the rectangle), so the new width is 8 (because $24 \div 3 = 8$). The width went from 5 to 8, for an increase of 3.

15. **C.** Using ol' SOH-CAH-TOA, because $\sin B = \dfrac{\text{opposite}}{\text{hypotenuse}} = \dfrac{12}{13}$ and $\cos B = \dfrac{\text{adjacent}}{\text{hypotenuse}} = \dfrac{5}{13}$, you can label the sides of the triangle like this:

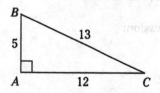

The tangent is of a different angle, but the principle is the same:

$$\tan C = \frac{\text{opposite}}{\text{adjacent}} = \frac{5}{12}$$

16. 96. This problem is easy if you remember an easy trick: *total = number × average*. In this case, the total must equal $4 \times 90 = 360$. Adding up Samira's first three scores gives you 264, and $360 - 264 = 96$.

17. 7. Remember the distance formula? It tells you that the distance between two points, (x_1, y_1) and (x_2, y_2) is $\sqrt{(x_2 - x_1)^2 + (y_2 - y_1)^2}$. Substituting your numbers, you get

$$10 = \sqrt{([-2]-[4])^2 + (p-[-1])^2}$$
$$= \sqrt{(-6)^2 + (p+1)^2}$$
$$= \sqrt{36 + (p+1)^2}$$

Square both sides, and $100 = 36 + (p+1)^2$. Now solve for p:

$$64 = (p+1)^2$$
$$8 = p + 1$$
$$7 = p$$

18. 84. You could try to figure out what a and b equal, but you don't need to. The key to getting this question right is remembering the formulas discussed in Chapter 8 — specifically, the one that says that $(a-b)^2 = a^2 - 2ab + b^2$. You know that $a - b = 8$, so $(a-b)^2 = a^2 - 2ab + b^2 = 64$. You're being asked for $a^2 + b^2$, which is $(a^2 - 2ab + b^2) + 2ab$, or $64 + 2(10) = 84$.

19. 360. The total surface area is the sum of the area of the square and the area of the four triangles. The square is easy: It's $10 \times 10 = 100$. The triangles are tougher. They don't have a height of 12. Twelve is the height of the pyramid, but the triangles are slanted. However, you can find the height of the slanted triangles by using the Pythagorean Theorem, as shown in the following diagram:

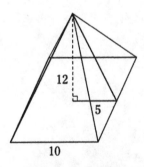

That little triangle in the diagram is a right triangle. One leg is 12, the height of the pyramid. The second leg is half the width of the square, or 5. This is a common right triangle, the 5-12-13 triangle. (If you didn't remember this one, you could have figured it out with the Pythagorean Theorem.)

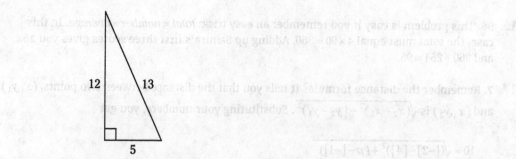

The hypotenuse, 13, is the altitude of each of the tilted triangles that make up the sides of the pyramid. Because the triangle's area is $\frac{1}{2} \times base \times height$, each triangle's area is $\frac{1}{2} \times 10 \times 13 = 65$. The four triangles together have an area of $4 \times 65 = 260$. Adding in the 100 from the base gives you 360.

20. **C.** If a equals 2 or more, then all the answer choices are true. However, if a equals 1, or a number less than 1, such as $\frac{1}{2}$, most of answer choices become false. This question is an old SAT trap: Numbers between 0 and 1 (such as fractions) behave in funny ways. The only statement that is true for all positive numbers, whether fraction or whole, is Choice (C): Twice any positive number must be bigger than the original number.

21. **D.** Because there are parallel lines in this problem, you need to look for angles that are congruent. You can find them by looking for lines that make a Z or a backward Z. Looking first at the bigger triangles, you can mark the diagram as follows:

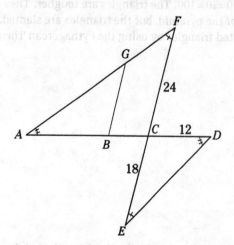

Notice that the two angles in the middle are vertical, so they're also equal. This is a picture of similar triangles: Angle F matches angle E, angle A matches angle D, and angle C is the same for both triangles. Therefore, you can use a ratio to figure out the length of AC:

$\frac{AC}{CD} = \frac{CF}{CE}$ and $\frac{AC}{12} = \frac{24}{18}$, which reduces to $\frac{AC}{12} = \frac{4}{3}$

Be careful that you match up the right parts when writing a ratio. Anyway, cross-multiplying your ratio tells you that $3(AC) = 48$, and $AC = 16$. Now, because $GB \parallel EF$, triangle ABG is similar to ACF as well. And, because $AG = GF$, the line GB cuts triangle ACF in half. That means that AB is half of AC, or 8.

22. **3.** Find the value of $\sin\theta$ and multiply it by 5. If the coordinates of point P are (4,3), the diagonal is 5 (as in, 3-4-5 right triangle). Use the SOH from SOH-CAH-TOA to get that $\sin\theta = \frac{opposite}{hypotenuse}$, which in this case is $\frac{3}{5}$. Multiply this by 5 for an answer of 3.

Module 2

1. D. You don't need to know what x and y equal in this problem. Look at the angle marked c in the following diagram. You know that c and z are vertical angles, which means that their measures are equal. Also, a, c, and b form a straight line, so $a + c + b = 180°$. Therefore, $a + b + z = 180°$.

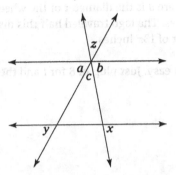

2. B. Walking out the door with skis, the customer is charged \$25. That is the y-intercept of the graphed line. Each day the customer holds the skis (whether they're used or not) is another \$20 charge, but that's represented by the slope of the line, not the y-intercept.

3. A. This question is based on the rules of graphed figures. From the graph, $f(x)$ is another name for the y-value based on x. A higher x-value moves the point farther to the right. In the graph, $f(x + 4)$ reads the value inside the parentheses (usually x, but in this case $x + 4$) as four spaces farther to the right than it actually is, so the graph moves four spaces to the left to compensate.

4. A. Do you remember your special triangle ratios? If not, it's okay: They're in the pop-up when you click Reference on the math portion of the SAT. First, spot the common right triangles by breaking up the 75° angle at the bottom right into 45° and 30° angles. The top right triangle is a 45-45-90 triangle, which makes both of its legs equal to 14. The bottom leg is also the hypotenuse of the 30-60-90 triangle at the bottom. In a 30-60-90 triangle, the hypotenuse must be twice the shortest leg, which is j. Therefore, j is 7.

5. C. If you forgot the equation for the volume of a cylinder, check the pop-up when you click the Reference button: the equation is right there for everyone else who also forgot. This formula, $V = \pi r^2 h$, basically states that volume is the base times the height — in this case, 20 square centimeters times 10 centimeters, for a volume of 200 cubic centimeters. Subtract the 78 cubic centimeters of iced tea, and the 122 cubic centimeters of ice cubes make up the remaining volume.

6. D. Because the answer is in minutes, start by turning 3 hours into 180 minutes. You know that k percent of these 180 minutes is going to be used for math. Remember that k percent means $\frac{k}{100}$. Taking a percent of a number involves multiplication, so your answer is $180 \times \frac{k}{100}$, or $\frac{180k}{100}$.

7. A. You need the areas of rectangle *BDEF* and triangle *BCD*. For the rectangle, you need the length of segment *BD*, which is also part of triangle *ABD*. Because you have two sides of right triangle *ABD*, use the Pythagorean Theorem to find the length of the third side, which is your target, *BD*: $4^2 + 8^2 = (BD)^2$, so $BD = \sqrt{80}$, or $4\sqrt{5}$. The area of the rectangle is $4\sqrt{5} \times 2\sqrt{5} = 8 \times 5 = 40$. The area of triangle *BCD* is $\frac{8 \times 4}{2} = 16$. Subtract the two, and $40 - 16 = 24$.

8. B. The circumference of the wheel is πd, where d is the diameter of the wheel. Because $d = 26$ inches, the circumference is 26π inches. The logo traveled half this distance, so divide the circumference by 2, for an answer of 13π inches.

9. A. Forget the online calculator — this one is easy. Just plug in 8 for t and the numbers work themselves out:

$$p(8) = \frac{20,000(2)^{\frac{8}{4}}}{8}$$
$$= \frac{20,000(2)^2}{8}$$
$$= \frac{20,000(4)}{8}$$
$$= \frac{80,000}{8}$$
$$= 10,000$$

10. A. Make a table for this one, dividing the sample by 2 for every 20 years:

Year	2000	2020	2040	2060	2080	2100
Sample	50	25	$\frac{25}{2}$	$\frac{25}{4}$	$\frac{25}{8}$	$\frac{25}{16}$

The final answer is $\frac{25}{16}$ grams.

11. D. A circle with the equation $(x - 4)^2 + (y - 1)^2 = 9$ has a center of $(4,1)$ and a radius of 3, so it certainly extends down 2 from the center and covers point $(4,-1)$. However, it is entirely to the right of the *y*-axis, placing Choices (A), (B), and (C) outside the circle.

12. D. A slope of $-\frac{1}{3}$ means that the line goes down 1 unit for every 3 units it moves to the right. Because *M* is on the *x*-axis, the line has gone down 2 units by the time it reaches *M*, so it must have moved 6 units to the right. That means that *M* is at $(5,0)$. *M* is the midpoint, which means that it's halfway to *P*. So, to get to *P*, move another 2 units down and 6 units right, which puts you at $(11,-2)$.

13. C. Because $b + c = x$, $b = x - c$. Substitute $(x - c)$ for b in the first equation, and write $a(x - c) = n$, which is Choice (C).

14. D. Possible numbers for *g* include 3, 6, 12, 15, 21, and so on. If you try multiplying these numbers by 7 and then dividing by 9, you discover that the remainder is always 3 or 6. Because 3 isn't one of the answer choices, the correct answer is 6. Note that the problem asks for which *could* be the remainder.

15. 6. Trial and error can work, but algebra is more reliable. Darren earns 15 dollars per hour on weekdays and $1\frac{1}{2} \times 15 = 22.50$ dollars per hour on weekends. If d equals his weekday hours and e equals his weekend hours, then $15d + 22.5e = 315$. Because $d + e = 18$ (his total hours), use substitution: $d = 18 - e$, so place $(18 - e)$ for d in the other equation:

$$15d + 22.5e = 315$$
$$15(18 - e) + 22.5e = $$
$$270 - 15e + 22.5e = $$
$$270 + 7.5e = 315$$
$$7.5e = 45$$
$$e = 6$$

He worked 6 hours during the weekends. Just like that.

16. 40. Sixty-five percent chose history or English, leaving 35 percent for other subjects. This 35 percent represents 14 students, so the question is, "35 percent of x is 14?" Set it up like this and solve for x:

$$\frac{14}{x} = \frac{35}{100}$$
$$35x = 1{,}400$$
$$x = 40$$

17. 6. Copy down the equation and solve for x. First square both sides, and when you remove the absolute value, remember the expression has both the positive and negative values:

$$\sqrt{|x+3|} = 3$$
$$|x+3| = 9$$
$$x + 3 = 9, -9$$
$$x = 6, -12$$

Because $x \geq 0$, it can only be 6.

18. 1 or 3. Because both expressions equal y, set the expressions equal to each other and solve for x:

$$x^2 - 2x + 6 = 2x + 3$$
$$x^2 - 4x + 3 = 0$$
$$(x - 3)(x - 1) = 0$$
$$x = 1, 3$$

Because x could equal 1 or 3, type in either 1 or 3, and either answer is considered correct.

19. 520. If the fee for each person is the same amount, and the difference in the total cost between 8 people and 10 people is $50 (because), then each addition of 2 people adds $50 to the total price, and each person costs an extra $25. So 10 people cost $320, and the additional 8 people add $200 to the price (because $8 \times 25 = 200$). Add the new $200 to the existing $320 for 10 people, and 18 people cost $520.

20. C. Direct proportion problems require a ratio — in this case, the ratio of volume to temperature. Thus, you can write $\frac{cc_1}{K_1} = \frac{cc_2}{K_2}$ and $\frac{31.5}{210} = \frac{x}{300}$. Cross-multiply to get $210x = 9,450$, and divide by 210 to get $x = 45$.

21. B. This scatter plot shows a negative trend, so the line of best fit would go roughly from the top left to the bottom right. However, point D is significantly lower than the rest of the points. If you try drawing a line between A and D, or B and D, you'll see that it's really not that close to a lot of the points. However, the line from A to C is a good approximation of the scatter plot as a whole, as you can see in this diagram.

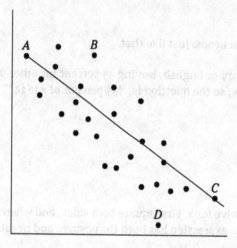

22. 500. Siva's two investments total $1,200, so set x as the amount earning 5 percent and $(1,200 - x)$ as the amount earning 7 percent. Five percent of x plus 7 percent of $(1,200 - x)$ equals $74, so set the equation up like this:

$$5\%(x) + 7\%(1,200 - x) = 74$$

Turn 5% and 7% into decimals 0.05 and 0.07, respectively, and solve for x:

$$0.05(x) + 0.07(1,200 - x) = 74$$
$$0.05x + 84 - 0.07x = 74$$
$$-0.02x = -10$$
$$x = 500$$

Because x represents the number of dollars earning 5 percent, the answer is 500.

Answer Key

Section 1: Reading and Writing, Module 1

1.	D	8.	C	15.	A	22.	A
2.	B	9.	A	16.	C	23.	D
3.	A	10.	D	17.	C	24.	C
4.	B	11.	A	18.	A	25.	A
5.	D	12.	B	19.	B	26.	B
6.	A	13.	D	20.	B	27.	D
7.	A	14.	C	21.	D		

Section 2: Reading and Writing, Module 2

1.	A	8.	C	15.	C	22.	A
2.	D	9.	A	16.	B	23.	B
3.	A	10.	B	17.	C	24.	C
4.	B	11.	A	18.	D	25.	C
5.	C	12.	C	19.	B	26.	B
6.	C	13.	B	20.	B	27.	A
7.	D	14.	A	21.	D		

Section 3: Math, Module 1

1.	B	7.	A	13.	C	19.	360
2.	C	8.	C	14.	B	20.	C
3.	B	9.	C	15.	C	21.	D
4.	C	10.	A	16.	96	22.	3
5.	D	11.	D	17.	7		
6.	A	12.	D	18.	84		

Section 4: Math, Module 2

1.	D	7.	A	13.	C	19.	520
2.	B	8.	B	14.	D	20.	C
3.	A	9.	A	15.	6	21.	B
4.	A	10.	A	16.	40	22.	500
5.	C	11.	D	17.	6		
6.	D	12.	D	18.	1 or 3		

Chapter 15

How Did You Do? Scoring Your Practice SAT

Two and a half hours of work, and you're still not finished! After each practice SAT, calculate your scores with these steps.

On the actual SAT, the algorithm varies slightly per exam, and the adaptive modules may be weighted differently (see Chapters 1 and 2 for more on how this works), so 90 correct answers on one exam may yield a slightly different score from 90 correct answers on another.

TIP

Finding Your Reading and Writing Score

Convert the number of questions you answered correctly to your SAT Reading and Writing score:

1. **Count up the number of Reading and Writing Test questions that you answered correctly, from both modules.**

2. **Use this table to convert that number to your estimated Reading and Writing Test Score.**

Number of Correct Answers	Reading and Writing Test Score
0	200
1	200
2	200
3	200
4	200

Number of Correct Answers	Reading and Writing Test Score
5	200
6	210
7	220
8	230
9	240
10	260
11	290
12	310
13	340
14	360
15	380
16	390
17	410
18	420
19	430
20	440
21	440
22	450
23	460
24	470
25	470
26	480
27	490
28	510
29	520
30	530
31	530
32	540
33	550
34	560
35	560
36	570
37	580
38	580
39	590

Number of Correct Answers	Reading and Writing Test Score
40	600
41	610
42	620
43	640
44	650
45	660
46	680
47	700
48	710
49	720
50	730
51	740
52	760
53	780
54	800

This is your SAT Reading and Writing score. Nice! Write the number down. Note that the more answers you get right, the more each one increases your score.

Finding Your Math Test Score

Convert the number of questions you answered correctly to your SAT Math test score:

1. **Count up the number of Math Test questions that you answered correctly, for both modules.**

2. **Use this table to convert that number to your estimated Math Test Score.**

Number of Correct Answers	Math Test Score
0	200
1	200
2	200
3	200
4	200
5	200
6	220
7	240
8	270

Number of Correct Answers	Math Test Score
9	300
10	320
11	330
12	340
13	350
14	360
15	370
16	380
17	390
18	410
19	430
20	450
21	460
22	470
23	480
24	490
25	500
26	520
27	540
28	560
29	570
30	590
31	610
32	620
33	630
34	640
35	650
36	660
37	680
38	690
39	710
40	740
41	760
42	770
43	790
44	800

This is your SAT Math score. Excellent! Write the number down. Note here also, the more answers you get right, the more each one increases your score.

Recording Your Overall Scores

Review the answers you missed to find your strengths and weaknesses. Also note whether you ran out of time or energy. Be sure to work on any problem areas, so your next attempt at the practice SAT will result in a higher score.

TIP

Don't worry so much about one score. Take two or three practice exams, and you'll see your scores improving! It's not where you are — it's the direction you're going. Usually all the mistakes happen in the first practice, so check your mistakes, see what happened, and skip those mistakes on the next round.

Like anything in the world that you do, you get better at it with practice. Get that practice out of the way here, now, so you improve *before* the real exam.

First practice exam

Date Taken _____

Reading and Writing Test Score _____ (200–800)

Math Test Score _____ (200–800)

Composite Test Score _____ (400–1600)

Second practice exam

Date Taken _____

Reading and Writing Test Score _____ (200–800)

Math Test Score _____ (200–800)

Composite Test Score _____ (400–1600)

Third practice exam

Date Taken _____

Reading and Writing Test Score _____ (200–800)

Math Test Score _____ (200–800)

Composite Test Score _____ (400–1600)

Fourth practice exam

Date Taken _____

Reading and Writing Test Score _____ (200–800)

Math Test Score _____ (200–800)

Composite Test Score _____ (400–1600)

5

The Part of Tens

Chapter 16

Ten Mistakes That Others Make That You Won't

E veryone makes these mistakes. Everyone except *you*, that is. Most test-takers make these mistakes, look back on them, think about them, learn, try again, and finally get things right. That's *them*. You, however, can skip over most of that by knowing in advance what *not* to do.

You Won't Cheat

Cheating on the SAT simply doesn't work, so don't even consider it. They're on to you. When you get to the testing center, and before you begin your test, the proctors separate you from anything that you can possibly use to cheat, including your phone, wristwatch, water bottle, jacket, and hat. On top of that, you're monitored by the proctor while taking the test. Any semblance of privacy goes right out the window. How would you cheat anyway? You can't check any answers or write all the math formulas on anything accessible during the test. Besides, the SAT tests your critical-reasoning and problem-solving skills, which you can't fake by cheating.

You Won't Neglect Your Break

During this ordeal, you have a 10-minute break, which is your chance to use the restroom, get some water, and have a snack. Don't waste this precious time in the vending machine line. Instead, prepare for your break by bringing a water bottle and a healthy snack so you can use your 10 minutes well. Don't drink too much water, though — you can't pause the exam to run to the restroom.

Don't plan on studying during your break, either. The review of any SAT-prep materials during the break can be considered cheating.

You Won't Pack Sugary Snacks

Pack a water bottle and healthy snack for your break. Water is best — not soda or juice — and the snack should be healthy, like a sandwich or nutrition bar, but not sugary, so no candy bar. Make sure whatever you bring doesn't have to go in the fridge.

You Won't Panic Over the Time Limit

Some test-takers fret over the clock. The key to success is to be aware of the clock while remaining calm. Practice working with a timer, so you're used to the timer on the SAT exam screen. As you get used to practicing with the clock, you become more comfortable working with it on exam day.

If you practice and prepare, the clock won't matter as much, anyway. When you know what to do, you answer most questions quickly and easily, with time remaining to review and best-attempt the few that you're not sure of.

TIP

The mistakes you make while relaxed are different from the mistakes you make while under pressure from the clock. Practice with a timer to get used to the time-limit pressure and become aware of the mistakes you'll make — and fix them *before* the test.

You Won't Run Out of Steam

The SAT also tests your stamina. Most students can't maintain this level of intense concentration for two-plus hours, so they burn out halfway through. Students have told me that halfway through a practice exam, they're so exhausted that they're just answering C, C, C . . . Obviously, this isn't an effective strategy — but at least they discover this during a practice test.

To build your stamina, keep practicing and stop when you get tired. Do this a few times, and eventually you'll go the full distance without fail.

You Won't Rush Through the Questions

Some students think that they need to rush through the questions to make the time limit. This is true, if you want to get them all wrong by missing details and making mistakes. I'd rather you get half the questions right and run out of time than miss them all by rushing through them. But that won't happen anyway: The SAT gives you enough time to answer all the questions correctly and calmly — if you don't get stuck.

REMEMBER

Remember the Other Golden Rule: *The secret to working fast and getting the answers right isn't rushing — it's knowing what you're doing.* The way you know what you're doing is by learning what's on the exam and practicing it.

You Won't Get Stuck on a Question

You get slightly over one minute per question. Imagine this: You encounter a tricky question that takes you five minutes, but you get it *right! Yes!* Then you run out of time before getting to the last four questions. So who won: you or that tricky question? Probably the question.

Don't let this happen. Instead, after about a minute, move on. Mark off any clearly wrong answers, guess one that *could* be correct, or even just mark an answer as a guess, mark the question for review, and *move on*. You can come back to it later, or if you don't get the chance, at least you may have guessed it right. This way you don't miss out on a bunch of questions at the end.

You Won't Stress Over the Answers

The SAT contains some seemingly difficult questions. You don't have to get them all: Do the best you can, score in the high percentiles, and get into that university, even with a scholarship! No one expects you to get a perfect score, so you shouldn't either.

REMEMBER

The SAT is only one of many parts of the application process. Your GPA, admissions essays, and any other relevant character-building experience (such as sports participation, job experience or volunteer work, or leadership training) also count toward your chances of admission. Turn to Chapter 1 for more on how your SAT score fits within the application process.

You Won't Change Your Morning Routine

The SAT is stressful enough. The last thing you need is to add more anxiety to the whole nerve-racking experience by changing your morning routine. If you normally have one glass of juice, should you have an extra glass for more vitamins or only half a glass so you don't have to run to the restroom? Should you have eggs for more protein or just toast to avoid the food crash? Here's a suggestion. *Do what you normally do.* It works every other day, and it'll work today. Don't change your routine.

TIP

If you're tempted to try an energy drink or something unusual for an enhanced test-taking experience, *try it first on a practice test!* Make sure this new mix doesn't upset your stomach or give you a headache. You don't need that distraction.

You Won't Dwell on Previous Modules

When guessing on a question and marking it for review, let it go until the end of the module so you can focus on the other questions at hand. When you reach the end of the module (but before moving on to the next one or before the time expires), you may return to the questions you skipped or marked and check or change your answers.

When you move on to the next module, however, that's it: You can't go back to a previous module. You have no choice but to move forward, so don't add to your anxiety by focusing on past questions that you can do nothing about.

Chapter **17**

Ten Ways to Get the Most from Practice SATs

Sitting through the actual SAT is kind of like being on stage. No matter how well you know the song or the routine, the first time you get up there is a new experience and your performance can go south. However, the second time is *always* much better. Students tell me again and again that the second time they took the SAT went *way* better than the first time, partly because they had more practice but also because the second time, they were *used* to it.

This may be how the testing process goes, but you can narrow that gap and make your first SAT go much better by using the practice exams to prepare for the testing experience. Here are ten ways to get the most from these practice SATs.

Practice an Entire SAT Exam in One Sitting

How well you can answer the questions doesn't matter if you can't maintain your energy for the length of the exam. When you're in a pressure cooker like the actual exam, your brain is in overdrive. You need to become used to working intensely for over two hours in one stretch so you can go the distance on exam day.

Practice Not Making Mistakes under Pressure

Did you spend 10 minutes on a question and not finish one of the modules? Did you get flustered and choke, thus losing your ability to focus, before the exam was over? Did you get lost in the app, unable to find the question you wanted to return to? Do you know better than to make these mistakes? Of course, you do, but this happens to everyone, especially under pressure.

Only by falling into a trap do you learn how to avoid it. Work out the bugs on a practice SAT. Make these mistakes at home, when it doesn't matter, instead of on the actual exam, when it's life or death (or a scholarship).

Practice with the Bluebook App

If you place Ernest Hemingway in front of Microsoft Word, would he be able to write anything? Probably not, even though he's one of the most noted authors of our time. For him, the problem wouldn't be the writing; it would be the app. The same applies to you: You can answer the questions, but the app is another story. How do you mark questions to return to? How do you annotate the reading? How do you find the math formulas? What does that button do? The app is easy to learn, but you have enough on your mind during the exam. Master the app *before* the exam.

TIP

Practice with the Bluebook app from www.collegeboard.com. It's free and looks and feels exactly like the real thing, providing you with a genuine simulation.

Practice with Others in the Room

Nothing is more distracting on your SAT than hearing someone using scratch paper, sighing, clicking keys, cursing, or (if they use *Digital SAT Prep 2025/2026 For Dummies*) chuckling confidently while working the exam. Get used to distractions by taking your practice SAT with friends or others who are also taking the SAT and therefore need to practice, and make sure they're taking the same practice exam that you are. The sounds as they work and sigh and groan or pat themselves on the back (because they also used *Digital SAT Prep 2025/2026 For Dummies*) become less of a distraction as you get used to the noises and the now-present feeling of competition.

Practicing with your friends is the best way to improve, and some of the key advantages are described separately in this chapter. For one thing, it also helps your friends improve their scores while you improve yours. Yes, the SAT is competitive, but with 2 million test-takers in the running, your handful of friends won't tip the scales — in fact, it's better if they have the chance to join you in college.

Practice as a Dress Rehearsal

Play by the rules of the testing center. No phone, hat, drink, snack, neck pillow, or anything that brings a modicum of comfort is allowed within reach in the exam room. Your break is short, and your scratch paper is limited. If this is not something that you're used to, it'll drive you nuts on exam day, so make sure it's a road that you've been down before, and it won't be as bad.

Do you get thirsty? Hungry? Uncomfortable? Chilly? What do you wish you had: water, a sandwich, a power bar, coffee, aspirin? Keep these things in mind and plan accordingly to pack them. On test day, you'll have access to your personal belongings during the break, so bring these things in a bag and be prepared for a quick refreshment.

Practicing with friends helps with this as well. Take whatever steps you can to make the testing experience as familiar and comfortable (or less *uncomfortable*) as possible.

Practice Your Competitive Edge

The practice test doesn't matter, so why try hard? In the second hour of the practice, you're exhausted, and you just want to get through it — and that's okay, because it's a practice test, right?

Wrong. If you've never tried as hard as you can for over two hours, you won't do it easily on exam day. You may intend to, but working at half effort on the practice exam is a hard habit to break, and it carries to the real thing.

It's like running a race by yourself versus running a race against someone else: You try harder when others are in the game, but you're not used to it if you never practice like that. One way to get around this is by recording your scores and trying to beat your last performance. Another way is to try to beat your friends' scores. This is another advantage of taking the practice exam with your friends who are also taking the same practice exam. Try to beat their scores to make it real and competitive, and you'll bring this edge to the actual exam.

Practice Your Test-Taking Strategies

Sure, this book is chock full of strategies. You know the fine points of knocking out the fast questions first, guessing on any question that stalls you for more than a minute, using the review screen as your roadmap, and crossing off wrong answers in the Reading and Writing — well enough to teach them. But can you make these work at game time?

As you take the practice SATs, focus on your strategies. You'll find what works and what doesn't, or you'll find your own take on an established strategy. Finding and honing the strategies that work for you is an important part of your prep process, but do this *before* test day.

One thing you could do is go through a practice SAT that you've already worked. Because the questions are familiar to you, you can focus more on the overall strategies.

Practice Managing Your Time

All the test-taking strategies are important, but time management overshadows everything. It doesn't matter if you know the *best* way to approach a question if the clock beats you to it. I have students telling me all day long that they forgot this strategy or that time-management tip. I tell them, "Great, glad you caught that . . . on a *practice* test."

Brush up on the time management tips, along with other test-taking strategies, in Chapters 3 and 6, the respective introductory chapters to the Reading and Writing and Math chapters. Practice those strategies and make them work for you on a *practice* test so that time management is one less thing to distract you on the *real* test.

Practice Finding Your Areas of Focus

Do you struggle more with the Science or Social Studies questions? Do you handle triangles better than you do exponents? Do you lose steam (causing your performance to drop) during the second hour? Do you run out of time? With these practice SATs, you can get a sense of how you work and where you need to focus, and *then* you can close those gaps. *You cannot fix your gaps unless you find them first.* There are no truer words.

Review your Practice SAT Answers and Explanations

After taking a two-hour practice SAT, the last thing you probably want to do is spend time reviewing it, so take a well-deserved break and save the answers and explanations for later. But be sure to review them: not only to review your areas of focus, but also to strengthen your grasp on all the topics.

After you've taken the practice exam and had a break, take the following steps to review:

1. Identify which questions you answered incorrectly.

2. Read the answer explanations and review any relevant material so you're prepared for a similar question next time.

3. Fully close that gap by revisiting that chapter or section in this book that covers the topic.

TIP

Here's another thing you can do. While you're taking the practice exam, mark any questions you're not sure of, and read the explanations for those answers after the exam. This way, even if you guessed correctly or took too long on it, you'll review that question along with the ones that you missed.

Index

Symbols and Numerics

' (apostrophe), 45
: (colon), 45
; (semicolon), 44
3:4:5 triangle, 138
3-D shapes, drawing, 147–151
30-60-90 triangle, 138–139
45-45-90 triangle, 138

A

absolute value, solving, 98–100
acute angle, 132
adaptive, 9
admission ticket, 19
adverse conditions, 20
Agricultural Health Study (AHS), 187
algebra
  about, 72
  setting up equations, 107–114
  solving for more than one *x*, 98–107
  solving for *x*, 93–98
angles, drawing, 132–135
answers and explanations
  Reading and Writing section, 65
  reviewing, 284
  stressing over answers and explanations, 279
  typing answers, 71
apostrophe ('), 45
applying strategies, 52
arc, of circles, 145
area, of circles, 144
arguments, identifying, 32
arithmetic mean. *See* mean

Autobiography of a Yogi (Yogananda), 180
average. *See* mean
axis of symmetry, 124

B

Bacteria in Daily Life (Frankland), 46
bar graphs, measuring, 163
Bedouins (Huneker), 234
big picture, 33
Biology For Dummies, 2nd Edition (Kratz and
    Siegfried), 177, 230, 237
Birdsall, William W. (author)
  Library of the Best American Literature, 228,
    235
Bluebook app, 282
Bohemians of the Latin Quarter (Murger), 184
breaks, 277
Brenner, Jessica (author)
  College Admission Essays For Dummies, 13
Briand, Paul I., Jr. (author)
  *Daughter of the Sky: The Story of Amelia
    Earheart*, 174
A Brief History of the Olympic Games (Young),
    235

C

CAH, solving right triangles with, 152–154
calculating area of triangles, 137
calculators, 72
capitalization, 40
catalyst, 32
Cather, Willa (author)
  O Pioneers, 176
cause and effect, identifying, 30

Cheat Sheet (website), 3

cheating, 277

chord, of circles, 143

circle charts, measuring, 164

circles
  drawing, 143–144
  drawing parts of, 145–147
  graphing, 125–127

circumference, of circles, 143

College Admission Essays For Dummies
  (Brenner), 13

College Board
  Customer Service, 10
  website, 14

College Board Services for Students with
  Disabilities, 11

colon (:), 45

complementary angle, 133

completing the text, 58–59

composite numbers, 74

composite score, 14

compound interest, 110–112

cones, drawing, 149–150

consecutive numbers, 74

context, words in, 45

contrast transitions, 41

control group, 32

conversions, simplifying, 80–81

coordinate geometry, graphing, 114–130

coordinate plane, 114

Crime: It's Causes and Treatment (Darrow), 179

Critical Reading questions, 24

Crowder, David A. (author)
  Sherlock Holmes For Dummies, 58–59

cube roots, simplifying, 86–88

cubes
  surface area of, 148–149
  volume of, 148

cylinders, drawing, 149–150

D

The Dancing Mouse: A Study in Animal Behavior
  (Yerkes), 26–30

D'Arrigo, Rosanne (author)
  Dendroclimatic Studies: Tree Growth and
  Climate Change in Northern Forests, 237

Darrow, Clarence (author)
  Crime: It's Causes and Treatment, 179

Darwin, Charles (author)
  On the Origin of Species, 183

data, interpreting, 55–56

Daughter of the Sky: The Story of Amelia Earheart
  (Briand, Jr.), 174

Davi, Nicole (author)
  Dendroclimatic Studies: Tree Growth and
  Climate Change in Northern Forests, 237

"The Deadliest Atlantic Tropical Cyclones,
  1492-1996," 52–53

The Decline and Fall of the Roman Empire
  (Gibbon), 46

degree measure, 146

Democracy in America (Tocqueville), 235

Dendroclimatic Studies: Tree Growth and Climate
  Change in Northern Forests (D'Arrigo, Davi,
  Jacoby, Wilson, and Wiles), 237

detail questions, 27–28

diameter, of circles, 143

Dickens, Charles (author)
  Great Expectations, 187

difference of squares, solving, 103–105

Doyle, Steven (author)
  Sherlock Holmes For Dummies, 58–59

drawing
  angles, 132–135
  basic shapes, 132–147
  circles, 143–144
  cones, 149–150
  cylinders, 149–150
  geometry, 131–158
  overlapping shapes, 144–145
  parallelograms, 140–143

parts of circles, 145–147

rectangles, 140

spheres, 150–151

squares, 140

3-D shapes, 147–151

trapezoids, 140–143

triangles, 135–139

trigonometry, 131–158

E

either/or, 42

Eligibility Form, 12

Eliot, George (author)

Middlemarch, 53–54

endurance, 278

English Grammar For Dummies (Woods), 41

English Grammar Workbook For Dummies (Woods), 41

equations, setting up, 107–114

equilateral triangle, 135

exponents, simplifying, 81–86

expressions, solving, 105–107

F

factored form, 122

factors, 73

Fakim, Gurib (author)

Novel Plant Bioresources, 61–62, 230

financial help, 12

First Woman, 173

focus, areas of, 284

foreign students, 12–13

formats, for questions, 51–60

formulas, 70–71

45-45-90 triangle, 138

fractions, solving for *x* in, 96–97

Frankland, Percy (author)

Bacteria in Daily Life, 46

Fulton, Frances I Sims (author)

To and Through Nebraska, 31

functions

about, 72

graphing, 127–130

future value (FV), 109

G

general form, of equation of a circle, 126–127

"Genetics," 225

geometry

about, 72, 131

coordinate, 114–130

drawing, 131–158

Gibbon, Edward (author)

The Decline and Fall of the Roman Empire, 46

grammar, 40–41

graph data, measuring, 163–168

graphing

circles, 125–127

coordinate geometry, 114–130

functions, 127–130

inequalities, 120–121

lines, 115–118

measuring multiple graphs, 166–168

parabolas, 121–125

two lines, 118–120

GRE For Dummies (Woldoff and Kraynak), 228

Great Expectations (Dickens), 187

Green Book, 191

Gurib-Fakim, Ameenah (author)

Novel Plant Bioresources, 61–62

H

"History & Culture," 240

Holmes, Hannah (author)

The Secret Life of Dust, 54–55

homophones, 40

Huneker, James (author)
  Bedouins, 234
"Hurricane Information," 63
hypotenuse, 155–157

I

i (interest rate), 109
icons, explained, 2
identifying
  arguments, 32
  cause and effect, 30
  objects, 44
  subjects, 44
imaginary *i*, simplifying, 88–90
imaginary numbers, 75
incomplete sentences, 40
in-context vocabulary, 37–39
inequalities, graphing, 120–121
inference questions, 28–29
Inherit the Wind (play), 238
integers, 74
interest, 109, 110–112
interest rate *(i)*, 109
interpreting
  data, 55–56
  research questions, 59–60
interrupters, 42
Into the House of the Ancestors (Maier), 48
irrational numbers, 74
isolating pronouns, 44
isosceles right triangle, 138
isosceles triangles, 135, 136

J

Jacoby, Gordon (author)
  Dendroclimatic Studies: Tree Growth and Climate Change in Northern Forests, 237
joining

sentences, 44
transitions, 41
Jones, Rufus M. (author)
  Library of the Best American Literature, 228, 235

K

Kew Gardens (Woolf), 34
Kratz, Rene (author)
  Biology For Dummies, 2nd Edition, 177, 230, 237
Kraynak, Joe (author)
  GRE For Dummies, 228

L

Labour Policy - False and True (Macassey), 174
learning disabilities, 11–12
"Leave it to Beaver: Partners Collaborate on Beaver Dam Analog Project," 185
Library of the Best American Literature (Birdsall and Jones), 228, 235
Life on the Mississippi (Twain), 237
The Life of Ludwig van Beethoven (Thayer), 239
line graphs, measuring, 164
lines
  graphing, 115–118
  graphing two, 118–120
lists, 43
literature, reading passages in, 33–35
Livingstone, David J. (author)
  A Practical Guide to Scientific Data Analysis, 236
Loon, Hendrik Willem van (author)
  The Story of Mankind, 48

M

Macassey, Lynden (author)
  Labour Policy - False and True, 174
Maier, Karl (author)
  Into the House of the Ancestors, 48

main idea questions, 28–29
Math section
  answer keys
    Practice Exam 1, 220
    Practice Exam 2, 267
  finding scores for, 271–272
  number of questions and timing for, 9
  question answers and explanations
    Practice Exam 1, 209–219
    Practice Exam 2, 258–266
  questions
    Practice Exam 1, 193–202
    Practice Exam 2, 242–250
mean, measuring, 159–160
measuring
  bar graphs, 163
  circle charts, 164
  graph data, 163–168
  line graphs, 164
  mean, 159–160
  median, 160–161
  mode, 160–161
  multiple graphs, 166–168
  pie charts, 164
  probability, 159–168
  range, 161–162
  scatter plots, 165–166
  statistics, 159–168
median, measuring, 160–161
"Meteors & Meteorites," 63–64
Middlemarch (Eliot), 53–54
misplaced modifiers, 40
mistakes, avoiding, 277–279, 281–282
mode, measuring, 160–161
modifiers, misplaced, 40
modules, dwelling on previous, 279
morning routine, 279
multiples, 73

Murger, Henri (author)
  Bohemians of the Latin Quarter, 184
  My Heart Leaps Up When I Behold (poem), 35–36

N

narrative, visualizing, 34
neither/nor, 42
noun-pronoun agreement, 42–43
Novel Plant Bioresources (Fakim),
  61–62, 230
numbers
  about, 72
  setting up sum of, 108–109
  simplifying, 73–75
  solving for *x* with, 93–94

O

O Pioneers (Cather), 176
objects, identifying, 44
obtuse angle, 133
On the Origin of Species (Darwin), 183
online format, 8–9
operations, 72
opposing ideas, 31
order of operations, 75
overall structure of the text, 53–54

P

paired conjunctions, 43
paired reading, 54–55
parabolas, graphing, 121–125
parallel structure, 40, 43–44
parallelograms, drawing, 140–143
percents, simplifying, 76–78
photo ID, 19
physical issues, 12
Pi, 143

pie charts, measuring, 164

Planning for Beavers Manual: Anticipating Beavers when Designing Restoration Projects, 229

planning prep time, 15–18

Play icon, 2

poetry, reading passages in, 35–36

polygons, 141

Pope, Alexander (poet), 185

A Practical Guide to Scientific Data Analysis (Livingstone), 236

Practice Exam 1

  about, 171–172, 203

  Math section

    answer key, 220

    question answers and explanations, 209–219

    questions, 193–202

  Reading and Writing section

    answer key, 220

    question answers and explanations, 203–209

    questions for, 173–192

  tips for, 281–284

Practice Exam 2

  about, 221–222, 251

  Math section

    answer key, 267

    question answers and explanations, 258–266

    questions, 242–250

  Reading and Writing section

    answer key, 267

    question answers and explanations, 251–258

    questions for, 223–241

  tips for, 281–284

prep time, planning, 15–18

present value (PV), 109

prime numbers

  about, 74

  simplifying, 76

principal, 109

probability

  about, 72

  measuring, 159–168

projections, simplifying, 90–92

pronoun cases, 44

pronouns, isolating, 44

PSAT/NMSQT, 20

publications

  Autobiography of a Yogi (Yogananda), 180

  Bacteria in Daily Life (Frankland), 46

  Bedouins (Huneker), 234

  Biology For Dummies, 2nd Edition (Kratz and Siegfried), 177, 230, 237

  Bohemians of the Latin Quarter (Murger), 184

  A Brief History of the Olympic Games (Young), 235

  College Admission Essays For Dummies (Brenner), 13

  College Board Services for Students with Disabilities, 11

  Crime: It's Causes and Treatment (Darrow), 179

  The Dancing Mouse: A Study in Animal Behavior (Yerkes), 26–30

  Daughter of the Sky: The Story of Amelia Earheart (Briand, Jr.), 174

  "The Deadliest Atlantic Tropical Cyclones, 1492-1996," 52–53

  The Decline and Fall of the Roman Empire (Gibbon), 46

  Democracy in America (Tocqueville), 235

  Dendroclimatic Studies: Tree Growth and Climate Change in Northern Forests (D'Arrigo, Davi, Jacoby, Wilson, and Wiles), 237

  English Grammar For Dummies (Woods), 41

English Grammar Workbook For Dummies (Woods), 41

GRE For Dummies (Woldoff and Kraynak), 228

Great Expectations (Dickens), 187

Green Book, 191

"History & Culture," 240

Into the House of the Ancestors (Maier), 48

"Hurricane Information," 63

Kew Gardens (Woolf), 34

Labour Policy - False and True (Macassey), 174

"Leave it to Beaver: Partners Collaborate on Beaver Dam Analog Project," 185

Life on the Mississippi (Twain), 237

The Life of Ludwig van Beethoven (Thayer), 239

"Meteors & Meteorites," 63–64

Middlemarch (Eliot), 53–54

Novel Plant Bioresources (Fakim), 61–62, 230

O Pioneers (Cather), 176

On the Origin of Species (Darwin), 183

Planning for Beavers Manual: Anticipating Beavers when Designing Restoration Projects, 229

Punch: Volume 118, Nos. 3052-3077, 234

The Secret Life of Dust (Holmes), 54–55

Sherlock Holmes For Dummies (Doyle and Crowder), 58–59

A Short History of the World (Wells), 223

The Story of Mankind (Loon), 48

To and Through Nebraska (Fulton), 31

Travels in the Upper Egyptian Deserts (Weigall), 47

U.S. History For Dummies (Wiegand), 57

The Wiley-Blackwell Companion to Sociology (Ritzer), 227

"Women in the Civil Rights Movement Historic Context Statement and AACRN Listing Guidance," 239

Punch: Volume 118, Nos. 3052-3077, 234

punctuation, 40–41, 44–45

PV (present value), 109

pyramids
  surface area of, 148
  volume of, 147

Pythagorean Theorem, 137

Q

quadratic equations, solving, 100–103

quadrilateral, 140

questions
  Critical Reading, 24
  detail, 27–28
  formats for, 51–60
  getting stuck on, 279
  inference, 28–29
  main idea, 28–29
  number of, 9
  Reading and Writing section, 26–30, 46–48, 61–64
  reading passages, 30–36
  Research and Graphics, 24
  rushing through, 278
  sentence completion, 23–24
  Standard English convention, 24
  timing for, 9
  writer's purpose, 29–30

quotations, using for support, 57–58

R

radians, solving, 154–157

radicals, solving for x in, 95–96

radii, of circles, 143

radius, of circles, 143

range, measuring, 161–162

rates of change, setting up, 112–114

rational numbers, 74

ratios, simplifying, 78–80

Reading and Writing section
  about, 23–24
  answer key
    Practice Exam 1, 220
    Practice Exam 2, 267
  answer strategies, 25–26
  finding scores for, 269–271
  number of questions and timing for, 9
  practice questions, 26–30, 46–48, 61–64
  question answers and explanations, 49–50, 65
    Practice Exam 1, 203–209
    Practice Exam 2, 251–258
  questions
    Practice Exam 1, 173–192
    Practice Exam 2, 223–241
  reading passage practice, 30–36
  reading strategies, 24–25
reading passages, practicing with, 30–36
real numbers, 75
reciprocal fractions, solving for *x* in, 97–98
recording overall scores, 273
rectangles, drawing, 140
rectangular solids, drawing, 147
registering, 10
regular shape, 140
Remember icon, 2
Research and Graphics questions, 24
research questions, interpreting, 59–60
rhombus, 141
right angle, 132
right triangles
  about, 136, 138–139
  solving with SOH CAH TOA, 152–154
rise over run, 116
Ritzer, George (author)
  The Wiley-Blackwell Companion to Sociology, 227

S

SAT
  day of, 18–19
  math (*See also* Math section)
    about, 69–70
    formulas, 70–71
    topics overview, 71–72
    typing answers, 71
  night before, 18
  scoring, 14
  what it looks for, 13–14
  when to take, 10–11
scatter plots, measuring, 165–166
science, reading passages in, 32–33
score report, 14
scoring, 14
  finding Math section scores, 271–272
  finding Reading and Writing section scores, 269–271
  recording overall scores, 273
The Secret Life of Dust (Holmes), 54–55
sector, of circles, 146
semicolon (;), 44
sentence completion questions, 23–24, 37–39
sentences
  joining, 44
  underlined, 52–53
setup
  equations, 107–114
  interest, 109–112
  rates of change, 112–114
  stories, 107–108
  sum of numbers, 108–109
Shakespeare, William (poet), 175
shapes
  drawing basic, 132–147
  drawing overlapping, 144–145
  3-D, 147–151

Sherlock Holmes For Dummies (Doyle and Crowder), 58–59

A Short History of the World (Wells), 223

Siegfried, Donna (author)
  Biology For Dummies, 2nd Edition, 177, 230, 237

similar triangles, 137

simple interest, 110–111

simplifying
  about, 73
  conversions, 80–81
  cube roots, 86–88
  exponents, 81–86
  imaginary *i*, 88–90
  numbers, 73–75
  order of operations, 75
  percents, 76–78
  prime numbers, 76
  projections, 90–92
  ratios, 78–80
  square roots, 86–88

snacks, 19, 278

social studies, reading passages in, 30–32

SOH, solving right triangles with, 152–154

solving
  absolute value, 98–100
  difference of squares, 103–105
  expressions, 105–107
  for more than one *x*, 98–107
  quadratic equations, 100–103
  radians, 154–157
  right triangles with SOH CAH TOA, 152–154
  trigonometric equations, 157–158
  trigonometric problems, 151–158
  unit circles, 154–157
  for *x*, 93–98

Sonnet 73 (poem), 175

"Sound and Sense" (poem), 185

special needs accommodations, 11–12

spelling, 40

spheres, drawing, 150–151

square roots, simplifying, 86–88

squares, drawing, 140

Standard English convention questions, 24

standard form
  about, 122
  of equation of a circle, 125–126

statistics
  about, 72
  mean, 159–160
  measuring, 159–168
  median, 160–161
  mode, 160–161
  range, 161–162

stories, setting up, 107–108

The Story of Mankind (Loon), 48

strategies
  applying, 52
  reading, 24–25
  for success, 15–20

strengthening a claim, 56–57

subjects, identifying, 44

subject-verb agreement, 42

success strategies, 15–20

sum of numbers, setting up, 108–109

supplementary angle, 133

support, using quotations for, 57–58

surface area
  of cubes, 148–149
  of pyramids, 148
  of rectangular solids, 147

T

tangents, of circles, 144

Technical Support (website), 3

test-taking strategies, 283

Thayer, Alexander Wheelock (author)
  The Life of Ludwig van Beethoven, 239

there/here, 42

30-60-90 triangle, 138–139

3:4:5 triangle, 138

3-D shapes, drawing, 147–151

time management
  importance of, 278
  practicing, 283
  with reading strategies, 24–25

timing, for questions, 9

Tip icon, 2

To and Through Nebraska (Fulton), 31

TOA, solving right triangles with, 152–154

Tocqueville, Alexis de (author)
  Democracy in America, 235

transitions, 41

transversal angle, 134–135

trapezoids, drawing, 140–143

Travels in the Upper Egyptian Deserts
  (Weigall), 47

triangles. *See also* right triangles
  calculating area of, 137
  drawing, 135–139
  right, 138–139

trigonometric equations, solving,
  157–158

trigonometric problems, solving, 151–158

trigonometry
  about, 72, 131
  drawing, 131–158

Twain, Mark (author)
  Life on the Mississippi, 237

U

undefined numbers, 75

underlined sentence, 52–53

unit circles, solving, 154–157

U.S. History For Dummies (Wiegand), 57

V

variables, 32

verb matching, 42–43

verb tension, 43

verbs, wrong-tense, 40

vertex form, 122

vertical angles, 133–134

visualizing narratives, 34

volume
  of cones, 150
  of cubes, 148
  of cylinders, 149
  of pyramids, 147

W

Warning icon, 2

water bottle, 19

weakening a claim, 56–57

websites
  College Board, 14
  *College Board Services for Students with
    Disabilities*, 11
  Eligibility Form, 12

Weigall, Arthur Edward Pearse (author)
  Travels in the Upper Egyptian Deserts, 47

Wells, H. G. (author)
  A Short History of the World, 223

when to take, 10–11

Whitman, Walt (poet), 228

whole numbers, 73

Wiegand, Steve (author)
  U.S. History For Dummies, 57

Wiles, Greg (author)
  *Dendroclimatic Studies: Tree Growth and
    Climate Change in Northern Forests*, 237

The Wiley-Blackwell Companion to Sociology
  (Ritzer), 227

Wilson, Rob (author)
  *Dendroclimatic Studies: Tree Growth and
    Climate Change in Northern Forests*, 237

Woldoff, Ron (author)
  GRE For Dummies, 228

"Women in the Civil Rights Movement Historic
  Context Statement and AACRN Listing
  Guidance," 239

Woods, Geraldine (author)
  English Grammar For Dummies, 41
  English Grammar Workbook For Dummies, 41
Woolf, Virginia (author)
  Kew Gardens, 34
word choice, 34
words in context, 45
Wordsworth, William (poet), 35–36
writer's purpose questions, 29–30
wrong-tense verbs, 40

X
x
  solving for, 93–98
  solving for more than one, 98–107

Y
y, solving for *x* with a, 94–95
Yerkes, Robert M. (author)
  The Dancing Mouse: A Study in Animal Behavior,
    26–30
Yogananda, Paramhansa (author)
  Autobiography of a Yogi, 180
Young, David C. (author)
  A Brief History of the Olympic Games, 235

About the Author

Ron Woldoff completed his dual master's degrees at Arizona State University and San Diego State University, where he studied the culmination of business and technology. After years as a corporate consultant, Ron opened his own company, National Test Prep, where he has helped students reach their goals on the GMAT, GRE, SAT, ACT, and PSAT. He created the programs and curricula for these tests from scratch, using observations of the tests and feedback from students. Ron has also taught his own GMAT and GRE programs as an adjunct instructor at both Northern Arizona University and the internationally acclaimed Thunderbird School of Global Management, as well as SAT and ACT at various high schools. Ron lives in Phoenix, Arizona, with his lovely wife, Leisah, and their three amazing boys, Zachary, Jadon, and Adam. You can find Ron on the web at http://testprepaz.com.

Dedication

This book is humbly dedicated to all those whom I've helped reach their goals. You have taught me as much as I have taught you.

—Ron Woldoff

Author's Acknowledgments

I would like to thank my friends Lionel Hummel and Jaime Abromovitz, who helped me get things going when I had this wild notion of helping people prepare for standardized college-admissions tests. I would like to thank my friend and former high school teacher Ken Krueger, who guided me through the business side of test prep. And more than anyone else, I would like to thank my best friend and wife, Leisah, for her continuing support and for always being there for me.

For this project, shout out to Tim Gallan for his help in bringing yet another manuscript through editing and production — definitely a good working partner. Also, hat tip to copy editor Marylouise Wiack and technical editor Amy Nicklin, who reviewed my work and kept me honest and on track — not always easy to do. Big thumbs up to Elizabeth Stilwell, our acquisitions editor, who was ultimately responsible for trusting me to revise this edition and for handling all the little things to keep it going.

For previous contributors, I would like to acknowledge Suzee Vlk, who held the reins on the *SAT For Dummies* series before handing them to Geraldine Woods, my co-author in crime on previous editions, along with Peter Bonfanti and Jane Burstein, who also lent to the success of this product. This book reflects all of your voices and talent.

Publisher's Acknowledgments

Acquisitions Editor: Elizabeth Stilwell

Development Editor: Tim Gallan

Copy Editor (previous edition): Marylouise Wiack

Technical Editor (previous edition): Amy Nicklin

Production Editor: Kumarasamy Saikarthick

Cover Image: © Courtney Hale/Getty Images

Leverage the power

Dummies is the global leader in the reference category and one of the most trusted and highly regarded brands in the world. No longer just focused on books, customers now have access to the dummies content they need in the format they want. Together we'll craft a solution that engages your customers, stands out from the competition, and helps you meet your goals.

Advertising & Sponsorships

Connect with an engaged audience on a powerful multimedia site, and position your message alongside expert how-to content. Dummies.com is a one-stop shop for free, online information and know-how curated by a team of experts.

- Targeted ads
- Video
- Email Marketing
- Microsites
- Sweepstakes sponsorship

20 **MILLION**
PAGE VIEWS
EVERY SINGLE MONTH

15
MILLION
UNIQUE
VISITORS PER MONTH

43%
OF ALL VISITORS
ACCESS THE SITE
VIA THEIR MOBILE DEVICES

700,000 NEWSLETTER
SUBSCRIPTIONS
TO THE INBOXES OF
300,000 UNIQUE INDIVIDUALS EVERY WEEK

# of dummies

Custom Publishing

Reach a global audience in any language by creating a solution that will differentiate you from competitors, amplify your message, and encourage customers to make a buying decision.

- Apps
- Books
- eBooks
- Video
- Audio
- Webinars

Brand Licensing & Content

Leverage the strength of the world's most popular reference brand to reach new audiences and channels of distribution.

For more information, visit dummies.com/biz

PERSONAL ENRICHMENT

Staying Sharp dummies

9781119187790
USA $26.00
CAN $31.99
UK £19.99

Facebook dummies
Carolyn Abram

9781119179030
USA $21.99
CAN $25.99
UK £16.99

Guitar dummies
Mark Phillips
Jon Chappell

9781119293354
USA $24.99
CAN $29.99
UK £17.99

Investing dummies
Eric Tyson, MBA

9781119293347
USA $22.99
CAN $27.99
UK £16.99

Beekeeping dummies
Howland Blackiston

9781119310068
USA $22.99
CAN $27.99
UK £16.99

Digital Photography dummies
Julie Adair King

9781119235606
USA $24.99
CAN $29.99
UK £17.99

Meditation dummies
Stephan Bodian

9781119251163
USA $24.99
CAN $29.99
UK £17.99

Pregnancy ALL-IN-ONE dummies
6 Books in one!

9781119235491
USA $26.99
CAN $31.99
UK £19.99

Samsung Galaxy S7 dummies
Bill Hughes

9781119279952
USA $24.99
CAN $29.99
UK £17.99

iPhone dummies
Edward C. Baig
Bob "Dr. Mac" LeVitus

9781119283133
USA $24.99
CAN $29.99
UK £17.99

Crocheting dummies
Karen Manthey
Susan Brittain

9781119287117
USA $24.99
CAN $29.99
UK £16.99

Nutrition dummies
Carol Ann Rinzler

9781119130246
USA $22.99
CAN $27.99
UK £16.99

PROFESSIONAL DEVELOPMENT

Windows 10 dummies
Andy Rathbone

9781119311041
USA $24.99
CAN $29.99
UK £17.99

AutoCAD dummies
Bill Fane

9781119255796
USA $39.99
CAN $47.99
UK £27.99

Excel 2016 dummies
Greg Harvey, PhD

9781119293439
USA $26.99
CAN $31.99
UK £19.99

QuickBooks 2017 dummies
Stephen L. Nelson, MBA, CPA, MS in Taxation

9781119281467
USA $26.99
CAN $31.99
UK £19.99

macOS Sierra dummies
Bob "Dr. Mac" LeVitus

9781119280651
USA $29.99
CAN $35.99
UK £21.99

LinkedIn dummies
Joel Elad, MBAe

9781119251132
USA $24.99
CAN $29.99
UK £17.99

Windows 10 ALL-IN-ONE dummies
10 Books
Woody Leonhard

9781119310563
USA $34.00
CAN $41.99
UK £24.99

SharePoint 2016 dummies
Rosemarie Withee
Ken Withee

9781119181705
USA $29.99
CAN $35.99
UK £21.99

Fundamental Analysis dummies
Matt Krantz

9781119263593
USA $26.99
CAN $31.99
UK £19.99

Networking dummies
Doug Lowe

9781119257769
USA $29.99
CAN $35.99
UK £21.99

Office 2016 dummies
Wallace Wang

9781119293477
USA $26.99
CAN $31.99
UK £19.99

Office 365 dummies
Rosemarie Withee
Ken Withee
Jennifer Reed

9781119265313
USA $24.99
CAN $29.99
UK £17.99

Salesforce.com dummies
Liz Kao
Jon Paz

9781119239314
USA $29.99
CAN $35.99
UK £21.99

Coding dummies
Nikhil Abraham

9781119293323
USA $29.99
CAN $35.99
UK £21.99

dummies.com

dummies
A Wiley Brand

Learning Made Easy

ACADEMIC

Algebra I
Mary Jane Sterling

9781119293576
USA $19.99
CAN $23.99
UK £15.99

Basic Math & Pre-Algebra
Mark Zegarelli

9781119293637
USA $19.99
CAN $23.99
UK £15.99

Calculus
Mark Ryan

9781119293491
USA $19.99
CAN $23.99
UK £15.99

Chemistry
John T. Moore, EdD

9781119293460
USA $19.99
CAN $23.99
UK £15.99

Physics I
Steven Holzner, PhD

9781119293590
USA $19.99
CAN $23.99
UK £15.99

1,001 Practice Questions SAT
Ron Woldoff

9781119215844
USA $26.99
CAN $31.99
UK £19.99

Organic Chemistry I
Arthur Winter

9781119293378
USA $22.99
CAN $27.99
UK £16.99

Statistics
Deborah J. Rumsey, PhD

9781119293521
USA $19.99
CAN $23.99
UK £15.99

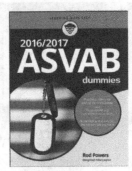

2016/2017 ASVAB
Rod Powers

9781119239178
USA $18.99
CAN $22.99
UK £14.99

1,001 Practice Questions Praxis Core
Carla Kirkland
Chan Cleveland

9781119263883
USA $26.99
CAN $31.99
UK £19.99

Available Everywhere Books Are Sold

dummies.com